Television and
the Socialization of
the Minority Child

Television and the Socialization of the Minority Child

EDITED BY

Gordon L. Berry
Claudia Mitchell-Kernan

University of California, Los Angeles
Los Angeles, California

1982

ACADEMIC PRESS
A Subsidiary of Harcourt Brace Jovanovich, Publishers
New York   London
Paris   San Diego   San Francisco   São Paulo   Sydney   Tokyo   Toronto

ACADEMIC PRESS, INC.
111 Fifth Avenue, New York, New York 10003

United Kingdom Edition published by
ACADEMIC PRESS, INC. (LONDON) LTD.
24/28 Oval Road, London NW1 7DX

Library of Congress Cataloging in Publication Data
Main entry under title:

Television and the socialization of the minority child.

Includes bibliographies and index.
1. Television and children. 2. Minorities in tele-
vision--United States. 3. Socialization. I. Berry,
Gordon L. II. Mitchell-Kernan, Claudia.
HQ784.T4T447   305.2'3   81-22795
ISBN 0-12-093220-2   AACR2

To our children,
Gordon, Steven, and Cheryl Berry
and
Claudia and Ryan Kernan

Contents

∃
Sherryl Browne Graves

The Impact of Television on the Cognitive and Affective Development of Minority Children   37

ⅠⅠ

TELEVISION, MINORITY CHILDREN, AND PERSONAL IDENTITY ISSUES

Ⅼ
Jeanne Spurlock

Television, Ethnic Minorities, and Mental Health: An Overview   71

Ⅼ
Ruby Takanishi

The Influence of Television on the Ethnic Identity of Minority Children: A Conceptual Framework   81

Gloria Johnson Powell

TELEVISION, SOCIALIZATION, AND SELECTED CONCERNS ABOUT SPECIFIC MINORITY GROUPS

Molefi K. Asante

Patti Iiyama
Harry H. L. Kitano

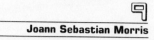
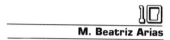
IV

TELEVISION, MINORITY CHILDREN, AND PERSPECTIVES FROM RESEARCH AND PRACTICE

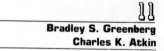

12

George Comstock
Robin E. Cobbey

Television and the Children of Ethnic Minorities:
Perspectives from Research 245

13

Oscar Katz

The Television Industry and Socialization:
A Perspective 261

List of Contributors

Numbers in parentheses indicate the pages on which the authors' contributions begin.

M. Beatriz Arias (203), School of Education, Stanford University, Stanford, California 94305

Molefi K. Asante (135), Department of Speech Communication, State University of New York at Buffalo, Buffalo, New York 14226

Charles K. Atkin (215), Department of Communication, Michigan State University, East Lansing, Michigan 48824

Gordon L. Berry (1), Graduate School of Education, University of California, Los Angeles, Los Angeles, California 90024

Robin E. Cobbey (245), Source Telecomputing Corporation, McLean, Virginia 22101

George Comstock (245), S. I. Newhouse School of Public Communication, Syracuse University, Syracuse, New York 13210

Aimée Dorr (15), Graduate School of Education, University of California, Los Angeles, Los Angeles, California 90024

Sherryl Browne Graves (37), Maracaibo, ZULIA, Venezuela, South America

Bradley S. Greenberg (215), Department of Communication, Michigan State University, East Lansing, Michigan 48824

Patti Iiyama (151), Center for Afro-American Studies, University of California, Los Angeles, Los Angeles, California 90024

Oscar Katz (261), Creative Consultant, Television and Motion Pictures, Beverly Hills, California 90211

Harry H. L. Kitano (151), Departments of Social Welfare and Sociology, University of California, Los Angeles, Los Angeles, California 90024

Claudia Mitchell-Kernan (1), Center for Afro-American Studies and Department of Anthropology, University of California, Los Angeles, Los Angeles, California 90024

Joann Sebastian Morris (187), American Indian Educational Commission, Los Angeles, California 90012

Gloria Johnson Powell (105), Division of Mental Retardation/Child Psychiatry, Department of Psychiatry and Child Psychiatric Outpatient Department, Neuropsychiatric Institute, University of California, Center for the Health Sciences, Los Angeles, California 90024

Jeanne Spurlock (71), American Psychiatric Association, Washington, D.C. 20009

Ruby Takanishi (81), Department of Psychology, Teachers College, Columbia University, New York, New York 10027

Preface

There has been much research conducted, many reports written, and myriad opinions expressed about the influence of television on the socialization of children in our society. Many social observers, while studying the role of this medium in the lives of children growing up during the 1980s, have also offered observations about the unique impact of television on selected minority group children. *Television and the Socialization of the Minority Child* was written to bridge the gap between the vast amount of general literature concerning television and social behavior and the increased attention social scientists are giving to the special issues of minority-group socialization in a television-oriented culture.

In attempting to meet our general goal of relating what is known about television and social behavior to issues and problems in the socialization of the ethnic minority child, we have chosen to focus our attention on Afro-Americans, American Indians, Asian Americans, and Hispanics. The book is intended to advance understanding of television and the socialization of ethnic minority children through three interrelated strategies. First, the contributors have been especially attentive to the problem of developing conceptual frameworks to help clarify the impingement of television on the psychosocial development of minority children. Second, the individual chapters explore and define selected research issues relating to ethnicity as a variable in television's impact on social behavior. Third, and of critical importance, the contributors identify and develop research methodologies that are capable of illuminating how and in what ways television exerts a socializing influence on minority children.

A powerful motivation for the development of this book was the recognition that the viewing of television has a tremendous potential to affect the social, cognitive, and affective learning of children. We are also acutely aware that television's role in the socialization of both nonminority children and minority children is not adequately understood. Although the techniques and processes by which television exerts an influence on child socialization remain imperfectly understood, concern for the ways its effects may be differentially realized or experienced according to viewer characteristics, such as ethnicity, was an important point of departure for this book.

We have met goals established for the book because of the excellent work of the contributors, who brought a multidisciplinary view to the material from such fields as communication, education, linguistics, history, psychiatry, sociology, and the television industry. It was according to these varied perspectives that we organized the volume into four major parts. These parts, although different in focus, are closely interrelated. Part I establishes a basic framework for the rest of the book by focusing on concepts and theories related to television and the socialization process. It provides a conceptual overview of television and its role in the socialization of the minority child, and it identifies broad cognitive and affective developmental issues as areas of special concern in relating the effects of the medium to some of the special needs of minority children. Attention is focused on minority children and personal identity issues in Part II. The chapters in this part examine the influence of television on mental health, identity formation, and self-concept development. In part III, the discussion turns to special socialization concerns television poses for Afro-American, American Indian, Asian American, and Hispanic children. The issues range from minority portrayals to linguistic concerns, and how the medium influences the outlook and values of minority children. Part IV deals with a number of important questions related to the minority child, television, and selected research issues. This concluding section looks at the specific findings of the available literature as a basis for offering projections for important areas of research in the future. Of special importance is the unique perspective it provides from a person who has been an executive in a major network and associated with many aspects of research in the media field.

We feel that this material is important because it attempts to pull together a number of diverse ideas and research notions in order to form a more coherent body of information. The volume is also important because it offers some practical and theoretical issues for consideration to a broad audience of people interested in television and socialization. It is our hope that the book will serve as a resource to stimulate further research and inquiry into the areas of television, ethnicity, and human behavior. Equally important, we trust that the material will be used by students, researchers, teachers, parents, special interest groups, and those professionals involved directly with the media industry. In the final analysis, we feel that the special focus on the minority child in this book may well serve to expand our knowledge concerning the impact of television on all children.

This book grew out of an invitational conference convened by the Center for Afro-American Studies at the University of California, Los Angeles and funded by a grant from the National Institute of Mental Health (1 R13 MH-30164-01). We gratefully acknowledge the support of those two organizations. Our special thanks to CAAS staff members, Anita Martinez for secretarial assistance and Althea Silvera for bibliographic help. We also thank Kay Lyou for her editorial assistance in connection with several of the papers and Juanita Ware who helped to coordinate the conference. We especially express our appreciation to Richard Allen, Carolyn B. Block, Rene Cardenas, James P. Comer, Seymour Feshbach, Roger Fransecky, Neal Gordon, Karen Hill-Scott, Cheryl Metoyer-Duran, Andrea Rich, Morris Rosenberg, and Marilyn F. Solomon who participated in the conference as discussants for the papers presented in this book. Although their papers were not included, their thoughts certainly are part of the total content of this volume.

Television and
the Socialization of
the Minority Child

Gordon L. Berry
Claudia Mitchell-Kernan

Introduction

TELEVISION AS A SOCIALIZING FORCE WITHIN A SOCIETY OF MASS COMMUNICATION

Television as a Communicator

Within a relatively short period of time, television has become a major force in our media-oriented society. It is significant to note, however, that television follows a chain of other print and electronic media associated with communication. Whereas many of the earlier media brought with them their special impact on society, it has been the communicative power and seductive force of television that has generated widespread concern about and interest in its influence on society.

Not only is there a television in almost every American home (U.S. Commission on Civil Rights, 1977), according to Gerbner and Signorielli (1979) television is in the average home over 6 hr a day and "presents a window to a world in which the typical viewer lives and learns more than 30 hours a week [p. 1]." Both the number of television sets and the hours of usage are increasing, and there is some indication that audiences are turning to television as a major source of validating

1

TELEVISION AND
THE SOCIALIZATION OF THE MINORITY CHILD

information and perhaps even beliefs and values. It is therefore not surprising that social observers, especially those concerned with the development of children, have turned their attention to examining the role of television within the broad context of the socialization process in our society.

One must study television within the framework of communication because its attributes are part of that process. Communication, narrowly viewed, is the art of transmitting information, ideas, and attitudes from one person to another (Emery, Ault, & Agee, 1974). Hiebert, Ungurait, and Bohn (1974) see communication as a part of a process with a series of actions that are always in motion; it is not a static entity fixed in time and space, but a dynamic process used to transfer meaning, transmit social values, and share experiences (p. 6).

In a society that relies increasingly on mass media for communicating, television has assumed increasing importance in the transmission of meaning, ideas, information, and values and its impact on the socialization process cannot be ignored. By *socialization* we mean the processes by which children learn and internalize the ways of their society (Havighurst & Neugarten 1962). It is, in addition, those processes by which members of the society acquire certain modes of thinking and behavior through social influences. Significantly, through its potential to transmit the values of the culture, television becomes a meaningful agent in the socialization of the child alongside the family, the school, religious institutions, the peer group, and other community-based institutions. Paraphrasing Nicholas Johnson (1977), television is more than a casual communicator, it is the greatest communications mechanism ever designed by man; it provides us with an unending stream of information, opinion, aesthetic taste and moral values. These multiple roles of television within the communications system place the medium within the dynamics of the socialization process and offer profound implications for research and pragmatic actions concerning its effects.

Television as a Socializer

The complexity of what is being communicated by an "unending stream" of attitudes, messages, and value transmissions presented on television was certainly at the core of the push to study this medium and its effects on children. Initially, the direction of much of the attention came from the federal government. During the early period of the 1970s the concern was with the medium's power to influence aggressive behavior and the impact on viewers of large cumulative levels of violence.

The relationship between the exposure to violent programming and subsequent aggressive behavior remains an important issue of great controversy. It is clear, however, that the issues of television's impact on American society and social life go beyond this important issue of violence. There is the need to consider other aspects of the medium's messages, especially those factors that relate to the socialization functions of television broadly conceived; including its impact on identity formation, self-esteem, cognitive development, moral development, and cultural awareness.

Individual behaviors and attitudes do not develop as discrete entities but are integrated into an holistic developmental pattern. It is likely that one cannot separate aggresive patterns of behavior from self-esteem and other psychological characteristics of the individual as if these learned behaviors developed discretely within the psycho-social development of an individual. We know from the principles of child development that the behavior and attitudes of children reflect patterns of early environmental experiences and exposure. Surveys of viewing patterns of children, including the age at which television viewing begins, alert us further to the potential socialization functions of television. Comstock (1975), synthesizing the findings of a number of studies, points out that:

1. Children typically begin viewing television regularly 3 or 4 years before entering the first grade.
2. Most children watch some television every day, and most watch 2 hr or more per day.

The statistics on the television viewing patterns of children have stimulated much interest in groups other than those traditionally concerned with socialization issues and child development. Even the medical profession is beginning to become interested in exploring the influences of television on the child. Dr. Thomas Elmendory, past-President of the California Medical Association, stated, "The medical profession is now deeply concerned about the effects of television on the young today [Los Angeles Times, 1976]." The challenge to learn and understand the power of this medium as a socializer is now conceived of as a multidisciplinary endeavor.

A conception of television as a socializer of children is not without precedent. Regarding the question of television's impact on children's outlook and values, Himmelweit, Oppenheim, and Vince (1966), in an early study conducted in England, undertook to examine the circumstances under which such impact might occur. Their research suggested that several principles can be formulated regarding the conditions under which television will have maximal effect on the child's values:

1. If the values or views recur from program to program
2. If the values are presented in dramatic form so that they evoke primarily emotional reactions
3. If they link with the child's immediate needs and interests
4. If through friends, parents, or immediate environment the viewer is not already supplied with a set of values which would provide a standard against which to assess the views offered by television

Leifer, Gordon, and Graves (1974) suggest that children change their attitudes about people and activities to reflect those encountered in television programs. They concluded that television is not only an entertainer of children, it is also an important socializer of them.

When a medium such as television has the power to transmit and reflect the values of an individual's sociocultural environment and when, as Leifer *et al.* suggest, it serves as a normative reference point, it assumes some of the characteristics of an agent of socialization. If the premise that television has some of these characteristics is accepted, it becomes crucial to examine television's impact on the hearts and minds of those who are subjected to its influences.

Television and Ethnicity

Few people would deny that it is important to study television in terms of its influence on all children. Some studies suggest, however, that there is a special need to learn more about the special effects of the medium on some minority and low-income children. Such children appear to watch more television than higher socioeconomic level children, and this seems especially true of black low-income children. Since many minority children are overrepresented in the lower socioeconomic groups, the findings may apply to minority groups other than blacks. However, even if children from American Indian, Asian-American, Afro-American, and Hispanic groups vary in their level of television viewing, the history of the portrayals and accuracy of the presentation of their cultures through all the media raises other profound psychosocial issues concerning what they are learning from the values transmitted by a medium such as television.

Alvin Poussaint (1974) studied some of the special power of television in terms of what minority children might learn about themselves and their families. In considering one aspect of its socializing influence, he observed that television offers a potential challenge to the guidance of the home environment, which may be particularly acute in the case of some minority children because their sense of self is affected by how they view their environment both through direct involvement and through television, newspapers, or other media presentations. In addition, psychologists studying child development have long recognized that modeling behavior for all children can include selected visual cues and images such as those offered on television. The modeling potential of television can be especially important for minority children who grow up in a society that does not always know how to practice its professed racial equality. Television's ability to transmit cues that may or may not reflect the values best able to aid minority children in a wholesome pattern of growth and development should therefore not be minimized. It is important, therefore, to explore medium's special influences on minority children and its impact on any culturally special aspects of their lives.

It is clear that television plays a major and as yet poorly understood role as an agent of socialization for minority and all American children. Television viewing provides a setting with tremendous potential for social and cognitive, or substantive learning. It may prove useful, therefore, to develop conceptual frameworks that provide a place for television as an agent of socialization among other agents, such as the family, the school, and the peer group who are traditionally given recognition in terms of their effects on psychosocial development.

The focus on ethnicity in the book is theoretically and methodologically motivated. We are on the threshold of understanding the techniques and processes by which television functions as a socializing agent. Attention to the ways in which television's effects may be differentially realized according to viewer characteristics such as ethnicity provides one avenue to clarify the means by which it impinges on the psychosocial development of children.

In spite of the uniformity of television's message to its audiences, there are research findings that suggest that its impact may not be uniform on viewers. Concern regarding the differential impact of television on children with different characteristics is aroused, first of all, by research findings indicating that some children view television considerably more than others: for example, the Comstock (1975) finding that television viewing is greater for young persons who are black, are from families of lower socioeconomic status, and are lower in academic achievement and measured IQ. Research findings such as those of Greenberg and Dominick (1969) and Gerson (1966), which suggest that some minority and low-income children may be especially susceptible to the socializing influences of television offer an equally compelling reason for the focus on ethnicity.

TOWARD A CONCEPTUAL FOCUS FOR THE STUDY OF TELEVISION, SOCIALIZATION, AND ETHNICITY

There are additional conceptual and theoretical reasons for considering ethnicity as a variable in television's socializing influence. The ethnic groups that are the specific focus of this book, American Indians, Asian Americans, Afro-Americans, and Hispanics occupy a special status within our societal system of stratification. These groups have historically been targets of prejudice and discrimination to a far greater extent than America's more privileged and assimilated ethnic groups. Members of these groups have not been able to enjoy access to the rewards of our society on an equal footing with other Americans and have been the victims of both institutionalized and informal practices of social, political, and economic domination. This special status often entails orientations that may dispose members of these groups to perceive, conceptualize, and evaluate experiences in ways that are different from the way majority group members treat the same experiences. Members of minority groups, for example, frequently express dissatisfaction with the image of their group that is presented on television. For at least some members of minority groups, stereotypic television portrayals present yet another instance of how ethnic minorities are ill-treated by majority group members, who are viewed as primarily responsible for the images presented. It should be noted that the perpetuation of stereotypes is a concern of most of the contributors to this volume and a special focus of a number of the papers. Similarly, the lack of visibility of some ethnic groups on television is likely to be highly salient for members of those groups and much less so for majority group members.

There are yet other reasons for viewing ethnicity as a significant variable in the socializing functions of television. Not only do the ethnic groups we mentioned occupy a special niche within American social structure, they are each, to some extent, culturally distinctive as well.

It is not our view that ethnic categories bind culturally homogeneous groups. In a highly complex society such as our own, there are many assimilative forces that reduce the degree to which any formerly distinct ethnic group maintains its distinctive cultural characteristics. Nevertheless, each of these groups is characterized by a number of distinctive cultural characteristics that differentiate it from other segments of the society. Each group is characterized by its own special institutional profile, which may include differences in language, religious practices, values, recreational patterns, as well as patterns of family life.

One problem in identifying television as a probable cause of some behavior or attitude is that television exerts its influence as a socializing agent simultaneously with other agents of socialization, such as the family, the school, and the peer group. If television viewing is regarded as a significant setting in which learning, broadly speaking, takes place, its effects must be assessed in terms of the way its influence combines and interacts with that of the more traditional agents of socialization that are demonstrably culturally organized and known to vary in significant ways across ethnic groups.

Unlike the experiences provided by the family, the school, and the peer group, the set of experiences provided by television is uniform for all viewers, with, of course, viewing patterns mediating the degree to which different individuals and groups are provided with a common set of experiences. In spite of this, there are compelling reasons not to expect television's impact to be uniform on all children: This is precisely because it is only one of a number of significant socialization experiences that may differ across ethnic groups.

Given diversity in the broader socialization context, it is not unreasonable to assume that different socialization experiences will produce different patterns of receptivity to the socialization potential of television. In short, although the message may be the same, its meaning may be very different according to the characteristics of the viewer. It is our view that ethnicity may be a significant viewer characteristic and may channel the way in which messages transmitted by the media are perceived, conceptualized, and evaluated.

It is important to emphasize that "American Indian," "Asian American," "Afro-American," and "Hispanic" are labels that circumscribe large population aggregates within which there is a tremendous amount of internal sociocultural variation. Notwithstanding, we regard culture as a useful rubric within which to consider a complex array of behavioral, attitudinal, and valuational characteristics that serve to differentiate each of the groups above from other societal segments.

Although children in our society acquire a good deal of shared culture, the distinctive sociocultural patterns of major ethnic groups form a background for the acquisition of different sets of attitudes and beliefs, values, standards of conduct, and perhaps even, strategies for learning (cf. Cole, Gay, Glick, and Sharp, 1971).

In sum, the social histories of Afro-American, Hispanic, American Indian, and Asian-American children depart from those of other segments of the society. Each of these groups exposes its children to different patterns of behavior and of reinforcement and, perhaps, to different opportunities for learning and discovery. It is not that ethnic identity strictly determines the learning experiences of children, but rather that ethnic identity is associated with patterns of experience that exhibit significant common denominators from the perspective of socialization. These shape the manner in which the socialization potential of television is realized.

Specific Considerations

There are probably many areas of psychosocial development in which the socialization functions of television may be differently realized according to ethnicity. The areas of cognitive development, language development, moral development, identity formation, and self-concept suggest themselves, for a number of reasons, as targets for investigation.

For example, within the institutional profile of each of the ethnic groups under consideration, linguistic differences loom large as an area of contrast with the dominant group. In the case of American Indians, Asian Americans, and Hispanics bilingualism is a major characteristic of the language portfolio of the group. In the case of blacks, dialect differences and bidialectism are equally distinctive features of the linguistic repertoire of their communities.

Significant segments of the American Indian, Asian-American and black populations exhibit degrees of mastery of Standard English that fall short of the level of competency required by many mainstream institutions. The mass media may be a significant avenue of exposure to Standard English for children of these groups. From the perspective of the reward structure of our society, Standard English is the socially dominant and prestigious linguistic code. The presentation of dialect differences in situations likely to invite invidious comparisons has the potential to shape the values and attitudes of children toward the language variety spoken in their communities.

In the area of identity formation, many studies suggest that ethnicity is a significant correlate to the child's acquisition of a healthy self-concept (Guggenheim, 1969; Long & Henderson, 1968; Williams & Byars, 1968). To the extent that television influences children's ideas about their groups, it probably figures as part of the environmental feedback that shapes their views of themselves. Although some studies (Banks & Grambs) appear to reverse earlier findings regarding the connection between ethnicity and self-esteem, in the past it appeared that black children incorporated many of the societally prevalent attitudes toward their ethnic group. This in turn seemed to produce feelings of inferiority and low self-esteem and even unrealistic perceptions of their own physical characteristics (Clark & Clark, 1947). Although the mass media today accords ethnic groups more respect than formerly, television is probably a source of environmental feedback regarding the place of one's group in the social structure. It also no doubt serves as a means by which minority children learn the societally prevailing attitudes toward their ethnic group.

It is not possible to know in advance precisely how television may differentially affect human development within and across ethnic groups. Our purpose in preparing a book on television and ethnicity is to bring together the work of a group of scholars whose research in child development and television and social behavior holds promise for improving our understanding of this important topic.

Although the approaches of the contributing authors differ, a number of recurring questions provide unifying themes for the chapters in this volume. What is the role of television in shaping the values, beliefs, attitudes, and actions of minority children? What information is given through television that might influence children's feelings, attitudes, and behavior toward their ethnic group and the broader community? What role, subtle or overt, does television play in shaping the social behavior of minority children? What role does television play in shaping children's views of themselves. How and in what ways does television convey to children majority group attitudes toward their ethnic group? What is the importance of television in the lives of minority groups? What are television's strengths, weaknesses, and values to ethnic minorities? What improvements can or should be made regarding the medium's treatment of minorities?

The contributors to this volume discuss a variety of conceptual and methodological problems involved in identifying television as a cause of children's behavior or as a source of their beliefs, values, and attitudes. Clear-cut answers to the questions posed are therefore rare. Not surprisingly, concern with issues of conceptualization and measurement are also a prominent feature of this book.

While television's positive contributions to children's learning receive attention, there is apparent throughout the book an obvious sense of uneasiness about what the literature suggests may be the special vulnerability of some low-income and minority children to television's messages and images that may impact negatively on their psychosocial development.

The social and behavioral scientists who have contributed to the book display acute awareness of the distance that must be traveled before definitive answers can be supplied for a number of the suggested linkages between television and social behavior. The evaluation of research findings and careful thinking reflected in this book should serve, however, to heighten awareness of relationships that may exist between what children are exposed to via television and what they learn and believe.

REFERENCES

Banks, J.A. & Grambs, J.D. Black self-concept implications for education and the social science (Eds.), New York: McGraw-Hill, 1972.

Clark, K.B., & Clark, M.P. Racial identification and preferences in Negro children. In T.M. Newcomb & E.L. Hartley (Eds.), Readings in social psychology. New York: Holt, 1947.

Cole, M., Gay, J., Glick, J., & Sharp, D.W. The cultural context of learning and thinking. New York: Basic Books, 1971.

Comstock, G.A. Television and human behavior: The key studies. Santa Monica, California: Rand Corporation, 1975.

Emery, E., Ault, P.H., & Agee, W.K. Introduction to mass communications. New York: Dodd, Mead, 1974.

Gerbner, G., & Signorielli, N. Women and minorities in television drama, 1969–1978. Philadelphia: University of Pennsylvania, Annenberg School of Communications, 1979.

Gerson, W. Mass media socialization behavior: Negro–white differences. Social Forces, 1966, 45, 40–50.

Greenberg, B., & Dominick, J. Racial and social class differences in teenagers' use of television. Journal of Broadcasting, 1969, 13, 3331–3344.

Guggenheim, F. Self-esteem and achievement expectations for White and Negro children. Journal of Projective Techniques and Personality, 1969, 33, 63–71.

Havighurst, R.J., & Neugarten, B.L. Society and education. Boston, Massachusetts: Allyn & Bacon, 1962.

Himmelweit, H.T., Oppenheim, A.N., & Vince, P. Television and the child: An empirical study of the effects of television on the young. London: Oxford Univ. Press, 1966.

Hiebert, R.E., Ungurait, D.F., & Bohn, T.W. Mass media: An introduction to modern communication. New York: David McCay, 1974.

Hearing on Television violence open. Los Angeles Times, Part I, August 18, 1976, pp. 3; 26.

Johnson, N. What can we do about television? In M.C. Emery & T.C. Smythe (Eds.), *Readings in mass communication, concepts, and issues in mass media.* Dubuque, Iowa: W.C. Brown, 1977.

Leifer, A.D., Gordon, N.J., & Graves, S.B. Children's television: More than mere entertainment. *Harvard Educational Review*, 1974, 44(2), 213–245.

Long, B.H., & Henderson, C.H. Self-social concepts of disadvantaged beginners. *Journal of Genetic Psychology*, 1968, 113, 41–52.

Poussaint, A.F. Building a strong self-image in the black child. *Ebony*, August 1974, pp. 138–143.

U.S. Commission on Civil Rights. *Window dressing on the set: Women and minorities in television.* Washington, D.C.: U.S. Govt. Printing Office, 1977.

Williams, R.L., & Byars, H. Negro self-esteem in a transitional society: Tennessee self-concept scale. *Personnel and Guidance Journal*, 1968, 47, 120–125.

TELEVISION AND ITS
SOCIALIZING INFLUENCES ON
MINORITY CHILDREN

Aimée Dorr

Television and the Socialization of the Minority Child

I must at the outset expose my discomfort in considering the role of television in the socialization of American minority children. Recognizing that all minority groups are not the same and all individuals in a group are not the same, I still assert that minority status in our society is likely to include some experiences that a relatively well-protected white, such as I, can only dimly imagine or understand. This is not to suggest that understanding can come *only* from the members of an ethnic group. There are obviously many commonalities across groups; moreover, an "outsider's" perspective is sometimes enlightening. Nonetheless, understanding of the values, functions, dynamics, and place of any group must be at least partially derived from the insights and work of members of that group. For these reasons I am glad that this chapter stands as one of many, most from scholars who belong to American minority groups.

I have somewhat delimited the three broad constructs—television, socialization, and minority children—with which this chapter deals. *Television* refers almost exclusively to entertainment programs, the commercials accompanying them, and the few bi- or multi-cultural series designed to teach and/or alter attitudes and behaviors. This omits

15

such programming as news, documentaries, and public affairs, which—although they too surely can socialize—is infrequently viewed by children. *Minority* refers to American "peoples of color." Although minorities are represented in all segments of society, compared to the white majority they will, on the average, be poorer, less well educated, less powerful, of lower status, (sub)culturally different, and physically differentiable. *Socialization* refers to the learning of information, cognitive processes, values, attitudes, social roles, self-concepts, and behaviors that are generally accepted—or expected—within one or many segments of American society (Berger & Luckmann, 1967). Even with these limitations, my perspective is rather broad. Other chapters are more specific in the kinds of television, minority groups, and socialization considered.

In my expansive sweep, I will seek to make a distinction between *process*, the rules or procedures by which one chooses what to watch, understands it, or learns from it, and *outcome*, the result of the application of these rules or procedures. Since processes can only be applied to available programming, I will broadly review its characteristics and speculate on what their consequences may be for minority children. I will then become even more expansive in order to consider the interactive influences of television and other socialization agencies and the interactive nature of majority–minority group relations. All of this is preceded by a section on the limitations of existing research, limitations that allow one to speculate but not to become much of an authority.

LIMITATIONS OF EXISTING RESEARCH

Although the amount of research on television and socialization has burgeoned (Murray, 1980), there is still little that concerns itself with American minority children. Comstock's (1975) 450-study annotated bibliography listed only about 55 that included minorities. Of these, roughly 30 focused on children. Adding more recent work still does not permit us to say much authoritatively about television's role in socializing minority children.

We can be encouraged that more work is being done now, but we must still be concerned that much of it is conceived and directed by whites. I have already stated that "outsiders" may provide valuable perspectives on another group. Without negating this, I want to describe two potential dangers. One is that whites may interpret results using whites and all they stand for as the desirable norm.[1] To the extent that white and minority cultures differ, such interpretation may be denigrating to the minority group. An anecdote from my house-hunting days is illustrative. One foray took us to an attractive neighborhood which was fully integrated. The realtor commented that this caused problems because the Asian Americans studied *too much*, thereby making it unreasonably difficult for white children. This is not the usual complaint one hears from whites encountering school de-segregation, but it once again assumes "white is right."

A second potential danger—one that is more difficult to spot in re-search reports—is that whites may select issues, designs, stimuli, mea-sures, or subjects in ways that produce results to the disadvantage of minorities vis-à-vis whites. Three brief examples should illustrate the point. The first is an interview that I developed with a black female and a white male colleague. It elicited good information from whites and blacks, but not from Puerto Ricans, despite our use of well-trained bilingual Puerto Rican interviewers. We all agreed Puerto Ricans could think and talk about the issues being studied, so our interview must have been inappropriate in its approach. A second example is con-sumer education curricula designed by the Urban League for low-income citizens, especially minorities, city dwellers, and youth. In con-trast to many such efforts, they were demonstrably successful (Martin, 1977), probably because the designers knew the audience well. A third example is the report that black children derived significantly fewer messages from an episode of *Fat Albert* than did white children (CBS, 1974). The conclusion was based on a contrast of both lower- and middle-class black children with middle-class white children. If, how-ever, one uses the published data tables to examine ethnic differences within social class (only possible for middle-class children), one finds that black and white children performed similarly.

A third limitation of existing research is that it has focused primarily on blacks, at present the most numerous minority group. Obviously, they cannot stand for all others. Moreover, black samples and all other minority samples are more likely than white samples to be lower in social class, with all that implies about education, occupation, income, and residence. Although it is self-evident, it is probably worth saying that ethnicity and social class are not equivalent. There are circum-

[1]These potential dangers occur whenever one group, however designated, studies another. For simplicity, and because it is the most common pertinent occurence for this chapter, I have limited my discussion to whites studying minorities. Such a limitation should not imply to the reader that I believe only whites are subject to these failings.

stances under which it would be appropriate to describe broad ethnic differences, sweeping social class into them, but for most research questions it is better to look at the separate contributions of class and ethnicity. Similarly, it would be appropriate in at least some cases to separate ethnic groups by place of origin (e.g., "Cubans," "Puerto Ricans," "Chicanos," and "Latin Americans" rather than the all-encompassing "Hispanics"), by current geographical area of residence (e.g., Chicanos from Texas, California, and Chicago), and by urban, suburban, and rural residence.

A fourth limitation of existing research is the preponderance of correlational rather than true or quasi-experimental designs. Both have merit in studying an issue, and some issues are better studied by one approach than another. Still, delineating the processes by which television programs are chosen, understood, and effective requires experimental work to demonstrate causation and correlational work to demonstrate existence in the real world. To date, we have too much of the latter and too little of the former.

The fifth and final limitation, which to some extent may be a cause of the fourth, is in the issues studied thus far. The lion's share has been about program content, viewing patterns, and content preferences. There are only a few studies of the processes by which television does or does not socialize minority children, of the effects of the programming children watch, of the effects of entertainment programming, and of the effects of giving time to watching television rather than to other leisure activities.

These limitations of the existing research present obvious possibilities for future research. It is to be hoped that this volume will be a rich stimulus to such activity. In the meantime, the limitations leave me cautious in assessing our understanding of the role of television in socializing minority children.

PROCESS AND OUTCOME

Socialization is a process. It is the set of paradigms, rules, procedures, principles, or whatever that govern perception, attention, choices, learning, development, and the like. It has an outcome or a series of outcomes. It produces someone with a taste for high culture or popular culture, someone who speaks colloquial Spanish and academic English, someone who chooses a Volkswagen over a Mercedes. Outcomes are obvious and interesting. They often allow the inference of process. I place most importance on such elucidation of process, since it provides the basic understanding necessary to make predictions or to take action in any particular situation.

Evidence about Processes

The process for which there is evidence over the largest number of minority groups is that of learning cognitive or social material or having one's behavior influenced simply by watching televised material; that is, *observational learning.* There is evidence that this process occurs among American Indians, blacks, Cambodians, Chicanos, Chinese Americans, Chinese Vietnamese, Cubans, Japanese, Lao Hmongs, Puerto Ricans, Vietnamese, and whites (Ball & Bogatz, 1970, 1973; Ball, Bogatz, Kazarow, & Rubin, 1974; Drabman & Thomas, 1977; Henderson & Swanson, 1977; Henderson, Zimmerman, Swanson, & Bergan, 1974; Johnston, Ettema, & Davidson, 1980; LaRose, 1980; Mays, Henderson, Seidman, & Steiner, 1975; Nelson & Napior, 1976; Shapiro, 1975; Williams & Van Wart, 1974) and no evidence that it differs in any substantial way, as a process, among these groups.

For example, black, Hispanic, and white children all learned cognitive material from watching *Sesame Street,* learned more when they watched more, and learned more of what the series emphasized (Ball & Bogatz, 1970; Bogatz & Ball, 1971). American Indian children of the Papago tribe learned to perform Piagetian-type tasks from watching televised lessons (Henderson *et al.,* 1974; Henderson & Swanson, 1977). In a different vein, aggressive episodes on television or videotape stimulated aggressive behavior in black children (Drabman & Thomas, 1977) in much the same way they did for white children (cf. Leifer, Gordon, & Graves, 1974; Liebert, Neale, & Davidson, 1973). Thus, observational learning is the one process for which there is evidence from a number of different minority groups.

The ways in which the characteristics of a visual display direct a child's attention to a particular part of the screen also seem to be similar among the ethnically mixed groups that have been studied. That is, we find that all members of an ethnically mixed group of children are more likely to look at people than at objects, at larger images, at movement, at the center of the screen, and so on (Flagg, Fenton, & Grady, 1978; Flagg, Housen, & Lesser, 1978). The suggestion here is that the basic perceptual processes that determine attention operate similarly for children from different ethnic groups.

The third process that may be the same for all children is that their prior understanding of or experience with a given topic influences their understanding when the topic is presented on television. We have relatively clear evidence for this with black and white children (Flagg, Housen, & Lesser, 1978; Newcomb & Collins, 1977) and American Indian children (Nelson & Napior, 1976) and indications of this for two Asian-American groups, blacks, three Hispanic groups, American Indians, and whites (Nelson & Napior, 1976). For example, when children are in the early grades of elementary school they seem to understand better a television program that portrays a family from the same social class as the child viewer rather than one portraying a family from a different social class (Newcomb & Collins, 1977).

A fourth process for which there is evidence of cross-ethnic similarity is that of choosing television programs to watch. Both black and white children seem to prefer programs with more rather than less action and/or humor and with main characters similar to themselves (Atkin, Greenberg, & McDermott, n.d.; Fletcher, 1969; Greenberg & Atkin, 1978; Lyle & Hoffman, 1972b; Murray, 1972). At the same time, the television diets of both groups do not evidence substantial selectivity in choosing from the menu television makes available to them. In some ways they are watching television rather than programs (Greenberg & Atkin, 1978; Lyle & Hoffman, 1972a, 1972b).

Just as children seem to prefer programs with main characters similar to themselves, they also tend to pay more attention to these characters and/or to choose them as models—at least, we have evidence that black (Atkin, Greenberg, & McDermott, 1979; Lyle & Hoffman, 1972b; Nelson & Napior, 1976) and Hispanic (Nelson & Napior, 1976) children do. Choices of models are especially complicated for minority and female children because all children like to choose as models those they consider powerful, successful, and/or in command of resources (cf. Bandura, 1969) as well as demographically similar to themselves. It is a fact of society and of television that minorities and women are less likely than white males to be powerful and successful (cf. U.S. Commission on Civil Rights, 1977, 1979). Thus, making a choice is generally easier for a white male child than it is for any other child, but in all cases the preferences that guide selection are similar.

Finally, television viewers, whatever their ethnicity, may be more accepting of material that conforms to their values, attitudes, and needs than of material that does not. For example, authoritarian viewers of whatever ethnicity are more likely to like, feel sympathetic toward, and agree with Archie Bunker than are nonauthoritarian viewers, whatever their ethnicity (Brigham & Giesbrecht, 1976; Surlin & Tate, 1976; Vidmar & Rokeach, 1974). In this case, personality traits of viewers that cut across ethnic lines are more important determinants of responses to the characters than is ethnicity per se.

Thus, our available evidence—although I must emphasize that it is scant—suggests that the processes by which television programs are chosen, relevant information is identified, and learning (or performance) occurs are similar for all children. We need to explore these processes with more minority children, especially those other than blacks. My choice for research issues to emphasize would be those of model selection and of interactions between what children bring to the set and what the set "gives" to them. Both seem to me to have the greatest potential relevance in explicating the role of television in socializing American minority children.

Evidence about Outcomes

Whereas the processes by which children choose television and are affected (or not) by it may be similar for all children—and I emphasize that we do not really know this—the outcomes may differ. In fact, in some cases we have been able to infer the existence of a process precisely because outcomes are different. Despite the facts that outcome differences may demonstrate process and that known processes may be used to predict outcomes, the existing studies of process and outcome cannot always be related to each other. Only two of the outcome differences relevant to this chapter can be easily related to process.

The first of these is that black children watch more programming with black characters than do white children. Direct support for this comes from Atkin et al. (1979), Fletcher (1969), and Greenberg (1972), who each analyzed children's reports of the television programs they actually watched, and from CBS (1974), which analyzed children's reports of the frequency with which they watched *Fat Albert.* Support may also be inferred from other studies that contrast black and white viewing frequencies for different types of programs when it is known that black characters are especially common in one or another program type (Fletcher, 1969; Greenberg & Dominick, 1969). The obtained or inferred differences in frequency of viewing programs with black characters are predictable from knowing that children generally like to watch programming with characters similar to themselves and from assuming that ethnicity is a relevant dimension for determining similarity. Presumably, similar differences would be found for other minority groups if there was relevant programming available for them to watch.

Just as differences in viewing frequency can be predicted and found, so too can differences in stated program, character, and role model preferences. Program and character preferences have been demonstrated with black, Chicano, Indochinese, and white children, each of whom is more likely to list as favorites main characters of the same ethnicity or programs featuring such characters (CBS, 1974; Eastman & Liss, 1978; LaRose, 1980; Lyle & Hoffman, 1972a, 1972b). They may also be inferred from reported program-type preferences (Lyle & Hoffman, 1972a, 1972b; Surlin & Dominick, 1970). Preferences are not totally redundant with viewing patterns (Goodhardt, Ehrenberg, & Collins, 1975; Seagoe, 1951), so preference data adds evidence for the importance of ethnic similarity. So, too, do data on role model preferences in which blacks are more likely to choose to be like black characters than are whites (Atkin et al., 1979).

The remaining outcomes cannot yet be linked to processes. The first outcome is that minority children on the average spend more time watching television than do white children. This has been demonstrated with data for blacks (Greenberg & Dervin, 1972; Greenberg & Dominick, 1969; Lyle & Hoffman, 1972a, 1972b) and Chicanos (Lyle & Hoffman, 1972a, 1972b). The second is that minority children seem to ascribe more reality or credibility to television portrayals than do white children of the same age. Such differences have been reported for both black and Chicano children and adolescents (Atkin et al., 1979; Greenberg & Dervin, 1972; Greenberg & Dominick, 1969; Lyle & Hoffman, 1972a). It should be noted, however, that differences seem to diminish or disappear as children mature and that the way questions are asked seems to influence responses. In at least one study (Lyle & Hoffman, 1972a), tenth-grade Chicano girls from blue-collar families were considerably more skeptical of television's reality than were tenth-grade white girls from blue- or white-collar families; in our own work (Leifer, 1976) black adults ascribed less credibility to television portrayals than did whites.

Many of these ethnic differences are predictable from knowledge of the processes by which children select, interpret, and are affected by television. The rest might be predictable if we had knowledge of the relevant processes. Most, if not all, depend at least partially on the programming available. How can children show that they prefer to watch characters of the same ethnicity if there are at most two or three programs featuring them? How can white children show that they will choose black role models if black characters are rarely portrayed as competent, successful, and powerful? Knowing what is available and what the selection, attention, learning, and performance processes are for children with television would allow us to predict some of television's effects and to test for them. Lacking the research, we can make some interesting speculations. To do so, we need to describe the programming most minority children watch most of the time.

CHARACTERISTICS OF
TELEVISION CONTENT

This description of what "average" minority child viewers see on television must be considered a rough approximation at best. As are all content analyses, it is out of date. Still, the fare does not appear to change enough from year to year to make this a serious fault (Gerbner, Gross, Jackson-Beeck, Jeffries-Fox, & Signorielli, 1978; Greenberg, in press; Greenberg & Atkin, 1978; Lemon, 1977; U.S. Commission on Civil Rights, 1979). A potentially more serious problem is that the studies on which the description is based were done by adult content analysts who were mostly white and who sampled programs that do not conform to those in a child's diet.

We know that children of different ages see television programs differently (Collins, in press; Collins, Berndt, & Hess, 1974; Collins & Westby, 1975; Flapan, 1968; Leifer, Collins, Gross, Taylor, Andrews, & Blackmer, 1971; Noble, 1975), and there is reason to believe that minority and majority viewers also see things differently (contrast the analyses by Gerbner et al., 1978; Lemon, 1977; and Turow, 1974; with those by Pierce, 1980; and Rainville & McCormick, 1977). We also know that children's viewing patterns differ from adults and, within childhood, by age, sex, and ethnicity (e.g., Lyle & Hoffman, 1972a, 1972b). It is plausible to attribute these somewhat different viewing patterns to differences in program content and children's content preferences. For instance, younger children watch proportionally more cartoons because they are more attracted to action and change than to plot (more likely in cartoons than prime time); girls watch proportionally more family comedy because they prefer to see females as main characters (more likely in family comedy than action/adventure); and blacks watch proportionally more situation comedies because they prefer to see blacks as main characters (more likely in sitcoms than crime dramas). I have tried to adjust my description of television content to reflect such variations in minority children's viewing patterns; however, it still may not conform to what a minority child would see.

Numbers, Personalities, and
Roles on Television

Minorities are rarely part of television's social order. For example, an analysis of 1971 Saturday morning network programming revealed that 61% of all characters were white, 30% were not ethnically identifiable, and 9% belonged to minorities (Mendelson & Young, 1972). A similar analysis of 1974 programming revealed that of those with identifiable ethnicity, 82% were white and 18% belonged to minorities (Harvey, Poulos, & Liebert, 1975). Gerbner et al.'s (1978) analysis of 1977 prime time and weekend morning offerings revealed that, of those with identifiable ethnicity, 88% were white and 12% belonged to minorities. Similar figures for the 1975, 1976, and 1977 seasons have been reported by Greenberg, Simmons, Hogan, and Atkin (1979) and Greenberg (1980).

When minorities have been separated out by ethnicity, the majority have been black; they represented 78% of all minorities in Mendelson and Young (1972), 50% in Harvey et al. (1975), and 64–71% in Greenberg et al. (1979). This and the preceding data suggest that blacks may now be represented on television in numbers roughly proportional to their representation in the American population, although other American minority groups are still not well represented. However, an analysis of the programs and roles in which minority characters are likely to appear makes their presentation seem less equitable than one might conclude from the overall numbers.

Minority characters, really blacks, are most likely to appear in programming that is either almost or totally filled with minority characters (Fernandez-Collado, Greenberg, & Atkin, 1979). They are most common in situation comedies, with about 60% of all prime-time series black characters appearing there (re-analysis of data from Greenberg et al., 1978). Action/adventure and crime-drama series are unlikely to have a cast made up primarily of minorities, although a few have had a black lead (e.g., *Christie Love, Tenafly, Shaft,* and *Paris*). When minority characters appear in programming other than a black series, they are likely to be few in number and to play minor rather than major roles. For example, another re-analysis of the Greenberg et al. (1978) data shows that of all black characters on 1977 prime-time and Saturday-morning series, only 39% are major characters; by comparison, 50% of *all* characters (including blacks) are major characters.

Thus, the television world for all children is predominantly filled with whites. Other analyses show that major characters are also most likely to be males, between the ages of 18 and 50, who operate in largely white, middle-class settings (Gerbner & Gross, 1980; Gerbner et al., 1978; Greenberg et al., 1978; U.S. Commission on Civil Rights, 1977, 1979). The only minorities who play any obvious role in television's world are black. Their presence has certainly increased in the past decade (U.S. Commission on Civil Rights, 1977, 1979), but in certain environments and not in others.

Just as minority representation on television has changed in the past decade, so too have the personality characteristics depicted. In the past, minorities—again, mostly blacks—were likely to be portrayed according to the negative stereotype as violent, victimized, incompetent, stupid, lazy, servile, humorous and the like (see U.S. Commission on Civil Rights, 1977, for a good summary of early studies). More recently, the portrayals are more positive (U.S. Commission on Civil Rights, 1977, 1979). Mendelson and Young (1972) found black characters endowed only with positive personality characteristics and white characters with both positive and negative characteristics. An analysis of nine series broadcast in mid-1974 (each having characters representing at least three of four demographic groups: black females, black males, white females, and white males) showed that blacks more than whites made reparations for bad behavior, resisted temptation, delayed gratification or persisted in tasks, and explained their feelings; they acted aggressively and altruistically less than whites did (Donagher, Poulos, Liebert, & Davidson, 1975). These and other studies show generally more positive personality characteristics for blacks than whites in recent seasons of television. It should, however, be noted that black characters are not uniformly "better," that there is a wide range of personality characteristics shown when all black characters are considered, and that minority portrayals still receive severe criticism.

It is important to note that portrayals of blacks and, probably, other minorities have not changed much in one significant area—their power in relationship to whites. Power relationships were once clear: Black characters had negative personality characteristics and almost uniformly subservient roles. Now we confine portrayals of black dominance largely to black series (Lemon, 1977). In interaction with whites, blacks are less dominant (Lemon, 1977) and black "leaders" have white co-leaders (Mendelson & Young, 1972); minority characters are more likely to be victimized and less likely to be killers (Gerbner & Gross, 1980) and are quite unlikely to be figures of authority or sources of information on educational shows (Mendelson & Young, 1972). A recent, richly illustrated paper on the many and subtle ways in which we can continue to demonstrate white supremacy on television makes these figures come alive (Pierce, 1980), and I recommend it to the interested reader.

The personality characteristics given to minority characters and the situations in which they are demonstrated are generally supportive of the current social structure. So, too, are the majority of social roles minorities, as opposed to whites, fill on television. Minorities generally fit our stereotypes of American society by being poor (Fernandez-Collado et al., 1979; Greenberg et al., 1978, 1979) and confined to their own ghetto. When minorities have more powerful roles, they are generally those that support the current social order (Clark, 1969). Blacks are police officers and teachers. They maintain the current laws of the land and they educate our children into our system. There are only infrequent glimpses of minorities who are middle- or upper-class, who live in or work for a social order that is more equitable for all, or who successfully challenge inequities.

Although in some ways one could argue that current portrayals of minorities present them as they usually are in our society—less powerful, poorer, and supportive of the social order—such portrayals ignore the substantial numbers of middle- and upper-class minorities who have achieved positions of power in America. They also fail to present positive role models to minority children and positive counters to the prevailing stereotypes held by whites. In an alternate perspective—one that accepts current portrayals as realistic—one can still fault these portrayals for ignoring attributes characteristic of traditional minority cultures in this country. Where are the bilinguals, the biculturals, those who speak Black English? We have come a long way since blacks were portrayed by whites or could only appear after receiving instruction on the limits of "blackness" a white audience would accept (U.S. Commission on Civil Rights, 1977). Yet we could go much further. Of course, some exceptions already exist at all hours of the day and night on virtually all stations. The most notable are specials, series produced with special funding (especially Emergency School Aid Act funding), and showcase (public relations) series.

POSSIBLE SOCIALIZATION EFFECTS

The preceding analysis of the television programs minority children watch and the simple fact that they spend many hours each day watching them together suggest certain consequences. In making these suggestions I will move far beyond any data we now have on the effects of watching television for either white or minority children. I will also momentarily ignore certain realities that ultimately must be considered in delineating television's role in socializing minority children. One is that television's social order is only one of many that all children experience. More on this later. The other is that children are not simple, passive acceptors of the television world. Like all of us, they bring to a program their own realities and their own way of making sense of it (for two quite different discussions of these ideas see Bandura, 1978, and Dorr, 1980). For example, some may look at a *Rebop* segment about a teenage Hispanic boy who helps his mother run a daycare center and feel he is a strong, attractive young man. Others may find him weak and unappealing because he does traditional women's work.

Since there are no current guides to what children of different ethnicities, social circumstances, ages, and so on will see in programming, I will speculate about television effects as though children see programs as the analysts and critics do. It is to be hoped that we will someday understand the ways in which various people make sense of what they see on television and what this means in terms of the effect it can have on them. This is a research area I certainly encourage. In the meantime, I will speculate as though all children see television as researchers and critics do.

The demographics of the world of entertainment television and the relative power and prestige given to whites there suggest much to minority children about their place in our society. Borrowing from Clark's (1972) suggestion that appearing on television represents a legitimation of a person or group, one would have to conclude that the exclusion of minorities from most programming, especially for all groups except blacks, suggests that they are not a legitimate part of our society. Their limited roles and circumstances suggest that only certain segments of minority cultures are relevant to the larger American society. Moreover, the predominance of minority characters in heavily or totally minority casts suggests that minorities should remain within, or are only important within, the context of their own minority group. Their occupational roles, actions within these roles, and lack of power in integrated settings suggest that in the larger American society "white is still right." Moreover, the current social order is one that everyone apparently seeks to maintain, even those who as a group suffer within it. If minority children see this place for themselves and take it seriously, it must have a chilling effect on their self-concepts and aspirations.

These same demographics and portrayals of relative power have implications for children who look to television for role models, which most seem to do at least some of the time (Greenberg, in press; Greenberg & Dervin, 1972). If minority children look for models of the same ethnicity as themselves, they find few to choose from on television. Those they do find have a limited range of personality characteristics, occupations, and social circumstances to emulate. If, on the other hand, they look for role models who are powerful and successful, then they would probably emulate white characters. These dual possibilities make it difficult to predict what specific attitudes and/or behaviors children may learn. If they look to minority characters as role models, then they might learn to be less knowledgeable, wealthy, assertive, or dominant than would white children, to defer to whites, or to accept largely white versions of their minority culture. If they look to white characters as role models, then they might learn white values and behaviors vis-à-vis work, money, aggression, competition, cooperation, family life, and so on. All of which may require giving up some distinctive elements of one's own ethnic culture. If children reject whites on television as role models and do not find members of their own ethnic group there to emulate, then perhaps they will turn more strongly to their own family and community for role models.

Turning from possible effects of television content to the simple act of viewing many hours a day, one confronts the possibility that the development of other skills and interests is affected. It is simple arithmetic plus the assumption—which is surely supportable—that the development of skills requires an investment of time. What, then, are minority children, and white children too, giving up when they spend hours each day watching television? Some children are probably giving up hours of exposure to real-life fighting, drug and alcohol use, and crime; for them, time with television is almost certainly a better alternative. But most children are probably giving up hours in which they could develop athletic, intellectual, artistic, interpersonal, mechanical, and manual skills. This implies another role for television in socializing children in addition to transmitting information, values, attitudes, and behaviors.

These possible socialization effects of television viewing are not really desirable in my value system. Consideration of them leads me to decry much of the television we currently make available to and attractive for our children, especially our minority children; to look for ways to make the few really fine series more readily available and attractive; and to look for ways to help minority children deal realistically and constructively with what they see on television. Any attempt to help children become more "literate" about television necessarily returns us to a recognition of the real-world context in which children view, understand, and may be affected by television. Since I have just presented some of the strongest possible effects of television and ignored the many other influences on children as they develop, I will be happy to turn to a more balanced view of television's role in socialization.

TELEVISION AND
ETHNIC ROLES IN CONTEXT

We would all be open to charges of lunacy if we laid solely at television's door the responsibility for our children's socialization. For almost all children opportunities abound for learning about themselves and society. There are families, communities, schools, formal and informal social organizations, radios, records, comics, magazines, books, newspapers, and films. These socialization agents have differing opportunities and methods available to them (see Leifer, 1975, for a comparison of families and television as socialization agents). They are likely to have different impacts in different areas of socialization. At present, we understand little about how various socialization agents interact to influence (or not) a child's development (see Dorr, 1978; McLeod, Fitzpatrick, Glynn, & Fallis, in press; and Moles, 1981; for a discussion of interpersonal influences on the viewing and effects of television). An important task of future research is to delineate these interactions.

To arrive at some understanding of the ways in which various socialization agents interact to influence children, we will need to identify the "messages" each agent delivers, the ways in which messages from different agents are congruent and incongruent, and the areas about which each agent delivers messages. Then we will need to determine the importance children give to these different messages and the credibility they give to each message source (probably topic specific). Finally, we will need to delineate the amounts and kinds of power each agent has to encourage or force adoption of its messages by children.

Television is likely to be relatively potent in those areas in which we do not have direct experience or strong tutelage by significant others (Hornik, Gonzalez, & Gould, 1980). It is heavily viewed and presents its messages in vivid and compelling ways. It is probably closer to watching real life, especially in series programming, than any other experience except watching real life. Since the real lives of most of us do not include much contact with many ethnic groups other than our own, television could be especially potent in filling our experiential gaps with these groups—to the extent that television includes them in its world (see Atkin et al., 1979 for evidence of this). Our essentially segregated society leaves this opening for television.

When people from different segments of society do finally get together, their roles are interactionally determined. To make it simpler for me to explore this final point, let me reduce my consideration to two groups: White people and minority people.[2] Let me also ignore the broader institutions and structure of our society and focus on the more

---

[2]Within this section I will emphasize what I believe is truly the interactive determination of social roles. To be comfortable with this emphasis, however, I must add here that I believe that a greater—but not total—responsibility for the social roles of minorities rests with white Americans rather than with minorities themselves. We have the lion's share of the power and resources and hence generally exert more influence over who gets to do and/or be what than do those with less power and fewer resources (that is, American minorities on the average).

personal encounters between these two groups. This chapter has been written as though minority children alone determined their personalities, roles, and statuses. Obviously, this is not entirely accurate. Social interaction and social structure are determined by all those who participate in them. To the extent that I expect individual blacks to behave like a "Tom, Buck, or Mammy" (to borrow from another author) I will probably elicit more of these types of behaviors from them than I would if I expected something different. Alternatively, to the extent that a black expects me to behave like a "Honky," I will probably behave more like that than I would if she or he expected something different from me.

With this perspective in mind, it becomes clear that we must worry about what American television teaches white children about minorities. Some of us must turn our focus around and ask what white children learn from television about blacks, Chicanos, Puerto Ricans, American Indians, Chinese Americans and so on. Are all blacks like J. J., Rerun, Fat Albert, or George Jefferson? Are all Asian Americans like Charlie Chan or Quincy's assistant, Sam? Are all American Indians shirtless savages who roam the Plains attacking white caravans, or are they all like Buffy St. Marie? If white children believe this is the case, how will they treat the real-life blacks, Asian Americans, or American Indians they encounter, and what behaviors will they bring out in minorities? Most white children, probably even more so than minority children, live in segregated communities in which they have little opportunity to learn firsthand about American minorities today. This must leave them more vulnerable to television's images of these groups than they would be if our society were more nearly integrated.

Given the structure of our communities and the nature of the minority portrayals white children see today, we really must concern ourselves with what whites learn to expect from minorities. In at least some circumstances, they create their social roles together, and both groups need to contribute to making these roles as desirable as possible to everyone. White children need to know that there are varieties of skills, interests, and personalities in each minority group, just as there are among whites, and to expect and accept that some of the time minority group members will be more intelligent, skillful, desirable, and/or powerful than will whites. Imagine what interethnic interactions would be like if whites began them with these expectations.

American television surely plays a role in socializing minority children today. Most of this chapter has focused on exploring what we now know about this role, on suggesting what the role may be, and on specifying areas in which we may wish to do more research about this role. This last section has moved to a consideration of the truly interactive nature of socialization and of the ways in which all of us create the social order. It is here that the most difficult and potentially important research needs to be done. Conceptual schemes and actual knowledge of these interactions are what we must hope ultimately to achieve, for it is only within them that we may be able to find ways in which television can promote better lives for all children—and for the adults into which they grow.

ACKNOWLEDGMENTS

My chapter has been improved by the comments of Carolyn Block, who served as discussant for it at the conference, and by ideas derived from the general discussion there.

REFERENCES

Atkin, C., Greenberg, B., & McDermott, S. *Race and social role learning from television.* Unpublished manuscript, Michigan State University, undated.

Atkin, C., Greenberg, B., & McDermott, S. Race and social role learning from television. In H. S. Dordick (Ed.), *Proceedings of the Sixth Annual Telecommunications Policy Research Conference.* Lexington, Massachusetts: Lexington, 1979.

Ball, S., & Bogatz, G. A. *The first year of* Sesame Street: *An evaluation.* Princeton, New Jersey: Educational Testing Service, 1970.

Ball, S., & Bogatz, G. A. *Reading with television: An evaluation of* The Electric Company. Princeton, New Jersey: Educational Testing Service, 1973.

Ball, S., Bogatz, G. A., Kazarow, K. M., & Rubin, D. B. *Reading with television: A follow-up evaluation of* The Electric Company. Princeton, New Jersey: Educational Testing Service, 1974.

Bandura, A. Social learning theory of identificatory processes. In D. A. Goslin (Ed.), *Handbook of socialization theory and research.* Chicago, Illinois: Rand McNally, 1969.

Bandura, A. The self system in reciprocal determinism. *American Psychologist,* 1978, *33,* 344–358.

Berger, P. L., & Luckmann, T. *The social construction of reality.* New York: Anchor, 1967.

Bogatz, G. A., & Ball, S. *The second year of* Sesame Street: *A continuing evaluation.* Princeton, New Jersey: Educational Testing Service, 1971.

Brigham, J. C., & Giesbrecht, L. W. *All in the Family:* Racial attitudes. *Journal of Communication,* 1976, *26*(4), 69–74.

CBS, Office of Social Research. *A study of messages received by children who viewed an episode of* Fat Albert and the Cosby Kids. New York: Author, 1974.

Clark, C. C. Television and social control: Some observations on the portrayal of ethnic minorities. *Television Quarterly,* 1969, *8,* 18–22.

Clark, C. C. *Television and the child.* Unpublished manuscript, Stanford University, 1972.

Collins, W. A. Cognitive processing and television viewing. In D. Pearl, L. Bouthilet, & J. Lazar (Eds.), *Television and behavior: Ten years of scientific progress and implications for the eighties.* Washington, D. C.: US Govt. Printing Office, in press.

Collins, W. A., Berndt, T. J., & Hess, V. L. Observational learning of motives and consequences for television aggression: A developmental study. *Child Development,* 1974, *45,* 799–802.

Collins, W. A., & Westby, S. D. *Children's processing of social information from televised dramatic programs.* Paper presented at the meeting of the Society for Research in Child Development, Denver, Colorado, April 1975.

Comstock, G. *Television and human behavior: The key studies.* Santa Monica, California: Rand Corporation, 1975.

Donagher, P. C., Poulos, R. W., Liebert, R. M., & Davidson, E. S. Race, sex, and social example: An analysis of character portrayals on inter-racial television entertainment. *Sociological Reports,* 1975, *37,* 1023–1034.

Dorr, A. *Television as a teacher: Interpersonal factors mediating viewing and effects.* Unpublished manuscript, Harvard University, 1978.

Dorr, A. When I was a child, I thought as a child. In S. B. Withey & R. P. Abeles (Eds.), *Television and social behavior: Beyond violence and children.* Hillsdale, New Jersey: Erlbaum, 1980.

Drabman, R. S., & Thomas, M. H. Children's imitation of aggressive and pro-social behavior when viewing alone and in pairs. *Journal of Communication,* 1977, *27*(3), 199–205.

Eastman, H. A., & Liss, M. B. *Ethnicity and children's television preference.* Unpublished manuscript, University of Southern California, 1978.

Fernandez-Collado, P. B., Greenberg, B. S., & Atkin, C. K. *The context, characteristics and communication behaviors of blacks on television.* Unpublished manuscript, Michigan State University, 1979.

Flagg, B. N., Fenton, T., & Grady, J. *The role of formal features in directing visual attention within a television presentation.* Unpublished manuscript, Harvard University, 1978.

Flagg, B. N., Housen, A., & Lesser, S. *Pre-reading and pre-science on Sesame Street.* Unpublished manuscript, Harvard University, 1978.

Flapan, D. *Children's understanding of social interaction.* New York: Columbia Univ. Press, 1968.

Fletcher, A. D. Negro and White children's television program preferences. *Journal of Broadcasting,* 1969, *13,* 359–366.

Gerbner, G., & Gross, L. The violent face of television and its lessons. In E. L. Palmer & A. Dorr (Eds.), *Children and the faces of television: Teaching, violence, selling.* New York: Academic Press, 1980.

Gerbner, G., Gross, L., Jackson-Beeck, M., Jeffries-Fox, S., & Signorielli, N. Cultural indicators: Violence Profile No. 9. *Journal of Communication,* 1978, *28*(3), 176–207.

Goodhardt, G. J., Ehrenberg, A. S. C., & Collins, M. A. *The television audience: Patterns of viewing.* Westmead England: Saxon House, 1975.

Greenberg, B. S. Children's reactions to television blacks. *Journalism Quarterly,* 1972, *49,* 5–14.

Greenberg, B. S. *Life on television: Content analyses of U.S. television drama.* Norwood, New Jersey: Ablex, 1980.

Greenberg, B. S. Television and role socialization. In D. Pearl, L. Bouthilet, & J. Lazar (Eds.), *Television and behavior: Ten years of scientific progress and implications for the eighties.* Washington, D.C.: US Govt. Printing Office, in press.

Greenberg, B. S., & Atkin, C. K. *Learning about minorities from television: The research agenda.* Paper presented at the conference on Television and the Socialization of the Minority Child, University of California, Los Angeles, April 1978.

Greenberg, B. S., & Dervin, B. *Use of the mass media by the urban poor.* New York: Praeger, 1972.

Greenberg, B. S., & Dominick, J. R. Racial and social class differences in teenagers' use of television. *Journal of Broadcasting,* 1969, *13,* 331–344.

Greenberg, B. S., Simmons, K. W., Hogan, L., & Atkin, C. K. *A three-season analysis of the demographic characteristics of fictional television characters.* Paper presented at the Sixth Annual Telecommunications Policy Research Conference, Airlie, Virginia, May 1978.

Greenberg, B. S., Simmons, K. W., Hogan, L., & Atkin, C. K. *Demographic attributes of fictional television characters for three seasons.* Unpublished manuscript, Michigan State University, 1979.

Harvey, S. E., Poulos, R. W., & Liebert, R. M. *The new children's season: A profile of the 1974–75 season.* Unpublished manuscript, Media Action Research Center, New York, New York 1975.

Henderson, R. W., & Swanson, R. *The effects of televised skill instruction, instructional system support, and parental intervention on the development of cognitive skills.* (Final report on Grant OCD-CB-479 from the Office of Child Development for the period 7/1/73–2/28/77.) Unpublished manuscript, University of Arizona, Tucson, Arizona Center for Educational Research and Development, 1977.

Henderson, R. W., Zimmerman, B. J., Swanson, R., & Bergan, J. R. *Televised cognitive skill instruction for Papago Native American children.* Unpublished manuscript, Arizona Center for Educational Research and Development, University of Arizona, Tucson, 1974.

Hornik, R., Gonzalez, M., & Gould, J. *Susceptibility to media effects.* Paper presented at the meeting of the International Communication Association, Acapulco, Mexico, May 1980.

Johnston, J., Ettema, J., & Davidson, T. *An evaluation of* Freestyle, *a television series to reduce sex-role stereotypes.* Unpublished manuscript, University of Michigan, Center for Research on Utilization of Scientific Knowledge, Institute for Social Research, 1980.

LaRose, R. *Formative evaluation report for* The New Americans. Unpublished manuscript, Applied Communications Networks, Los Angeles, California, 1980.

Leifer, A. D. Research on the socialization influence of television in the United States. *Fernsehen und Bildung,* 1975, *9,* 111–142.

Leifer, A. D. *Factors which predict credibility ascribed to television.* Paper presented at the meeting of the American Psychological Association, Washington, D. C., September 1976.

Leifer, A. D., Collins, W. A., Gross, B. M., Taylor, P. H., Andrews, L., & Blackmer, E. R. Developmental aspects of variables relevant to observational learning. *Child Development,* 1971, *42,* 1509–1516.

Leifer, A. D., Gordon, N. J., & Graves, S. B. Children's television: More than mere entertainment. *Harvard Educational Review,* 1974, *44,* 213–245.

Lemon, J. Women and blacks on primetime television. *Journal of Communication,* 1977, *27*(4), 70–79.

Liebert, R. M., Neale, J. M., & Davidson, E. S. *The early window: Effects of television on children and youth.* New York: Pergamon, 1973.

Lyle, J., & Hoffman, H. R. Children's use of television and other media. In E. A. Rubinstein, G. A. Comstock, & J. P. Murray (Eds.), *Television and social behavior* (Vol. 4). *Television in day-to-day life: Patterns of use.* Washington, D. C.: US Govt. Printing Office, 1972. (a)

Lyle, J., & Hoffman, H. R. Explorations in patterns of television viewing by preschool children. In E. A. Rubinstein, G. A. Comstock, & J. P. Murray (Eds.), *Television and social behavior* (Vol. 4). *Television in day-to-day life: Patterns of use.* Washington, D. C.: US Govt. Printing Office, 1972. (b)

McLeod, J. M., Fitzpatrick, M. A., Glynn, C. J., & Fallis, S. F. Television and social relations: Family influences and consequences for interpersonal relations. In D. Pearl, L. Bouthilet, & J. Lazar (Eds.), *Television and behavior: Ten years of scientific progress and implications for the eighties.* Washington, D.C.: U.S. Government Printing Office, in press.

Martin, W. *Final report of the Neighborhood Youth Consumer Education Project's Consumer Action Team Program* (Vol. 2). Unpublished manuscript, National Urban League, New York, 1977.

Mays, L., Henderson, E. H., Seidman, S. K., & Steiner, V. J. *An evaluation report on Vegetable Soup: The effects of a multi-ethnic children's television series on intergroup attitudes of children: Precis and overview.* Unpublished manuscript, Medgar Evers College, City University of New York, 1975.

Mendelson, G., & Young, M. *A content analysis of Black and minority treatment on children's television.* Boston, Massachusetts: Action for Children's Television, 1972.

Moles, O. *Family interaction and television viewing: Studies of low-income and minority families.* Paper presented at the meeting of the American Educational Research Association, Los Angeles, April 1981.

Murray, J. P. Television in inner-city homes: Viewing behavior of young boys. In E. A. Rubinstein, G. A. Comstock, & J. P. Murray (Eds.), *Television and social behavior* (Vol. 4). *Television in day-to-day life: Patterns of use.* Washington, D. C.: US Govt. Printing Office, 1972.

Murray, J. P. *Television and youth: 25 years of research and controversy.* Boys Town, Nebraska: Research Use and Public Service, 1980.

Nelson, B., & Napior, D. *Formative evaluation of the Rebop II pilot.* Unpublished manuscript, Abt Associates, Cambridge, Massachusetts, 1976.

Newcomb, A. F., & Collins, W. A. *Children's comprehension of family-role portrayals in televised dramas: Effects of SES, ethnicity and age.* Paper presented at the meeting of the Society for Research in Child Development, New Orleans, March 1977.

Noble, G. *Children in front of the small screen.* Beverly Hills, California: Sage, 1975.

Pierce, C. M. Social trace contaminants: Subtle indicators of racism in TV. In S. B. Withey & R. P. Abeles (Eds.), *Television and social behavior: Beyond violence and children.* Hillsdale, New Jersey: Erlbaum, 1980.

Rainville, R. E., & McCormick, E. Extent of covert racial prejudice in pro-football announcer's speech. *Journalism Quarterly,* 1977, 54, 20–26.

Seagoe, M. V. Children's television habits and preferences. *Quarterly Journal of Film, Radio, and Television,* 1951, 6, 143–153.

Shapiro, B. N. *Comprehension of television programming designed to encourage socially valued behavior in children: Formative research on Sesame Street programming with social and affective goals.* Unpublished manuscript, University of Massachusetts, Amherst, 1975.

Surlin, S. H., & Dominick, J. R. Television's function as a "third parent" for black and white teen-agers. *Journal of Broadcasting*, 1970, *15*, 55–64.

Surlin, S. H., & Tate, E. D. *All in the Family*: Is Archie funny? *Journal of Communication*, 1976, *26*(4), 61–68.

Turow, J. Advising and ordering: Daytime, primetime. *Journal of Communication*, 1974, *24*(2), 138–141.

U.S. Commission on Civil Rights. *Window dressing on the set: Women and minorities in television.* Washington, D.C.: US Govt. Printing Office, 1977.

U.S. Commission on Civil Rights. *Window dressing on the set: An update.* Washington, D.C.: US Govt. Printing Office, 1979.

Vidmar, N., & Rokeach, M. Archie Bunker's bigotry: A study in selective perception and exposure. *Journal of Communication*, 1974, *24*(1), 36–47.

Williams, F., & Van Wart, G. Carrascolendas: *Bilingual education through television.* New York: Praeger, 1974.

Sherryl Browne Graves

The Impact of Television on the Cognitive and Affective Development of Minority Children

There can be little doubt that television occupies a special and powerful position in our society today. It is a medium that carries messages and images that have gained some significant supporters, but more often than not, its offerings have been perceived as having some negative influences. No area has commanded more attention than has the influence of television on the affective and cognitive development of children and young people. This chapter shall, therefore, evaluate some of television's influences and its impact in the area of cognitive and affective development, with a special emphasis on the following questions: What effect does television have on the cognitive and affective development of minority children? Do minority children learn from exposure to television? Is television capable of influencing the emotional lives of American Indian, Asian-American, Afro-American and Hispanic children? Is television positive or negative to the development of a child?

Cognitive development in a child represents the unfolding process of how the mind works. Cognition refers to the "process or act of knowing, preceiving, or of gathering knowledge together. The faculty of apprehending, knowing, thinking, and information processing [Wilkening, 1973, p. 46]." For Piaget (Piaget & Inhelder, 1969), chil-

37

TELEVISION AND
THE SOCIALIZATION OF THE MINORITY CHILD

dren's intellects grow and develop through active interaction with their environment. This constant adjustment and readjustment to the contingencies of the real world serves as the foundation for the development of adult thinking. Whereas the field of cognitive development is a rich and complex one, most of the research on television and cognitive development is limited to the role of television in teaching specific information and to the role of television in aiding information processing skills.

Affective development, in contrast, looks at the emergence of "feelings, emotions or dispositions as a mode of mental functioning [Wolman, 1973, p. 11]." In affective development research, the recognition and development of emotions in children and the process by which children learn to positively or negatively evaluate the self and others are examined.

The nature and process of cognitive and affective development in minority children are important because of the peculiar place these children have within our culture. In general, with the exception of Asian-American children, minority children score lower on a wide variety of tests of intellectual performance (Hellmuth, 1967, 1968; Roberts, 1967). Sociocultural and economic disadvantage are frequently cited as the reason for the gap in cognitive performance between minority and majority children. In an investigation of measured differences in mental ability among different ethnic groups, Lesser and his colleagues (Lesser, Fifer, & Clark, 1967) discovered that "social class and ethnic group membership . . . have strong effects upon the level of (each of four) mental abilities [p. 96]."

Compensatory education programs like Head Start, Follow Through and Upward Bound were developed in light of the minority child's presumed different cognitive functioning. For Upward Bound, one of the critical guidelines was "to prepare students in the essentials of success in college. The curriculum should be aimed, therefore, toward these objectives: critical thinking, effective expression and development of positive attitudes toward learning (Office of Economic Opportunity, 1965, p. 8–9)." In a similar manner, professional and lay people have frequently expressed concern about the delicate emotional balance that minority children are forced to strike in a racist society (Grier & Cobbs, 1968; Harrison-Ross & Wyden, 1973; Roberts, 1967; Spurlock, 1973).

Television can be conceived of as an institution that both reflects and creates social reality. Clark (1972), Gerbner (1972), and Graves (1977) point out that television plays a role as an instrument of social and political oppression for the disaffected and disenfranchised in that the medium reflects the racism that pervades much of our society (Jones, 1972).

Clark (1972) suggests that television maintains and reinforces racism by failing to provide minority groups with legitimation through recognition and respect. By *recognition*, Clark means acknowledgment of a group's uniqueness and relevance. Recognition implies a conscious choice to acknowledge the existence and value of a group of people. The second element of legitimation, respect, involves message contents that share (a) the definition of an actor's behavior, (b) the assessment of an actor's behavior, and (c) the accountability of an actor's behavior. These issues are frequently raised when minorities criticize television's presentation of their groups. I often feel that people with an understanding of only the most superficial aspects of a minority group mistake this for empathy, knowledge, and expertise. Given this less than salutary picture of television in relation to racism, its role for affective development of minority children emerges as an important one.

To the extent that television elaborates the tendency to reduce traditional intellectual activity on the part of its viewers by substituting hours and hours of mindless distraction, it has been a subject of criticism (Leifer, Gordon, & Graves, 1973). In this context, television's impact on the intellectual functioning of American youth becomes a hotly debated issue. Reform-minded groups characterize their action programs against certain aspects of television as "a crusade to head off America's addiction to mindless programming ("Violence!" 1975)." According to many social critics, television is responsible for, or at least a heavy contributor to, the declining intellectual abilities of American children. The decline in national reading test scores and verbal and quantitative aptitude scores such as the SATs are frequently cited in support of this view (Winn, 1977).

Concern about television's influence on intellectual development and academic achievement is in part related to the fact that children are drawn to it and use it to a greater extent than they use formal classroom instruction (Liebert, Neale, & Davidson, 1973): "American children spend more time watching television than they spend in the classroom. We see few dropouts from the electronic school and very little television truancy. [Siegal, 1975, p. 18]."

In assessing how television influences minority children in the areas of cognitive and affective development, it is useful to present a framework for understanding the role that television plays in child development. The conceptual framework I will employ comes from the work of two colleagues and myself (Leifer *et al.*, 1973). It requires that one have information about television, children, and other socialization agents. Visually, one can think of the relationship of these three elements as three intersecting circles (see Fig. 3.1).

Television, children and other agents each have some characteristics and actions that do not directly influence the others. It is important, however, when thinking about the relationship of any two elements, to acknowledge the reciprocal interaction between them. This mutual interaction means that neither television nor the child is entirely active nor entirely passive. Television modifies the children, and the children modify their experience of television. Furthermore, one may have to consider that other agents are influencing the interaction between children and television.

Most of the research on children and television is not based on any particular conceptual or theoretical framework. One is faced with a rather haphazard patchwork of studies whose only commonality is its subjects' stimulus or response. Acknowledging these deficits in the literature, I will proceed to review that literature by examining sepa-

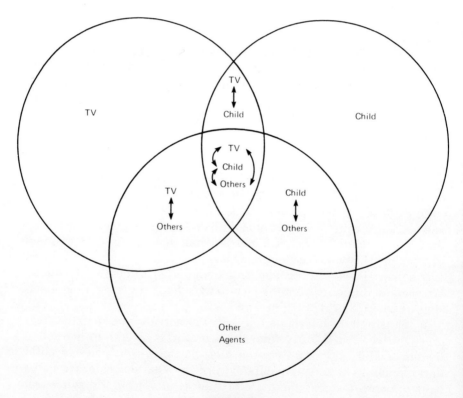

Figure 3.1.

rately research on television's impact on cognitive development and on affective development. Within each of these major divisions, research on television, children, and other agents will be presented in turn. Both major sections, cognitive development and affective development, will conclude with a summary and suggestions for future research. Throughout this chapter I will use the term *minority children* to refer to children of American Indian, Asian, Afro-American, and Hispanic descent.

COGNITIVE DEVELOPMENT

Television and Its Contribution to Minority Children's Learning and Cognitive Functioning

In this section I will examine four different issues. The first two subsections will provide reviews of research on educational and commercial television, respectively, with regard to their impact on learning and cognitive functioning. The third subsection will deal with evaluation of the impact of television on a specific cognitive ability, creativity. In the fourth subsection, research on television presentations of specific strategies for information processing will be presented. The focus of this last subsection is the television side of the television–child dyad and, in consequence, on the relationship between television content (stimulus) and cognition (response).

LEARNING FROM INSTRUCTIONAL AND
EDUCATIONAL TELEVISION

Instructional Television

Over the years, an extensive body of research into the use of television for instructional purposes has developed. Instructional television is usually produced by local or state agencies associated with the public education system. It is designed to either replace or enhance existing educational curricula in schools. Evaluations of instructional television present evidence on the ability of these systems to teach a variety of students a large number of different subjects. Several reviews (Chu & Schramm, 1967; Dubin & Hedley, 1969; May & Lumsdaine, 1958; Reid & MacLennan, 1967; Schramm, 1973) indicate that students ranging in age from preschoolers to adults can learn a variety of curricular materials, including mathematics, science, foreign languages, history, art, and social science, when television is the medium of instruction. From this research, one can conclude that instructional television is as effective at teaching as are live instructors.

Although most of this research does not include minority children as subjects, the strength of the findings across sexes, age groups, curricular material, and geographical locations strongly suggests that the impact would be the same for minority students.

Educational Television

Unlike instructional television, educational television is widely available on commercial and public television stations. It is usually produced by public television stations or private production groups like Children's Television Workshop (CTW). Furthermore, since educational television must compete for its audience with entertainment programming, the format of the programs is both entertaining and educational. Educational series seem to differ from instructional ones in that minority children are usually considered a major part of the target audience.

Sesame Street. With the introduction of *Sesame Street* by CTW in the late 1960s, a new era was born in the field of educational television. This highly entertaining series for preschool children was developed for at least two reasons (Palmer, Chen, & Lesser, 1976). First, there was a growing concern for the early cognitive stimulation of young children, especially those thought to be educationally deprived or disadvantaged. In effect, this translated into a concern for low-income and minority children, especially black and Hispanic inner-city preschoolers. Second, there was a growing recognition that television, which has access to a wide range of socioeconomic and cultural groups, was being underused as a deliberate educational intervention.

With 1½ years of planning prior to broadcast, the school-preparation curriculum of *Sesame Street* was born (Palmer *et al.*, 1976). The goals of the series included symbolic processes (recognition of letters, numbers, and geometric forms and their use), cognitive organization (perceptual discrimination, classifying, sorting, ordering, and understanding relationships among objects and events), reasoning and problem solving, and the child in relation to his or her social and physical worlds (Lesser, 1974).

At least seven studies have evaluated the ability of *Sesame Street* or *Plaza Sesamo*, the Latin American version, to achieve its stated goals (Ball & Bogatz, 1970; Bogatz & Ball, 1971; Cook, Appleton, Conner,

Shafer, Tomkin, & Weher, 1975; Diaz-Guerrero & Holtzman, 1974; Diaz-Guerreo, Reyes-Lagunes, Witke, & Holtzman, 1976; Kenny, 1975; Minton, 1975).

The Educational Testing Service (ETS) evaluated 2 years of *Sesame Street* to determine if subjects who viewed the series for an extended period learned more than those who did not. The immense popularity of the series, however, made it difficult to find a true none-viewing control group. The ETS then selected a design to manipulate viewing by encouraging the parents of experimental subjects to have their children watch the program at home or by selecting sites for experimental subjects in which the program was only available on cable or ultra high frequency (UHF) television. The samples included disadvantaged children from black, inner-city areas of Durham, North Carolina and Boston, Massachusetts; poor white areas of Boston, Phoenix, Arizona, and rural northern California; and poor Hispanic areas of Phoenix (Ball & Bogatz, 1970).

Learning was assessed by testing for the specific skills and information taught in the series. Some related tasks requiring generalization were also included in the pretest and posttest measure. The first-year results indicated that those who viewed more had increased their learning gains over a 6-month period relative to those who were not encouraged to view. Those who watched more gained more than those who watched infrequently or never. The second-year evaluation highlighted the generalization effect of the series when significant posttest differences between encouraged and control subjects were found on the Peabody Picture Vocabulary test (Bogatz & Ball, 1971).

Although there was evidence that encouragement to view had a general impact, not all subgroups were affected equally. For example, younger children (3-year-olds) gained more than older children (5-year-olds), and disadvantaged viewers who watched frequently gained as much as frequent viewers from advantaged homes. Among those who watched infrequently, however, disadvantaged preschoolers gained little compared with their middle-class counterparts.

Sesame Street demonstrated success in meeting a large portion of its stated goals. Many had hoped, however, that the series, like many educational interventions of the time, would serve to narrow the gap in measured cognitive functioning between minority and majority children. The ETS research, a reevaluation of the ETS data (Cook et al., 1975), as well as dissertation research on the series (Minton, 1975) all point out that *Sesame Street* did not close the gap.

One reason for this partial failure is that the program was viewed by advantaged and disadvantaged children alike. The re-analysis of the

ETS data offers another explanation. Cook *et al.* (1975) found that the children who viewed more gained more. Those who viewed more were more likely to be middle class. Furthermore, his analysis suggests that a large portion of the gain for frequent viewers was not caused by their viewing. His research suggests, moreover, that on the average, the advantaged group had larger gains than did the disadvantaged group.

In conclusion, one can say that the series did teach cognitive material to advantaged and disadvantaged children; however, different children were affected in different ways. In general, the more children watched, the more they learned.

Plaza Sesamo. Plaza Sesamo is a Hispanic, Spanish-language version of *Sesame Street.* It was adapted to Hispanic culture with the same general curriculum goals as the North American series. Two evaluations of this series were conducted on Mexican children (Diaz-Guerrero & Holtzman, 1974; Diaz-Guerreo *et al.,* 1976). Even though these studies are not on minority group samples, they do provide insight into the effectiveness of an educational television series on Spanish-speaking children. Furthermore, many Spanish-speaking children in the United States are of Mexican descent and have much in common with Mexican children.

Both evaluations of *Plaza Sesamo* were studies of 3- to 5-year-old Mexican children. Experimental groups viewed the series in a daycare setting, and control subjects viewed cartoons. The children were tested on skills specifically taught by the series and on general measures of cognitive ability indirectly related to the series' goals. They were tested prior to, during, and after exposure to the series. In the first, smaller experiment, subjects were also rated on a daily basis for their attention to the series.

The results of the two studies are as follows:

1. Children who watched more performed better on series-specific measures than did control subjects who watched cartoons.
2. The series was more effective with 4- and 5-year-olds than it was for 3-year-olds.
3. Urban children gained more after exposure than did rural children.
4. After only 7 weeks of viewing, differences between experimental and control groups were apparent.

The second study of *Plaza Sesamo,* a large-scale summative evaluation study, did not report evidence of generalization effects as did the earlier experimental study (Diaz-Guerrero & Holtzman, 1974). The larger study was plagued with problems of nonrandom attrition, excessive absenteeism among rural subjects, and the addition of new instruments to the study. Diaz-Guerrero et al. (1976) speculate, however, that the additional support and encouragement that resulted from the daily attention study in the first experiment substantially altered the treatment environment.

Research on the North American and Hispanic versions of Sesame Street indicates that the encouraged viewing of an entertaining educational television series resulted in the acquisition and partial generalization of symbolic processes, cognitive organizational skills, reasoning and problem-solving skills, and information gain from exposure to the series over an extended period of time. Not all children were affected equally, but those who viewed more tended to gain more. Age, place of residence, and socioeconomic status (SES) were sometimes related to the differences in effect. Although Sesame Street alone is not the solution to the problem of racial and socioeconomic differences in cognitive performance, it does provide the minority child with a positive learning experience. The series has been highly successful in attracting an audience of minority viewers (Greeley, 1974) and in teaching some cognitive skills and information (Liebert, 1977).

The Electric Company.   The Electric Company is another CTW production. Unlike Sesame Street, The Electric Company teaches elementary reading skills to first-graders at all levels of reading, to second-graders in the lower half in reading achievement, to third- and fourth-graders in the lowest quarter in reading achievement. A summative evaluation of The Electric Company was carried out by ETS in 400 classrooms at four sites (Ball & Bogatz, 1973). Males and females, black, Hispanic, and white North Americans were sampled. Some experimental subjects viewed the series in school, and others were encouraged to view at home. Control and home-viewing groups received their normal classroom reading instruction.

Only those children who watched the program in school showed improvement in reading that could be reasonably attributed to viewing The Electric Company (Ball & Bogatz, 1973). Although the school viewers improved more than controls did on tests of the series-specific content, there were few differences between these two groups on a standard measure of reading. Except for the worst readers, those in the bottom 10% of the initial reading distribution, all age, sex, and ethnic groups appeared to benefit equally from exposure to the series.

In summary, The Electric Company evaluations indicate that a television series can increase the reading skills of minority children during the elementary school years. Only the poorest readers were unaffected by exposure to the series. The series was most successful when viewed in a school setting.

Carrascolendas. *Carrascolendas* is a series for Chicano children that was developed in Texas. Its goals, to develop cognitive skills and to encourage positive attitudes in the context of a multinational cultural environment (Williams & Van Wart, 1974), are pursued by presentation of segments in both English and Spanish.

Three evaluations of the series' effectiveness were conducted between 1971 and 1974. In the first 2 years, Chicano children in Texas were the subjects; the 1974 studies included a national sample of Spanish-speaking children. All viewing took place in classrooms.

The evaluation battery included subtests in Spanish and in English on history–culture, self-concept, science, math, and language skills. The results of the Texas and national studies are as follows:

In the Texas study

• Gains were observed in the subtests in English on history–culture across 3 years of evaluation.
• There was evidence of Spanish and English language-skill gains in viewers as compared with nonviewers.
• Second-grade viewers gained the least, except in one English subtest.

The results of the national study are as follows:

• First-grade viewers gained more in four of five Spanish subtests.
• Kindergarten viewers gained more in three of five English subtests than did their nonviewer counterparts.

Carrascolendas, then, was effective in teaching better language fluency in both Spanish and English to Chicano children, and in transmitting information in English about history and culture. Though its success was partially tied to the use of television in a school setting, *Carrascolendas* illustrates that programming designed for a specific audience can enhance cognitive performance.

Villa Alegre. Bilingual Children's Television, a private production company, developed the Spanish–English series, *Villa Alegre,* for a 4- to 8-year-old audience. Unlike *Carrascolendas,* this series was intended for both Spanish-speaking and English-speaking audiences. Its curriculum concentrated on a number of cognitive areas, with particu-

lar emphasis on language usage in both English and Spanish (Bilingual Children's Television, 1973).

Formative evaluation studies were conducted (Bilingual Children's Television, 1973), and 4- to 8-year-old Spanish- and English-speaking children were tested. Both English and Spanish monolingual children gained most when the language segments were conducted in both languages. There was a slight tendency for Spanish monolinguals to do better than English monolinguals, a difference probably attributable to greater exposure to English for the Spanish monolinguals compared with a relative lack of exposure to Spanish for the English monolinguals. The effectiveness of television as a teacher for minority children when there is a clear and specific intent to convey information is illustrated by *Villa Alegre*.

After reviewing the research on instructional and educational television, one recognizes that minority children can acquire information and, in some cases, develop cognitive skills after exposure to programs designed to educate. The effect tends to be greater the longer the exposure to the material. Programs like *Carrascolendas* that are designed for a specific minority audience can be highly effective; programs that are directed toward a broader minority audience, for example, *Sesame Street*, *The Electric Company*, and *Villa Alegre*, have also been shown to be effective. There is, however, little evidence to demonstrate that the educational or instructional television available to the public-at-large is able to counteract the social, economic, and cultural forces that produce lower test scores in cognitive function for minority children, especially those who are economically disadvantaged.

LEARNING FROM ENTERTAINMENT TELEVISION

Instructional and educational television have been shown to have a positive impact on minority children's cognitive performance, but the time children spend viewing such programming is minimal (NBC, Social Research Department, 1976). It can be generally observed that children spend far more time watching regular network entertainment that may or may not have planned instructional and educational goals. (Nielsen Co., 1977). It is important then, to understand how general entertainment content may affect cognitive development.

In general, minority children have a higher exposure to entertainment television than their white peers (Greenberg & Dervin, 1970; Lyle & Hoffman, 1972a). For example, black children watch more television than white children (Greenberg & Dervin, 1970), and one study (Lyle & Hoffman, 1972a) found more viewing among Chicano girls than among their white peers. Because of uncontrolled socioeconomic class differences in the samples, it is not clear if the reported minority group differences are not, in fact, masking what are really socioeconomic class differences. Several studies also show that black preschoolers view *Sesame Street* in proportions equal to, if not greater than, white preschoolers (Cook et al., 1975; Greeley, 1974; Lyle, 1975).

There is relatively little research on the impact of entertainment television on minority audiences. Comstock (1975) reviewed over 2300 studies of television and human behavior and found only 51 that were relevant to minorities and the poor. These included studies in which minorities and the poor were the principal focus and studies in which SES or racial differences are judged to be a principal finding. One must look to the general effects of entertainment television for guidance on the possible and actual impact of this type of programming on minority children.

Entertainment television that is designed only to amuse still influences the acquisition of cognitive content (Leifer, Gordon, & Graves, 1974). From television, children learn about behavior both aggressive and prosocial (Leifer et al., 1974; Liebert et al., 1973) and about social roles (Frueh & McGhee, 1975; Graves, 1975; Peterson & Thurston, 1933; Pingree, 1975). Research on Hollywood-made films in the 1930s suggests that children can acquire "facts" after exposure to audiovisual stimuli (Holaday & Stoddard, 1933). On the positive side, adolescents learned about citizenship and the Constitution after viewing a special network program on the subject (Alper & Leidy, 1970). Comstock, Chaffee, Kalzman, McCombs, & Roberts state (1978) that it is impossible to argue that children's cognitions are unaffected by television.

Entertainment programming's most dramatic impact on cognitive development and learning is in the area of advertising. That children learn about products from exposure to advertisements is clear (Adler, Friedlander, Lesser, Meringoff, Robertson, Rossiter, & Ward, 1977): They pay attention to commercials (Levin & Anderson, 1976), learn slogans and jingles from televised ads (Lyle & Hoffman, 1972a), and are moderately likely to have more positive attitudes toward and desire for advertised products than for unadvertised ones (Atkin, 1975a, 1975b; Goldberg & Gorn, 1974; Robertson & Rossiter, 1977).

Whereas these are some of the general responses to advertising by all children, race has been found to be a variable mediating the impact of advertising on children (Adler et al., 1977). Because the problem of confounding race with SES is ever-present, one has to be cautious in interpreting the racial effects; nevertheless, research suggests that black and white children respond to commercials differently. Black children

pay less attention and have slightly lower levels of recall and information acquisition than their white peers.

In the area of endorsement effects, that is, how the product presenter affects viewer attitudes and behavior, racial cues are a complicated factor. Black children who are 10–12 years old have been found to be more influenced by black product presenters, according to Hyams, Tanner, and Rossiter (1975), and Robertson, Rossiter, & Brenner (1975). Atkin (1975a), however, found an apparently significant "cross race" effect for older black children. These subjects were affected more by white presenters than by black presenters. Prior socialization experiences, and the specific racial composition of the advertisement can be presumed to contribute to these contradictory findings on the influence of the race of the presenter on black children.

The impact of commercials on black children's nutritional and health values was the focus of Donohue's (1975) study. After exposure to commercials, Donohue found that first- to third-grade black children apparently felt that when a disruption in physical well-being occurs, the appropriate behavior is the taking of some medicine or pill to correct the imbalance. It appeared from this study that many children learn that there are pills and chemicals that will insure the continuance of good health when taken regularly. In another study, black children's value perceptions of specific commercials were appraised (Meyer, Donohue, & Henke, 1977b). Black and white children were shown two McDonald's commercials. The majority of black subjects reported that the fast food shown was more nutritious than the food served at home, whereas only 15% of the white subjects had this response.

Thus, television, whether it is designed to teach or entertain, can alter children's cognitions, but the extent of the learning and the specific conditions that best contribute to learning for various minority groups is not discernible from the existing literature.

TELEVISION AND CREATIVITY

Educators, parents, clergy, politicians, journalists, and social activists have all expressed concern about television's impact on cognitive development. In particular, it has been suggested that television's provision of both visual and auditory inputs may serve to diminish or at least to disrupt the creative process in children. Creativity is "the dynamic process of pursuing discovering and achieving new perceptions and solutions of problems [Wilkening, 1973, p. 53]."

The question arises: Does an audiovisual medium that can bring life to a child's fantasies stimulate or stifle the ability to discover and achieve new perceptions? The research on television and creativity is in its infancy, and minority persons have not served as subjects.

Singer and Singer (1973), along with others, have been engaged in a study of the natural development of fantasy play (see also Piaget, 1962) and a study of specific training procedures to encourage imaginative play (Freyberg, 1973; Marshall & Hahn, 1967; Singer & Singer, 1976; Smilansky, 1968). In a 1976 study, Singer and Singer investigated the relative effectiveness of adult intervention versus television's *Mister Rogers' Neighborhood* in encouraging fantasy play. White children were assigned to either an experimental group that saw the series for 30 min (E_1), an experimental group that watched for 30 min with an adult present (E_2), an experimental group that spent a 30-min session in directed play activities with an adult (E_3), or a control group that saw no television and received no make-believe training. All of the subjects were between 3 and 4½ years old. The subjects were rated on level of imaginative play. The results indicate that levels of imaginative play were highest with live adult training, lower for television with adult, lower still for television alone, and lowest for no treatment. That television alone was not stimulating was a bit surprising, since the curriculum for *Mister Rogers' Neighborhood* emphasizes make-believe in both its format and content. This study suggests that television, even when there is a conscious effort to promote imaginative thinking, is not altogether effective with preschoolers; adult intervention is preferable.

Meline (1976) investigated how different media (print, audiotape, and videotape) would affect children's ability to offer creative solutions to real social problems. Sixth- and seventh-grade white children were randomly assigned by grade and sex to one of three media treatment conditions and were given a test of four problems. The first problem was about cars and traffic and the need for finding other means of transportation in the future; the second was about new ideas for the recycling of waste materials; the third problem dealt with how one could get people to stop smoking; and the last was about improving the cities of the future. Sample solutions, either verbal or visual, were presented, and subjects were then asked to write their own responses. The results of the study indicate that children exposed to concrete videotape presentations consistently gave significantly fewer solutions that departed from the objects, people, actions, and events shown. Children who only heard samples named or described (the audiotape and print conditions) gave significantly more creative ideas.

Finally, Wade's (1971) study of television, creativity, and adolescents supports the idea that the more creative adolescent spends more time on activities other than television viewing. Some think that the activity of television viewing, which is passive, is itself detrimental to the cognitive developmental process.

The results of the research reviewed suggest that television is associated with lower levels of imaginative play and fewer creative responses to problems. Researchers already report a relative lack of these cognitive skills in minority children (Freyberg, 1973; Smilansky, 1968). Since minority children watch more television, one can theorize that their television experiences are, at best, not encouraging fantasy play or creativity, skills that are important to optimal cognitive functioning and tested intellectual performance.

TELEVISION AS A VIEWING ACTIVITY

Although television can provide its viewers with a highly varied and frequently rich visual and auditory experience, television viewing is basically a passive activity: One sits and waits to be entertained. It does not provide the child with many opportunities to manipulate objects, to act upon the environment, to practice relating to others, or to make many attempts at organizing thoughts and behaviors for desired outcomes. All of these activities are thought to be of crucial importance for optimal cognitive development (Piaget & Inhelder, 1969).

Television teaches visual information processing strategies, and these must surely affect the child's mental representations. Perhaps McLuhan (1964) has stated most radically the controversy about the internal processing of visual and auditory information for the child viewer. McLuhan describes television as a "cold" medium, one low in data and requiring high participation in contrast to film, which is "hot," requiring low participation. McLuhan feels that television demands participation and involvement, that it does not allow itself to recede into the background. Rather, McLuhan seems to suggest that television envelops and engages the individual through its images and projections (McLuhan & Fiore 1967).

Salomon (1972, 1976) has experimentally investigated audiovisual media's ability to explicitly model cognitive operations. In studies with Israeli 5- to 8-year-olds (1976) and with eighth- and ninth-graders, (1972), Salomon has shown that television can promote specific skills needed for accurate information processing.

Cognitive operations such as laying out solid objects and attending to details, were explicitly modeled in films that were viewed by unskilled junior high school students. Their learning of the skills was increased. Similarly, films that used visual techniques that caused the viewer to focus on details or on the laying out of a solid object positively affected the corresponding skills of junior high school students. Salomon's work in Israel with *Sesame Street* suggests that cognitive skill mastery in initially skillful children was augmented when the television format required use of those skills. For less skillful children, there was no proficiency gain if the film assumed that the viewer already had the skills. These subjects did improve when exposed to films that explicitly presented the information processing strategies (Salomon, 1976). Not only does television teach content, then, but it can be used to teach ways of processing information, especially when the strategies are dependent on a visual component. This is a new field of research, and the studies need to be replicated and expanded in terms of the content used, the subject groups sampled, and the response measures that are tested. Certainly, children who have been brought up on the visual vocabulary of commercials that include the abrupt zoom, elliptical editing, the absence of story lines, and flash cuts, have different ideas about how to organize visual experience than children who have been exposed only to print media.

To summarize, all types of television are able to alter learning and cognitive performance in minority children. Although instructional, educational, and advertising content succeed in inducing children to acquire and retain the information presented, the impact of television on creativity and on information processing skills may be more extensive and complex. We have only examined the characteristics of television that are related to learning; it is appropriate now to focus attention on the characteristics of children that may influence how television content and format are perceived.

Characteristics of Children That Influence the Impact of Television on Minority Children

Let us examine the child side of the television–child dyad shown in Figure 3.1, p. 40. Even though racial differences are important when examining the impact of television on children, it is clear that the literature is incomplete with respect to minority groups. Most of the research has dealt with black–white differences, although recently there have been studies isolating Hispanic–white differences. There is almost no information on the impact of television on American Indian and Asian-American children. A variety of studies indicate that the magnitude of television effects varies as a function of age (Collins, 1970, 1973; Collins, Berndt, & Hess, 1974; Collins & Westby, 1975; Leifer, Graves, & Gordon, 1975; Leifer & Roberts, 1972; Meyer,

Donohue, & Henke, 1977a; Ward, Reale, & Levinson, 1972), and researchers have begun to look at the way in which children of different age groups process information from television. Again, there is very little research in this area that has included minority children.

It is clear that children's skills in extracting and using information from television change qualitatively from preschool- to high-school-age. With increasing age, there is improvement in the ability to reconstruct causal sequences (Leifer, Collins, Gross, Taylor, Andrews, and Blackburn, 1971), to retain plot-line connections that have been interrupted by commercials (Collins, 1973), to remember more central plot incidences (Collins, 1970; Hale, Miller, & Stevenson, 1968; Hawkins, 1973; Leifer & Roberts, 1972), to understand main and subplots without confusion; to expect plot information to be presented linearly, and to anticipate the next event in a plot (Collins & Westby, 1975). Younger children pick up more irrelevant information (Collins, 1970; Hawkins, 1973) and are less able to understand motivations and consequences for characters' behaviors (Collins et al., 1974; Leifer et al., 1971; Leifer & Roberts, 1972).

The studies cited on age-related changes in cognitive processing of television included white subjects only. In a study by Newcomb and Collins (1977), lower- and middle-class black and white subjects were exposed to one of two situation comedies about a family whose SES was either congruent or incongruent with their own. It was found that both black and white middle-SES second-graders viewing the middle-class family showed higher scores on ability to infer causes, comprehension of peripheral content, and overall comprehension. Lower-SES children achieved higher information processing scores on the lower-class black family series. Preliminary data analyses suggest that there may be an interaction between social class and ethnicity on children's social comprehension of television.

Similarly, two studies of black children's responses to advertising suggest that black children interpret television advertising differently from white children (Meyer et al. 1977a, 1977b); the black subjects were less aware of the nature and intent of television advertising than white samples were (Bever, Smith, Bengen, & Johnson, 1975; Ward et al., 1972).

Meyer, et al. (1977a, 1977b) found that black children between 5 and 12 years of age did not understand that commercials are designed to sell a product; they thought that advertising is developed to help people or to teach people. No more than 56% of black subjects understood the purpose of commercials compared with 85–90% of a sample of white children (Ward et al., 1972). Black children were more likely than white children to believe that television commercials were always truthful (Bever *et al.*, 1975; Rossiter & Robertson, 1974; Ward *et al.*, 1972). When a subsample of 8-year-olds from this group were given a short instructional unit on television commercials, however, they responded with higher levels of understanding and higher levels of disbelief than their uninstructed black peers.

As a consequence of the failure to recognize the intent of advertising and their greater acceptance of it as truthful, black children may be more vulnerable to the influence of advertisers than are white children, and hence more open to messages about social roles.

The age and, most important, the cognitive level of a child, influence the effect of television; race is a useful predictor of level of cognitive awareness of the nature and intent of commercials. These appear to be the most salient child characteristics that have been isolated. Neither sex differences nor differences due to place of residence have been found.

The Role of Other Agents of Socialization

Other agents of socialization (individuals, groups, organizations, or other forms of media) vary along three dimensions: their socioeconomic and cultural characteristics, their content, and their form. The content characteristics of other agents may be similar to or different from the content characteristics of television. The socioeconomic and cultural characteristics partially predict what agents will do and how they will do it.

It is important to examine the role of other agents relative to the reciprocal relationship between television and children. That other agents do play an important role in mediating the impact of television on the learning and cognitive performance of minority children has been researched, and this work can be summarized as follows: If an adult watches a program with a child, the learning that takes place is enhanced.

There are a number of striking examples of the positive effect of adult co-viewing. Preschoolers who watched *Sesame Street* with their mothers learned more than those who watched alone (Ball & Bogatz, 1970; Cook *et al.*, 1975). The impact of *Plaza Sesamo* on the learning and cognitive performance of Chicano children was greater when adults were present Diaz-Guerrero *et al.* (1976) state: "It is fairly obvious that in the earlier study, more adults attending to children were present at more times, creating a subtly different atmosphere in the first experiment than in the second [p. 154]." *The Electric Company* evaluation (Ball & Bogatz, 1973) concluded that those children who viewed the series in school, under the supervision of a teacher, had greater improvement in reading performance than those who watched at home.

Research on television and creativity shows the importance of adult mediation of television on this special cognitive ability. Preschoolers who watched *Mister Rogers' Neighborhood* with an adult engaged in higher levels of imaginative play than did those who watched the program alone.

The effect is clear: Television plus an adult equals increased learning. What is not clear is why this is the case. Is the adult's presence a cue to the children to be more attentive? Does the adult's presence give television more saliency to the children? Does the adult co-viewer comment or gesture in some way in a manner that reinforces the content? These are just a few hypotheses that merit further investigation.

Suggestions for Future Research

There is ample evidence that television is capable of influencing learning and cognitive functioning of majority children, and some evidence for its ability to influence minority children. Television—educational, instructional, and commercial—can convey a wide range of cognitive content and can influence cognitive skills such as imagination and creativity. Furthermore, specific ways of information processing can be conveyed. Finally, the children's levels of cognitive development can dramatically influence how they experience television's myriad content.

My first thought about the type of research that is needed was, "We need more research in which minority children's experience of television is explored." There are several lines that seem to be worth pursuing. The variables form three clusters—subject variables, television stimulus variables, and learning process variables.

SUBJECT VARIABLES

One of the subject variables most important to the understanding of the impact of television on minority children is their racial and ethnic group status. Most research on television and learning that has included minority subjects has used predominantly black samples. Due to Spanish bilingual programming, Hispanic children have been assessed. We know very little about the impact of television on the learning and cognitive functioning of American Indian or Asian-American children. These children may have specific mental abilities that have been more highly trained than others as a consequence of their cultural milieu (Lesser *et al.*, 1967), and therefore may learn from television in a different way.

The second subject variable of importance is age. Since research on minority children has been relatively sparse, we know little about the interaction of the effect of age and ethnicity on the cognitive processing of television or the activity of television viewing. There may be important although subtle differences in the impact of age that could have important consequences for television's impact.

Another subject variable that is particularly relevant is the amount of viewing (and general viewing habits) of minority children. There is fairly consistent evidence that black children are generally heavy viewers, but there is little known about the amount of television other minority children view. There is evidence that suggests that the amount of viewing is related to the viewer's perceived reality of television (Gerbner & Gross, 1973; Greenberg & Reeves, 1976). The amount of viewing may also relate to the child's familiarity with the visual vocabulary of television, and this greater familiarity may serve to enhance learning. We know little about this relation.

In a similar vein, it may be important to know something about the nature of the child's viewing habits, that is, the type of programs the child selects. We know that viewing habits can be related to ideas about aggression, occupation, and foreign people (Gerbner & Gross, 1973); viewing habits surely have implications for how one learns from television.

A steady diet of crime-dramas or adventure shows may expose a child to a variety of visual techniques like zoom, slow motion, and flashback because these styles are particularly relevant to an action-oriented plot. A child who watches mostly situation comedies and game shows, on the other hand, may have exposure to very restricted visual techniques. The former child may become more skilled at decoding active visual presentations; the latter may be better able to learn through more static but highly verbal presentations. Viewing habits may influence the child's expectations about learning from television, so that a child whose viewing is mostly of educational programs may have developed a particular attentional set that facilitates learning from television.

Race, age, and viewing habits seem to be the most productive subject variables for initial investigation; however, there may be other viewer characteristics that are also important. For example, SES may prove to be a more relevant characteristic than race or ethnicity. In a variety of other areas of psychological research, it seems that uncontrolled SES variables are masked in a study of racial group differences, and that this masking stems, in large part, from the results of discrimination. A much larger proportion of minority people are at the lower SES levels, and a much larger proportion of whites are at higher SES levels. Since social class is an important variable, researchers in television and ethnicity should be sensitive to social class differences within minority groups as well.

Other subject variables that may prove interesting include sex of the viewer, place of residence, perceived reality of television, and use of nontelevision media. It is important to consider viewer characteristics when trying to unravel the mystery of the impact of television.

TELEVISION VARIABLES

There are two kinds of television variables that can be investigated—content variables and production technique variables. Most of the research in this area has focused on the impact of cognitive content variables (Ball & Bogatz, 1970, 1973; Bogatz & Ball, 1971; Chu & Schramm, 1967; Diaz-Guerrero et al., 1976). Although there may not have been much research in terms of linking selected content variables with the production variables, one can assume that "who" presents the content does have a direct relationship to the "what" issues involved in the production of the visuals and the related auditory devices employed. From research in advertising, for example, there is some evidence to suggest that the race of the communicator may play a role in the acquisition of product information (Hyams et al., 1975), and one can hypothesize that the race of the characters on the successful educational series like Sesame Street and Carrascolendas may be partially responsible for minority children's learning. Certainly, research on observational learning suggests that models who are more similar to viewers may lead to greater learning (Leifer, 1966; Maccoby & Wilson, 1957; Maccoby, Wilson, & Burton, 1958; Rosenkrans, 1967).

Studies of racial endorsement effects in commercials suggest both same-race and cross-race preferences for black children (Atkin, 1975b; Robertson et al., 1975). In a study of southern preschool black children (Neely, Heckel, & Leichtman, 1973), it was learned that black children were more likely to imitate the behavior of less attractive (punished) white models than they were to imitate attractive (rewarded) black models. These studies suggest that the race of the communicator is an important variable affecting learning. There is also evidence, however, that children will imitate a variety of models (Bandura, 1962; Stouwie, Hetherington, & Parke, 1970; Thelen & Fryrear, 1971). More research is needed to understand how these variables operate for black children. An investigation of the relative impact on minority children of majority, same-race minority, and other-minority presenters would be of special interest.

The second major area of investigation is on how the structural features of the medium—production techniques—affect learning (Dorr, 1977; Salomon, 1976). The structural features include things like type of visual slots, characteristics of the audio track, and pacing of the show. There has been very little investigation of the child's understanding of the visual grammar of television and of how this comprehension of the meaning of production techniques influences learning.

PROCESSES AFFECTING LEARNING

The final area of research that would be productive in understanding how present media affect the cognitive development and learning of minority children is the investigation of the processes that influence learning from television. The influence of adult encouragement to view or adult co-viewing seems to be an important area. The evaluations of *Sesame Street, Plaza Sesamo,* and *The Electric Company* (Ball & Bogatz, 1973; Diaz-Guerrero et al., 1976) suggest that adult encouragement to view facilitates learning in minority children. Several other studies with white children support the finding that adult co-viewing can increase learning. The Singers' work (1976) on imagination showed that an adult mediator plus a television program resulted in higher levels of imaginative play than did television alone. In a study of the responses of 8- to 10-year-old boys to television commercials (Prasad, Rao, & Sheikh, 1978), it was found that maternal advice was a more powerful influence than a commercial if the advertized product was moderately attractive. For highly desirable toys, maternal advice was ignored, and the commercial's ability to persuade was a more powerful influence. In another study (Corder-Bolz & O'Bryant, 1978), white male and female preschoolers were exposed to an entertainment program alone or an entertainment program with an adult co-viewer. In the television-plus-adult condition, children retained more information than did children in the television-alone condition.

There is evidence that adult co-viewing and adult commentary facilitate learning, but most of the research has been with preschoolers. More research is needed to determine if adult commentary and joint viewing has a similar impact across children of different ages and children of different racial and ethnic groups. The importance of understanding how much adult co-viewing and adult commentary can alter the television experience is crucial as one tries to use the medium in an effective and efficient manner.

Minority children, specifically black and Hispanic children, can and do learn cognitive content and cognitive skills from exposure to instructional, educational, and commercial television (Adler, *et al.*, 1977; Ball & Bogatz, 1970, 1973; Bogatz & Ball, 1971; Diaz-Guerrero & Holtzman, 1974). More research is needed to increase our knowledge of how content and production variables effect learning, how characteristics of minority children affect learning, and how other socialization agents can affect learning from television. Let us now turn to the issue of television's impact on the affective development of children.

AFFECTIVE DEVELOPMENT

Emotion Recognition

Little is known about television's influence on minority children's emotions, motivations, or feelings of self-confidence; there have been only a few isolated studies in these areas. Several television series have been developed with emotional content goals. For example, *Sesame Street* has specifically designed segments to help children's recognition of emotions such as happy, sad, or proud. *Mister Rogers' Neighborhood* focuses on the young child's emotional development; one segment of this series dealt with how one feels when a good friend moves away. A program entitled *Inside/Out*, developed by the Agency for Instructional Development, is a mental health series for older elementary-school-age children.

Very little evaluation research has been conducted on the emotional content of these programs. Preliminary evaluators of *Sesame Street* affect bits (Lasker & Bernath, 1974) suggest that preschool-age children can recognize simple emotions such as happy, sad, and mad, and that exposure through television increases their ability to recognize them in other situations. Although evaluations of *Inside/Out* have not been directed to its impact on the emotional development of viewers, there is evidence that older elementary school students and their teachers enjoy the programs, identify with the interpersonal and individual situations that are presented, and are provoked to stimulating discussions subsequent to viewing (National Instructional Television Center, 1973).

Research on motion pictures in the 1930s suggests that audiovisual stimuli can evoke strong emotional reactions in children, particularly in children under 12 years of age (Dysinger & Ruckmick, 1933). Osborne and Endsley (1971) studied the emotional reactions of young children to televised violence and found that preschoolers, some of whom were black, reacted more to films of human and cartoon violence than to nonviolent films. Children generally described human violence as scariest and recalled more details of films containing it. The children reported liking nonviolent cartoons best. Other research on television suggests that the emotional reactions of preschool children predicted subsequent aggressiveness. If the child responded favorably to the program, then the level of subsequent aggression was higher (Ekman, Liebert, Friesen, Harrison, Zlatchin, Malmstrom, & Baron, 1972).

Television and Self-Concept

There are several studies on television's impact on self-concept. The developers of *Carrascolendas* hypothesized that the self-concept of Chicano children exposed to a bilingual series that also focused on Mexican culture would be positively influenced, but research indicates that the series was not successful in this goal. The impact of film on black children's self-concept was also studied (Dimas, 1971): A 1-hr film featuring blacks in several social roles resulted in changes that could be interpreted as positive changes in self-concept.

There is a body of research on the impact of television on self-concept in which the children's willingness to imitate the same-race model was indirectly assessed and the nature of the children's attitudes toward their own minority group was evaluated.

In a study of the influence of the race of a televised role model on black children (Neeley et al., 1973), black preschoolers imitated white models, both positive and negative, more than they imitated black models. In a study of toy selection, Waters (1977) reports that black children imitated the toy selections of white models even when those toys were smaller and of inferior quality.

It should be noted, however, that research on *Sesame Street* (Bogatz & Ball, 1971), *The Electric Company* (Ball & Bogatz, 1973), *Carrascolendas* (Diaz-Guerrero et al., 1976), and *Villa Alegre* (Bilingual Children's Television, 1973) demonstrated that programs featuring positive minority models positively alter minority children's cognitive performance. The children accept and imitate the minority role models as models for their own behavior.

Studies of the racial attitudes of children exposed to television suggest how children may view themselves as minority group members. Research on *Sesame Street* (Bogatz & Ball, 1971), *Vegetable Soup*, a multiracial, educational series (Mays, Seidman, & Steiner, 1975), multiracial cartoons (Graves, 1977), and entertainment content (Leifer, Graves, & Phelps, 1976) show that the racial attitudes of black and white children can be altered after only 30 min exposure or after 2 years of exposure. In general, children's attitudes will change in the direction of the characterization of the minority actors, that is, positive racial attitudes are a consequence of exposure to positive racial presentations and negative racial attitudes are a consequence of exposure to negative presentations.

The research on television and affective development in minority children is sparse. Although television can influence the recognition of emotions and may cause emotional arousal, there is little to suggest that it can have a positive impact on self-concept. Still, television can alter attitudes toward one's own racial group in both positive and negative directions. It is not clear what determines the likelihood that a minority child will imitate the behavior of a minority role model.

Suggestions for Research

The need for research in this area is desperate. Innumerable papers have been written discussing the devastating effects of low self-concept, low self-esteem, and unclear racial identity on minority children. These characteristics place an undue roadblock in the developmental pathway of these children (Jones, 1972; Powell, 1973; Spurlock, 1973).

There are so many questions to be answered that I will only try to outline general areas of investigation that are likely to produce relevant research. As in the field of cognitive development, research is needed on the impact of television on the affective response of American Indian, Asian-American, Afro-American, Hispanic, children of both sexes and varying ages and socioeconomic backgrounds. Differences among the cultures of these groups would suggest that their affective worlds may have important, although perhaps subtle, differences.

On the television side of the dyad, it is important to understand the short-term and cumulative effects on affect of exposure to various types of television content. Does a particular diet of television predispose a child to particular emotional responses? Furthermore, what is the role of the structural, visual techniques in eliciting affective responses? Are zooms more likely to result in fear and anxiety than abrupt cuts?

The role of other agents must also be considered. What is the role of adult co-viewing in the relationship of television and affect? Is adult commentary sufficient to alter the effects of television on minority role model imitation or on attitudes toward one's own racial group?

CONCLUSIONS

Television is able to influence cognitive functioning and, it appears, affective responses. This is true for instructional, educational and commercial television. Although we know something about how blacks respond, we know nothing about the impact of television on American Indian and Asian-American children. Aside from the research on instructional television, we know little about what content or production techniques are most effective with different minority groups in terms of socialization issues. More varied television stimuli, more representative samples, more complex measures of dependent variables and, in general, research designs that derive from a clear theoretical perspective are needed.

Television can be a liberating force or it can be a stultifying one. It can aid in the growth and development of minority children or it can stifle, retard, and impede maturation. Adults have a responsibility to insure that television plays the most positive role possible in the lives of American Indian, Asian-American, Afro-American, and Hispanic, children. They deserve special attention and consideration because they are overburdened by the consequences of adult racist thinking. Through a more systematic examination of television in their lives, we may be able to help relieve the weight that has been tied around their necks.

REFERENCES

Adler, R.P., Friedlander, B.Z., Lesser, G.S., Meringoff, L., Robertson, T.S., Rossiter, J.R., & Ward, S. *Research on the effects of television advertising on children: A review of the literature and recommendations for future research.* Washington, D.C.: US Govt. Printing Office, 1977.

Alper, S.W., & Leidy, T.R. The impact of information transmissions through television. *Public Opinion Quarterly,* 1970, 33, 556–562.

Atkin, C.K. *Effects of television advertising on children, second year experimental evidence* (Unpublished Report No. 2). Michigan State University, 1975. a

Atkin, C.K. *Effects of television advertising on children: Content analysis of children's television commercials* (Unpublished Report No. 5). Michigan State University, 1975. b

Ball, S., & Bogatz, G.A. *The first year of* Sesame Street: *An evaluation.* Princeton, New Jersey: Educational Testing Service, 1970.

Ball, S., & Bogatz, G.A. *Reading with television: An evaluation of* The Electric Company. Princeton, New Jersey: Educational Testing Service, 1973.

Ball, S., & Bogatz, G.A. A reply. In T.D. Cook, H. Appleton, R.F. Conner, A. Shaffer, G.A. Tamkin, & S.J. Weber (Eds.) Sesame Street *revisited.* New York: Russell Sage Foundation, 1975.

Bandura, A. Social learning through imitation. In M.R. Jones (Ed.), *Nebraska Symposium on Motivation* (Vol. 10). Lincoln, Nebraska: Univ. of Nebraska Press, 1962.

Bever, T.G., Smith, M.L., Bengen, B., & Johnson, T.G. Young viewers troubling response to television ads. *Harvard Business Review*, 1975, *53*, 119–121.

Bilingual Children's Television. *A formative evaluation of Villa Alegre.* Unpublished paper, San Francisco: Bilingual Children's Television, 1973.

Bogatz, G.A., & Ball, S. *The second year of* Sesame Street: *A continuing evaluation*, Princeton, New Jersey: Educational Testing Service, 1971.

Chu, G.C., & Schramm, W. *Learning from television: What the research says.* Washington, D.C.: Nat. Assoc. of Educational Broadcasters, 1967.

Clark, C.X. Race, identification, and television violence. In *Television and social behavior* (Vol 5). Washington, D.C.: US Govt. Printing Office, 1972.

Collins, W.A. Learning of media content: A developmental study. *Child Development*, 1970, *41*, 1133–1142.

Collins, W.A. Effect of temporal separation between motivation, aggression and consequences: A developmental study. *Developmental Psychology*, 1973, *8*(2), 215–221.

Collins, W.A., Berndt, T.J., & Hess, V.L. Observational learning of motives and consequences for television aggression: A developmental study. *Child Development*, 1974, *45*, 789–802.

Collins, W.A., & Westby, S. *Children's processing of social information from televised dramatic programs.* Paper presented at biennial meeting of the Society for Research in Child Development, Denver, Colorado, April 1975.

Comstock, G. *Television and human behavior: The key studies.* Santa Monica, California: Rand Corporation, 1975.

Comstock, G., Chaffee, S., Katzman, M., McCombs, M., & Roberts, D. *Television and human behavior.* New York: Columbia Univ. Press, 1978.

Cook, T.D., Appleton, H., Conner, R.F., Shaffer, A., Tamkin, G.A., & Weber, S.J. Sesame Street *revisited.* New York: Russell Sage Foundation, 1975.

Corder-Bolz, C.R., & O'Bryant, S. Can people affect television? Teacher vs. program. *Journal of Communication*, 1978, *28*(1), 97–103.

Diaz-Guerrero, R., & Holtzman, W.H. Learning by televised *Plaza Sesamo* in Mexico. *Journal of Educational Psychology*, 1974, *66*, 632–643.

Diaz-Guerrero, R., Reyes-Lagunes, I., Witzke, D.B., & Holtzman, W.H. *Plaza Sesamo* in Mexico: An evaluation. *Journal of Communication*, 1976, *26*(2), 145–155.

Dimas, C. *The effect of motion pictures portraying black models on the self concept of black elementary school children.* Unpublished doctoral dissertation, Syracuse University, 1970.

Donohue, T.R. Effects of commercials on black children. *Journal of Advertising Research*, 1975, *15*, 41–47.

Dorr, A. *When I was a child, I thought as a child.* Unpublished paper, Harvard University, 1977.

Dubin, R., & Hedley, R.A. *The medium may be related to the message: College instruction by Television.* Eugene, Oregon: Univ. of Oregon Press, 1969.

Dysinger, W.S., & Ruckmick, C.A. *The emotional responses of children to the motion picture situation.* New York: Macmillan, 1933.

Ekman, P., Liebert, R.M., Friesen, W.V., Harrison, R., Zlatchin, C., Malmstron, E.J., & Baron, R.A. Facial expressions of emotion while watching televised violence as predictors of subsequent aggression. In G.A. Comstock, E.A. Rubinstein, & J.P. Murray (Eds.), *Television and Social behavior* (Vol 5). Washington, D.C.: US Govt. Printing Office, 1972.

Freyberg, J. Increasing imaginative play of urban disadvantaged kindergarten children through systematic training. In J.L. Singer (Ed.), *The child's world of make believe.* New York: Academic Press, 1973.

Frueh, T., & McGhee, P.E. Traditional sex-role development and amount of time spent watching television. *Developmental Psychology,* 1975, *11,* 109–110.

Gerbner, G. Violence in television drama: Trends and symbolic functions. *Television and social behavior* (Vol. 1). Washington, D.C.: US Govt. Printing Office, 1972.

Gerbner, G., & Gross, L. *The social reality of television drama.* Unpublished manuscript, Annenberg School of Communication, 1973.

Goldberg, M.E., & Gorn, G.J. Children's reactions to television advertising: An experimental approach. *Consumer Research,* 1974, *1,* 69–75.

Graves, S.B. *Racial diversity in children's television: Its impact on racial attitudes and stated program preferences of young children.* Unpublished doctoral dissertation, Harvard University, 1975.

Graves, S.B. *The psychological impact of black portrayals on television.* Unpublished paper, Social Science Research Council, New York, 1977.

Greeley, B. Black viewers tune in soul and Cronkite. *Variety,* September 18, 1974, p. 35.

Greenberg, B.S., & Dervin, B. *Use of mass media by the urban poor.* New York: Praeger, 1970.

Greenberg, B.S., & Reeves, B. Children and the perceived reality of television. *Journal of Social Issues,* 1976, *32,* (4), 86–97.

Grier, W., & Cobbs, Price M. *Black rage.* New York: Bantam, 1968.

Hale, G.A., Miller, L.K., & Stevenson, H.W. Incidental learning of film content: A developmental study. *Child Development,* 1968, *39,* 69–78.

Harrison-Ross, P., & Wyden, B. *The black child: A parent's guide.* New York: Berkeley, 1973.

Hawkins, R.P. Learning of peripheral content in films: A developmental study. *Child Development,* 1973, *44,* 214–217.

Hellmuth, J. (Ed.). *Disadvantaged child* (Vol. 1). New York: Brunner/Mazel, 1967.

Hellmuth, J. (Ed.). *Disadvantaged child* (Vol. 2): *Head Start and early intervention.* New York: Burnner/Mazel, 1968.

Holaday, P.W., & Stoddard, G.D. *Getting ideas from the movies.* New York: Macmillan, 1933.

Hyams, L., Tanner, S., & Rossiter, J.R. *Effects of race models on children's product preferences.* Paper presented at Conference on Culture and Communications, Temple University, Philadelphia, Pennsylvania, April 1975.

Jones, J.M. *Prejudice and racism.* Reading, Massachusetts: Addison-Wesley, 1972.

Kenny, D.A. *PANAL: Panal data analysis of the first year of Sesame Street.* Unpublished research report, Harvard University, Department of Psychology, 1975.

Lasker, H., & Bernath, N. *Status of comprehension study of* Sesame Street *affect bits.* Unpublished report to the Children's Television Workshop, Harvard University, 1974, 1–12.

Leifer, A.D. *The relationship between cognitive awareness in selected awares and differential imitation of a same-sex model.* Unpublished master's thesis, Stanford University, 1966.

Leifer, A.D., Collins, W.A., Gross, B.M., Taylor, P.H., Andrews, L., & Blackburn, E.R. Developmental aspects of variables relevant to observational learning. *Child Development,* 1971, *42,* 1509–1516.

Leifer, A.D., Gordon, N.J., & Graves, S.B. *Children and television: Recommended directions for future effort.* Report to the Office of Child Development, May 1973.

Leifer, A.D., Gordon, N.J., & Graves, S.B. Children's television: More than mere entertainment. *Harvard Educational Review,* 1974, *44,* 213–245.

Leifer, A.D., Graves, S.B., & Gordon, N.J. *When people think television is a window on their world.* Paper presented at Annual Meeting of the American Educational Research Association, Washington, D.C., April, 1975.

Leifer, A.D., Graves, S.B., & Phelps, E. *Monthly report of critical evaluation of television project.* Unpublished manuscript, Harvard University, Center for Research in Children's Television, 1976.

Leifer, A.D., & Roberts, D.F. Children's responses to television violence. In J.P. Murray, E.A. Rubinstein, & G.A. Comstock (Eds.), *Television and social behavior* (Vol. 2); *Television and social learning.* Washington, D.C.: US Govt. Printing Office, 1972.

Lesser, G., Fifer, G., & Clark, D.H. Mental abilities of children in different social and cultural groups. In J.I. Roberts (Ed.), *School children in the urban slum.* New York: Free Press, 1967.

Levin, S., & Anderson, D. The development of attention. *Journal of Communication,* 1976, *26,* 2.

Liebert, R.M., Neale, J.M., & Davidson, E.S. *The early window: Effects of Television on children and youth.* Elmsford, New York: Pergamon, 1973.

Lyle, J. *The people look at public television,* Washington, D.C.: Corporation for Public Broadcasting, 1975.

Lyle, J., & Hoffman, H.R. Children's use of television and other media. In E.A. Rubinstein, G.A. Comstock & J.P. Murray (Eds.). *Television and social behavior* (Vol. 4): Washington, D.C.: US Govt. Printing Office, 1972. (a)

Lyle, J., & Hoffman, H.R. Explorations in patterns of television viewing by preschool-age children. In E.A. Rubinstein, G.A. Comstock & J.P Murray (Eds.). *Television and social behavior* (Vol. 4): *Television in day-to-day life: Patterns of use.* Washington, D.C.: US Govt. Printing Office, 1972. (b)

Maccoby, E.E., & Wilson, W.C. Identification and observational learning from films. *Journal of Abnormal and Social Psychology,* 1957, *55,* 76–87.

Maccoby, E.E., Wilson, W.C., & Burton, R.V. Differential movie-viewing behavior of male and female viewers. *Journal of Personality,* 1958, *26,* 259–267.

McLuhan, M. *Understanding media: The extensions of man.* New York: Signet, 1964.

McLuhan, M., & Fiore, Q. *The medium is the message.* New York: Bantam Books, 1967.

Marshall, H., & Hahn, S.C. Experimental modification of dramatic play. *Journal of Personality and Social Psychology,* 1967, *5,* 119–122.

May, M.A., & Lumsdaine, A.A. *Learning from films.* New Haven, Connecticut: Yale Univ. Press, 1958.

Mays, L., Seidman, S.K., & Steiner, V.S. *An evaluation report on* Vegetable Soup: The effects of a multi-ethnic children's television series on intergroup attitudes of children. Unpublished manuscript, New York State Department of Education, 1975.

Meline, C.W. Does the medium matter? *Journal of Communication*, 1976, *26*(3), 81–90.

Meyer, T.P., Donohue, T.R., & Henke, L.L. Black children's perception of television commercials: A cognitive development study. *Journal of Advertising Research*, 1978, *18*(15): 51–62.

Meyer, T.P., Donohue, T.R., & Henke, L.L. Black and white children's value perceptions of specific adult and child-oriented television commercials. Unpublished manuscript, 1977.

Minton, J.H. The impact of *Sesame Street* on readiness. *Sociology of Education*, 1975, *48*, 141–151.

NBC, Social Research Department. *Public television*. New York: National Broadcasting Company, 1976.

National Instructional Television Center. Inside/out: A guide for teachers. Bloomington, Indiana: *Author*, 1973.

Neely, J.J., Heckel, R.V., & Leichtman, H.M. The effect of race of model and response consequences to the model on imitation in children. *Journal of Social Psychology*, 1973, *89*, 225–231.

Newcomb, A.F., & Collins, W.A. *Children's processing of television portrayals of black and white families*. Paper presented at Biennial Meeting of Society for Research in Child Development, New Orleans, Louisiana, March 1977.

Nielson Company, *National Audience Demographics Report*. New York: 1977.

Office of Economic Opportunity. *Upward bound*, Washington, D.C.: US Govt. Printing Office, 1965.

Osborne, D.K., & Endsley, R.C. Emotional reactions of young children to television violence. *Child Development*, 1971, *42*, 321–331.

Palmer, E.L., Chen, M., & Lesser, G.S. *Sesame Street:* Patterns of international adaptation. *Journal of Communication*, 1976, *26*(2), 109–123.

Peterson, R.C., & Thurstone, L.L. *Motion pictures and the social attitudes of children*. New York: Macmillan, 1933.

Piaget, J. *Play, dreams and imitation in childhood*. New York: Norton, 1962.

Piaget, J., & Inhelder, B. *The psychology of the child*. New York: Basic Books, 1969.

Pingree, S. *A developmental study of the attitudinal effects of nonsexist television commercials under varied conditions of perceived reality*. Unpublished doctoral dissertation, Stanford University, 1975.

Powell, G.J. Self-concept in white and black children. In C.V. Willie, B.M. Kramer, & B.S. Brown (Eds.), *Racism and mental health*. Pittsburgh, Pennsylvania: Univ. of Pittsburgh Press, 1973.

Prasad, V.K., Rao, J.R., & Sheikh, A.A. Mother vs. commercial. *Journal of Communication*, 1978, *28*(1), 91–96.

Reid, C., & MacLennan, D.W. *Instructional television and film: Summary of studies*. Washington, D.C.: US Office of Education, 1967.

Roberts, J.I. (Ed.). *School children in the urban slum*. New York: Free Press, 1967.

Robertson, T.S., & Rossiter, J.R. Children's responsiveness to commercials. *Journal of Communication*, 1977, *27*(1), 101–106.

Robertson, T.S., Rossiter, J.R., & Brenner, D. *Children's responses to commercials: A conjoint analysis*. Unpublished working paper, University of Pennsylvania, Wharton School, 1975.

Rosenkrans, M.A. Imitation of children as a function of perceived similarities to a social model of vicarious reinforcement. *Journal of Personality and Social Psychology*, 1967, *7*, 429–434.

Rossiter, J.R., & Robertson, T. Children's television commercials: Testing the defenses. *Journal of Communication*, 1974 (Autumn) *24*(4): 137–144.

Salomon, G. Can we affect cognitive skills through visual media? A hypothesis and initial findings. *Audiovisual Communication Review*, 1972, *20*, 401–423.

Salomon, G. Cognitive skill learning across cultures. *Journal of Communication*, 1976, 26(2), 138–144.

Schramm, W. *Big media, little media*. Stanford, California: Stanford University, Institute for Communication Research, 1973.

Siegal, A.E. Communicating with the next generation, *Journal of Communication*, 1975, 25(4), 14–24.

Singer, D.G., & Singer, J.L. Some characteristics of make-believe play in nursery school children: An observational study. In J.L. Singer (Ed.), *The child's world of make-believe*. New York: Academic Press, 1973.

Singer, J.L., & Singer, D.G. Can television stimulate imaginative play? *Journal of Communication*, 1976, *26*, 74–80.

Smilansky, S. *The effects of sociodramatic play on disadvantaged preschool children*. New York: Wiley, 1968.

Spurlock, J. Some consequences of racism for children. In C. Willie, Kramer, B.M., & Brown, B.S. (Eds.), *Racism and mental health*. Pittsburgh, Pennsylvania: Univ. of Pittsburgh Press, 1973.

Stouwie, R.J., Hetherington, E.M., & Parke, R.D. Some determinants of children's self-reward behavior after exposure to discrepant reward criteria. *Developmental Psychology*, 1970, *3*, 313–319.

Thelen, M.H., & Fryrear, J.L. Effect of observer and model race on the imitation of standards of self-reward. *Developmental Psychology*, 1971, *5*, 133–135.

Violence! *TV Guide*, June 14–20, 1975, pp. 4–7.

Wade, S.E. Adolescents, creativity, and media: An exploratory study. *American Behavioral Scientist*, 1971, *14*, 341–351.

Ward, S., Reale, G., & Levinson, D. Children's perceptions, explanations, and judgments of television advertising: A further exploration. In E.A. Rubinstein, G.A. Comstock, & J.P. Murray (Eds.), *Television and social behavior* (Vol. 4): *Television in day-to-day life: Patterns of use*. Washington, D.C.: US Govt. Printing Office, 1972.

Ward, S., & Wackman, D. Television advertising and intrafamily influence: Children's purchase influence attempts and parental yielding. In E.A. Rubenstein, G.A. Comstock, & J.P. Murray (Eds.), *Television and social behavior* (Vol. 4): *Television in day-to-day life: Patterns of use*. Washington, D.C.: US Govt. Printing Office, 1972.

Waters, H.F. What television does to kids. *Newsweek*, February 21, 1977, pp. 62–65.

Wilkening, H.E. *The psychology almanac*. Monterey, California: Brooks/Cole, 1973.

Williams, F., & Van Wart, G. *Carrasolendas: Bilingual education through television*. New York: Praeger, 1974.

Winn, Marie. *The plug-in drug: Television, children and the family*. New York: Viking, 1977.

Wolman, B.B. (Ed.). *Dictionary of behavioral science*. New York: Van Nostrand Reinhold, 1973.

TELEVISION, MINORITY CHILDREN, AND PERSONAL IDENTITY ISSUES

Television, Ethnic Minorities, and Mental Health: An Overview

To provide the reader with a common frame of reference, it is appropriate to first define the terms of the topic. I have elected to identify "ethnic minorities" as the four racial minorities in this country—American Indian, Asian American, Afro-American, and Hispanic. From the many definitions of mental health, I have selected that offered by Thomas and Comer (1973) as most pertinent to the issue presented in this volume: "Mental health includes people's feelings of worth in the context of the total cultural and social system as well as within the identifiable groups to which they belong [p. 165]."

The development of mental health or impairment is rooted in an individual's early life experiences. These experiences may be shaped and/or impinged on by a number of factors including the nature of prenatal care and early parenting. Of course, these factors are dependent on a number of others, both intrinsic and extrinsic to the parenting figures. A reference to the impact of black identity at different levels of development is illustrative. If the black child's parents have coped successfully with the discriminatory practices that they have experienced and feel reasonably comfortable about their racial identity, their children are more likely not to falter when they experience racist ac-

71

TELEVISION AND
THE SOCIALIZATION OF THE MINORITY CHILD

tions (Spurlock & Lawrence, 1979). Socioeconomic issues are significant variables. Davis (1968) noted that:

> The chances for successful negotiations of infantile stages of personality development are significantly decreased for the child of any family at the lowest end of the socio-economic scale and, since. . . . Negro families occupy a disproportionately large segment of the population at the end of scale there will be a larger proportion of Negro children emerging from infancy with specific vulnerabilities to later damaging experience [p. 95].

Chess and Hassibi (1978) note the potentially destructive impact of a number of spin-offs of existence in poverty all of which lend to feelings of hopelessness and powerlessness: insufficient diet that tends to produce a low energy level and reduced responsiveness to the environment; overcrowded housing; reduced or absence of public services; and substandard schools. Reports about the specific vulnerabilities of children from some minority groups abound; that is, single parenting, absent fathers, and/or multiple mothering. However, less attention has been given to the input of the extended family (often "adoptive"), which often greatly dilutes the negative impact of the environment. (Spurlock & Lawrence, 1979).

The development of self-esteem as it intertwines with social process (Thomas & Chess, 1980) warrants particular attention here. The stresses generated by societal values that are embedded in racial prejudices make a marked impact on the self-esteem of minority people. A major discriminatory practice is embedded, perhaps, in the misconception of homogeneity within minority groups and the stereotypes of color. For most minorities, these notions are reinforced by nearly all their daily experiences; television viewing is no exception.

THE IMPACT OF TELEVISION
ON ALL CHILDREN

The nature and intensity of the impact of television on the growing child has provoked numerous studies and debate. Perhaps the reader recalls a congressional subcommittee's investigation of delinquency in the early 1950s. In a review of the hearings, Bogart (1958) noted the existence of different opinions about the influences of television on children. He concluded that the aggressive impulses of children are rooted in their interpersonal relationship with parents and significant others and that television may influence the nature of the expression of psychological problems. In their review of studies of the effect of television on children, Efron and Hickey (1969) pointed to the inconclusiveness of much of the research. They suggested that research to support the hypothesis that imitation occurs in response to the actual viewing situation was lacking, although it had been observed in laboratory studies. On the other hand, Rothenberg (1975) pointed out that 50 studies yielded evidence that viewing of violence causes an increase in aggressive behavior in the young. It has also been noted that aggression displayed in television is more likely to disturb children and to be imitated by them when aggression is part of their real-life experience (Garry, 1967). Thus, children living in communities with high incidents of acts of violence are particularly vulnerable to television images of violence.

A former president of the Washington, D.C. Board of Education, Therman Evans, suggested that violence portrayed on television "should be of extreme importance for Black parents and Black people at least for two reasons . . . that Black-on-Black violence is epidemic [and] that this violence is being fostered by younger and younger members of our community" ["Media, violence and black people," 1976, p. A-11]. Reports of violence are a part of the daily newscasts, Evans said, citing a 6-year-old who suggested to her parents that the family not watch the news because "there's too many bad things happening [personal communication]."

A more recent account of charges and countercharges about the negative impact of television on the health of America's children is summarized by Keniston (1977):

> Television . . . illustrates the mixed blessing of technological change in American society. It is a new medium, promising extraordinary benefits: great educational potential, a broadening of experiences, enrichment of daily life, entertainment for all. But it teaches children the uses of violence, offers material consumption as the answer to life's problems, sells harmful products, habituates viewers to constant interaction and to other forms of learning [p. 55].

Some observers and critics are as concerned about the amount of time that children spend watching television as they are about the content of the material viewed. By the time average children are 16, they have watched from 12,000 to 15,000 hr of television. This is the equivalent of 15–20 months of watching, 24 hr a day (Bronfenbrenner, 1970). Literature related to children and television contains numerous references that illustrate that children in disadvantaged homes are exposed to more hours of television that those living in advantaged circumstances. Of particular concern is the finding that an excessive diet of television viewing impairs cognitive development (Singer, 1977).

The heaviest period of television viewing by children is during prime time. It should also be noted that many reruns are now programmed during prime time. Thus, children see more programs designed for adults that those especially developed for the younger generation. These viewing experiences expose them to commercials that express a powerful set of values. These advertisements seem to promise that for every ill there is a simple cure (Keniston, 1977). Of greater concern for some parents, clinicians, and researchers, is the resulting curtailment of active recreational activities, to say nothing of homework and/or self-directed reading. Siegel (1977) said that the profound significance of television is that as a source of general information it may have a greater impact on a child's social development than school.

THE IMPACT OF TELEVISION ON MINORITY CHILDREN

In a presentation to a group assembled for the National Conference on Human Experimentation, Yette (1976) spoke of "the mass media . . . systematically programmed to devalue Black and other colored peoples, and to foster self-hate and other destructive behavior patterns [p. 2]." He cited a number of incidents demonstrating the negative impact of television. Two excerpts are summarized for illustration. The first is a reported interview with newscaster John Chancellor: "While on leave from NBC to direct the Voice of American in 1966, Chancellor told Time magazine: 'It's a mistake to think that television alone makes up people's minds on broad questions. What it does is amplify their prejudices' [p. 15]." Second, Yette gave the following account of a reporter's description of the city of Chicago from a 1975 sequence from a *Today's Show* bicentennial program. It is a striking example of the amplification of prejudices by a television production.

> The camera panned the Chicago North Shore, the skyline off Lake Michigan, and the commercial opulence of Michigan Avenue. Then, to close his narration, to sum up his report . . . [he] said: "But there is a poor side, a corrupt side of Chicago." And, as he said "corrupt", the camera moved in from the richness of the North Shore, and focused up tight solely on the face of a small Black child, standing beside a fence that looked like it should have been taken from the set of either the *Sanford and Son* junkyard or the *Good Times* tenement [p. 18].

Here, the media of television served to reinforce the prejudice that black identity is characterized by corrupt behavior. Of significance is that the reporter's reference to corruption omitted any statement about the documented gangsterism and political "wheeling and dealing" that has been a part of the history of the city of Chicago.

Negative stereotypes of minorities are incorporated into history books used in secondary education and are seen in the films of the 1930s and in contemporary television productions. Attneave (1979) addressed this pattern in relation to American Indian children, saying: "The media reinforces negative stereotypes of American Indians, as well as many of the problems experienced by Indian children themselves. These derive in part from films, from television westerns, and from the vestigial animosities that remain between the conqueror and the defeated [p. 241]." Other examples of the perpetuation of negative sterotypes of minority populations are discussed in a report of the U. S. Commission on Civil Rights (1977). Filmmaker Irvin Paik is quoted as observing that Asians are usually depicted as servants, Karate experts, Fu Manchu type villains, or as Charlie Chan, the supergood, superwise, self-effacing detective (U. S. Commission on Civil Rights, 1977, p. 7). It was further noted that the roles of Asian males are seldom played by Asians and that these type of films have been an integral part of television programming. This pattern is similar to that followed in the production of the *Amos 'n' Andy* radio and television series. It has been suggested that the original actors, who also created the story, trained black actors to project the characters "in the nuances of the stereotype with which whites would be comfortable [Barnouw, 1970, p. 297]." The absence of any reference to the Hispanic population in the report's account of programming in the 1950s is puzzling. Reference is made to the racist coloring, as illustrated in commercials depicting this minority group in the 1960s. Mexicans were represented in the character of "Frito Bandido," who used a pair of six-shooters to steal corn chips. In spite of the numerous protests calling for the commercial to be banned, it appeared on the networks for 4 years.

However, news coverage during the 1960s gave television viewers an opportunity to see some of "good guys" who were also Afro-American. Viewers saw and heard Dr. Martin Luther King, Jr. calling for equal opportunities for black people through peaceful means. After Dr. King's assassination, the viewers also saw the destructive behavior of black people as the cameras zeroed in on the looting of buildings that had been broken into and often set ablaze. Some mental health professionals considered this behavior to be a defense mechanism—identification with the aggressor. The firearms and bombs once used against blacks had disappeared from the television screen; in their stead one saw bricks and matches used by those who had been discriminated against.

The Report of the National Advisory Commission on Civil Disorders (Kerner Commission, 1968) indicated both positive and objectionable impressions of the news coverage of the aftermath of the assassination. It was reported that twice as many "calm" television sequences were shown as "emotional" series (p. 369). On the other hand, it was reported that "live television coverage via helicopter of the 1965 Watts riot had been inflammatory [p. 372]." Furthermore, it was noted that the underlying slum problems were given little coverage as compared to that received by confrontation between blacks and whites.

EFFORTS TO CORRECT OVERSIGHTS
AND DISTORTIONS

The results of the television industry's efforts to eradicate the negative stereotypes of minorities has been sharply debated. This is illustrated in a critique of the seven-part series *Of Black America*, hosted by Bill Cosby and broadcast in the summer of 1968. The U.S. Commission on Civil Rights (1977) noted that the series "the first of its kind to explore in a serious manner the extent to which blacks had been ignored or degraded by white America, but CBS was criticized for employing few Blacks in the planning and production of the series [p. 10]." Hobson (1974) described the programs as having said much *about* black America but nothing "by, for and of" black America (p. 187). The network and the producers of the series *Julia*, in which Diahann Carroll starred as a widowed nurse and the mother of an elementary-school-age child, seriously set out to correct the stereotypes held about black people. However, this writer's immediate and sustained concern was that the stereotype of the fatherless black family had been sustained and that the real-life experience of the average black family had been "whitewashed." This impression has been eloquently expressed by Fife (1974):

> Giving the entire series the benefit of the doubt, there was nothing malicious about *Julia*. It was simply another bit of fluffy TV viewing. . . . It was not what blacks visualized when the Kerner Commission called for more positive black images in the media. *Julia's* main failings were based on what it omitted, and its basic approach to the presentation of black family life in the U.S.A. Though it had some gentle "kidding" jokes between Julia and her white associates, it didn't recognize the facts of black–white communication problems: everyone in the show operated on a fairly one-dimensional basis that excluded black identity [p. 13].

The increased visibility of blacks in more recent series has more frequently than not reinforced the negative stereotypes. *Hey, Baby I'm Back* is a case in point. Here again, the black father is presented as immature and irresponsible; the Sapphire image of the black woman is incorporated into the image of the maternal grandmother. No doubt, the series was written as comedy; the audience is heard "breaking up" with laughter in each segment that this writer has observed. But, as Yette (1976) has written: "Laughter is not always comedy; sometimes it is disguised tragedy poorly understood. Much of what now passes as Black television comedy is in the latter group. At worst, it is tragedy; at best, it is poor taste [p. 20]." *Good Times* and *The Jeffersons* are striking examples: "The victim of corruption both takes the blame for it, and is taught to enjoy (as in *Good Times*) and to participate (as in *The Jeffersons*) in the victim's role [p. 20]." However, it should be noted that some health and social problems have been realistically addressed on these programs. For example, the high rate of hypertension among blacks and the topic of equal employment opportunity has been dealt with on *Good Times*.

Topper Carew, a producer of children's programs, is quoted in a *Time* essay (Lance, "Blacks on TV: A disturbing image," 1978) as supporting the notion that programs about blacks are white properties. "They have a heavy black presence, that's all. They are White shows with Black people appearing on them [p. 101]." This kind of patterning is also observable in programs in which other minority groups are represented. In the real world, Asian Americans are well known for their competence in the sciences, but the role delegated to an Asian in *Quincy* is that of a technician; (who although competent, is given a subservient role). In the real world, Chicanos are not homogenous, but in the early episodes of *Chico and the Man* they were portrayed as uniformly lazy and slovenly. A different picture of Hispanic character was shown only after protests from Hispanic groups.

USE AND MISUSE OF TELEVISION VIEWING

Minority populations use and misuse television for some of the same reasons that the majority group use or misuse this medium. It should be noted that the conclusion of one study (Haskins, 1974) was that children of the white middle class have benefitted *more*, even though the program's goal was to aid children *who had been identified as disadvantaged*. Far too often, television watching is used as a baby sitter. It is also used as a method of rewarding children (i.e., a promise to stay up later to watch a particular program if chores are adequately and promptly done) and of punishing them (the banning of television watching for a designated period of time because of some misbehavior). For both adults and children, television is frequently used to dilute boredom and/or as a means of escape. The phenomena of addiction may well be related to the latter. This is vividly illustrated by the vast number of viewers of the day-time "soaps" and their need to be "filled in" if an episode is missed. It should be emphasized that men who are available for daytime viewing have been similarly affected; a similar patterning has also been noted in segments of the adolescent population.

For families struggling at the lower economic levels, television may be the only affordable entertainment. Certainly, it is a major source of entertainment, not only for sports enthusiasts but also for those who view situation comedies as pure entertainment. Some black viewers of *Good Times* are more amused by the antics of J.J. rather than troubled by the portrayal of a black adolescent as perpetually clowning.

Some minority parents, not unlike parents of the majority group, make use of some programming for educational purposes for their children by arranging for them to view such programs as *Sesame Street* and *Mister Rogers' Neighborhood*. A sizeable percentage of minority adults have taken advantage of courses offered by public television. *Roots* and *The Autobiography of Miss Jane Pittman* have met multiple needs, especially for black viewers.

The viewers' attempts to use television to dilute boredom and/or to escape real-life situations are particularly distressing. This pattern can be especially disastrous to children because excessive viewing retards their cognitive development. Both children and adults tend to deprive themselves of other economically affordable, growth-promoting activities.

SUMMARY

The cursory nature of this overview may well prompt some to charge it with oversights of importance. No attention has been given to the fact that the increased appearances of people of color in programming means that there has been a growing economic benefit to some. There is no question that economic security is an important factor in the development of and maintenance of mental health.

The fact that history repeats itself has been underscored. Examples have been cited to show that some gains have been made, but that the gains appear woven into a fabric of reinforcement of racial biases. In the long run, the mental health of all viewers is in potential jeopardy because of the ripple effects of ethnic and racial prejudices.

REFERENCES

Attneave, C.L. The American Indian child. In J.D. Call, J.D. Noshpitz, R.L. Cohen, & I.N. Berlin (Eds.), *Basic handbook of child psychiatry*. New York: Basic Books, 1979.

Barnouw, E. *The golden web: A history in the U. S., 1933–1953* (Vol. 2). London and New York: Oxford Univ. Press, 1970.

Bogart, L. *The age of television*. New York: Unger, 1958.

Bronfrenbrenner, U. *Two worlds of childhood: U.S. and U.S.S.R.* New York: Russell Sage Foundation, 1970.

Chess, S., & Hassibi, M. *Principles and practice of child psychiatry*. New York: Plenum, 1978.

Davis, E.B. The American Negro: From family membership to personal and social identity. *Journal of the National Medical Association*, 1968, 60, 92–99.

Efron, E., & Hickey, N. *TV and your child: In search of an answer*. New York: Triangle, 1969.

Evans, T.E. Media, violence and black people. *Washington Post*, August 4, 1976, A–11.

Fife, N.D. Black image in American TV: The first two decades. *The Black Scholar*, 1974, 6, 9–10.

Garry, R. Television's impact on the child. *Children and TV: Television's impact on the child*. Washington, D.C.: Association for Childhood Education International, 1967 (Bulletin 21-A).

Haskins, J. New Black image in the mass media: How educational is educational TV? *Freedomsways*, 1974, 14(3), 200–208.

Hobson, S.M. The rise and fall of Blacks in serious television. *Freedomsways*, 1974, 14(3), 185–199.

Keniston, K. (with the Carnegie Council on Children). *All our children: The American family under pressure*. New York: Harcourt Brace Jovanovich, 1977.

Kerner Commission. *Report of the National Advisory Commission on Civil Disorders*. New York: Bantam, 1968.

Morrow, L. Blacks on TV: a disturbing image. *Time*, March 27, 1978, pp. 101–102.

Rothenberg, M.B. Effects of television violence in children and youth. *Journal of the American Medical Association*, 1975, 234, 1043–1046.

Siegel, A. *Effects of television on children*. Paper presented at the Physician's Training Session on Television and Children, Chicago, Illinois, October 1977.

Singer, J.L. *TV imaginative play and cognitive development: Some problems and possibilities*. Paper presented at the Annual Meeting of the American Psychoanalytic Association, San Francisco, California, 1977.

Spurlock, J., & Lawrence, L. The black child. In J.D. Call, J.D. Noshpitz, R.L. Cohen, & I.N. Berlin (Eds.), *Basic handbook of child psychiatry*. New York: Basic Books, 1979.

Thomas, A., & Chess, S. The self and self-concept. *The dynamics of psychological development*. New York: Brunner/Mazel, 1980.

Thomas, C.S., & Comer, J.P. Racism and mental health services. In C.V. Willie, B.M.

Kramer, & B.S. Brown (Eds.), *Racism and mental health*. Pittsburgh, Pennsylvania: Univ. of Pittsburgh Press, 1973.

U. S. Commission on Civil Rights. *Window dressing on the set: Women and minorities in television*. Washington, D.C.: US Govt. Printing Office, 1977.

Yette, S.F. *The mass media v. the Black mind: Creating the behavior statistics*. Paper presented at the National Minority Conference on Human Experimentation, Reston, Virginia, January 1976.

Ruby Takanishi

The Influence of Television on the Ethnic Identity of Minority Children: A Conceptual Framework

Television is a pervasive presence during childhood in American society. Minority group children watch a great deal of television, as do their white counterparts. Several studies indicate that low-income black children and adolescents watch television more than do their white peers (Comstock, 1975; Dominick & Greenberg, 1970), and that they consider television a trusted and reliable source of information (Greenberg & Dervin, 1970). Data on the television-viewing behavior and preferences of Asian-American, Native-American, and Hispanic populations (Eslien, 1974) are virtually nonexistent.

Like television, race is also a pervasive fact of American childhood (Goodman, 1952). The racial awareness and ethnic group identification of children are influenced by a wide variety of individuals, including parents, siblings, peers, teachers, and other adults as well as by children's direct encounters with the environment. Television plays a potentially important role together with these socializing agents. However, its influence on ethnic identity and intergroup attitudes has not been widely investigated. Although the representation of blacks on television has increased in recent years (Bush, Solomon, & Hair, 1977), little is known about the impact of these representational shifts on ethnic identity. The relationship between television violence and ag-

TELEVISION AND
THE SOCIALIZATION OF THE MINORITY CHILD

gressive behavior remains the most heavily researched area in television's role as a socialization agent (Liebert & Schwartzberg, 1977).

Studies have explored the proportional representation and character images of minority groups on television (E. Barcus, 1971; F. E. Barcus, 1977; Mendelson & Young, 1972; Ormiston & Williams, 1973; Seggar, 1977). Minority groups have been traditionally underrepresented and presented in stereotyped roles (Clark, 1969; Seggar & Wheeler, 1973). In response to ethnic group militancy during the 1960s, blacks became somewhat more visible on television (Barcus, 1977; Bush *et al.*, 1977). However, serious questions have been raised about the manner in which they have been portrayed (Bond, 1975; Clark, 1969; Collier, 1974; Pierce, Carew, Pierce-Gonzalez, & Willis, 1977).

Barcus (1977) conducted an extensive content analysis of weekend and weekday afternoon commercial children's television. He found that representation of minorities was still sparse in 1975. Program characters were predominantly white (89% on weekends, 96% on weekday afternoons). Blacks constituted 7% and 3%, of the weekend and weekday programming, respectively. Other minorities were virtually nonexistent. Barcus concluded that white children view a world that is unrealistically populated with people like themselves, whereas minority children see a world in which they are, for the most part, invisible. Barcus's study is limited by the fact that children's television viewing is heaviest during prime time and late afternoon. The weekend, daytime "children's ghetto" represents less than one-fifth of children's total viewing time (National Science Foundation, 1977).

From the studies on ethnic representation and portrayals, some individuals have suggested that television must have deleterious effects on the self-concept and ethnic identity of minority children, particularly since negative images are so consistently presented on children's programming (Rutstein, 1974). Others suggest that the increased presence of black characters on television may lead to enhanced self-image and ethnic identity. Both suggestions are based on the assumption that television has a unidirectional effect on children's ethnic identity. In fact, there is a paucity of studies that have focused on the impact of television on children's ethnic identity. Studies of the social effects of television have been explored mainly at the surface level, for example, on sex- and race-role presentations (Liebert & Schwartzberg, 1977). None of the existing studies on television and its influence on ethnic identity have actually measured ethnic identity.

Furthermore, as Ball (1976) has detailed, the difficulty of conducting research on the effects of television, whatever the outcomes of interest, make it an undertaking in which we are unlikely to obtain clear and unequivocal results. In addition to the design and measurement problems involved in determining television's short- and long-term impact, television remains but one of the multiple socializing agents that influence the development of children in our society. Furthermore, we are only beginning to understand the complex processes by which television exerts its influences.

This chapter will focus on the potential impact of television on the development of ethnic identity in children from minority groups in terms of programming content, character portrayals, and ethnic representation. The influence of television on self-concept is the topic of Chapter 6, by Gloria Powell (this volume). For the purposes of this chapter, an *ethnic group* refers to a group of individuals who share sociocultural experiences and/or similar physical characteristics. Such groups may be viewed by their members and/or nonmembers as religious, racial, national, linguistic, and/or geographical (Dashefsky, 1976). What ethnic group members have in common is their ethnicity. *Ethnic identity* is defined as an attachment to an ethnic group and a positive orientation toward being a member of that group. In line with Blu (1977), each group defines itself partially in relation to others. The content or image of group identity affects both members' and nonmembers' views and actions toward each other.

Although the task of this chapter is to focus on the socializing influence of television on minority children, it is important to state from the onset that given the existing power relations in American society, it is equally important that studies examine the impact of television on how white children perceive and relate to minority people. Television can have a particularly powerful effect when children do not have direct experience with or other sources of information about people and events (DeFleur & DeFleur, 1967: Greenberg, 1972). In situations where children do not have much contact with minority individuals, there is some evidence that television could play an important role in their perceptions of and attitudes toward individuals from minority group backgrounds (Greenberg and Gordon, 1972).

A CONCEPTUAL FRAMEWORK FOR STUDYING THE INFLUENCE OF TELEVISION ON MINORITY CHILDREN

Research on the influence of television on the ethnic identity of minority children is very limited. There are both conceptual and methodological problems with the existing studies, which limits their generalizability and meaningfulness. In addition, some of the studies reflect an implicit bias about the nature of low-income black culture (see, for example, Hinton, Seggar, Northcott, & Fontes, 1974).

All the studies identified in this literature search were conducted on black people. This is understandable since blacks are portrayed on television significantly more than other minority groups, which remain largely invisible (Barcus, 1977). Hence it is difficult to determine the influence of content and images on nonblack minority group children. With the small number of research studies available on the effects of television on blacks, it is dangerous to generalize from this research to factors and processes that may be operating in other minority groups. Hence the comments in this chapter on the influence of television relate primarily to black populations. Some of the observations may be useful in examining television's influence on children from other minority groups, but generalizations should be made with extreme caution.

Since the studies are relatively limited in number, this chapter is organized around a conceptual framework for examining the potential influence of television on minority group children. Levels of analysis in the framework are described and accompanied by relevant literature.

Level I: The Social, Political, and Economic Context of Television

Television is one of the media of influence in a society and it exists within a complex network of social, political, and economic arrangements (Melody, 1973). Historical trends in the society also impact on television. In viewing television as a potential socializing agent, these contextual factors must be considered in conceptualizing research and in interpreting results. It is beyond the scope of this chapter to describe fully the sociopolitical context of television; however, excellent discussions are available (Bentzen & Brown, 1977–1978; Leifer, Gordon, & Graves, 1974; Melody, 1973).

Level II: Television as a Socializing Agent—Content-Stimulus Properties

Television exists within a societal context, and its potential influences are mediated by a number of competing socializing agents—

peers, schools, community institutions, parents, and other forms of media. Television influences by the content, portrayals, and images that it transmits. Studies that are based on a notion of "simple transmission" focus on the representation and images of blacks on television and how these have changed over time, with the implicit assumption that the presence of more blacks on television screens will have a positive effect on ethnic identity. Less attention has been focused on the latent qualities or hidden messages of these representations (Liebert & Schwartzberg, 1977) and on how these representations are perceived and interpreted by the viewers.

In general, the representation of blacks and other minorities has changed slightly since the 1960s. Barcus (1977) conducted an extensive survey of weekend and weekday afternoon commercial children's television to provide a foundation for further research and an assessment of changes. As Barcus himself recognized, his study was quantitative and did not include qualitative analysis of character portrayals. Barcus's sample consisted of Saturday and Sunday morning programs for children in Boston, Massachusetts, during April 1975. The monitoring of programming during after-school hours was undertaken in 10 independent stations across the United States.

Barcus and his associates found that the presentation of minorities was negligible. In after-school children's television, the characters were 96% white, 3% black, and 1% other minorities. These patterns were consistent over cartoon comedy, other comedy, action–adventure, and variety shows. In commercials, 95% of the individuals were white, 5% black, with other minorities nonexistent. Blacks appeared mainly on snack commercials. Black representation was higher (11%) on weekend noncommercial television. Finally, Blacks were portrayed mainly as children and teenagers, rather than adults.

Barcus (1977) concluded that although adult television has broadened its presentation of minorities, particularly of blacks, children's television lags behind. One-quarter of all weekday programming is out-dated, and sexual and racial stereotypes are prevalent. In comparing his 1975 findings with his earlier 1971 study, Barcus concluded that ethnic representation has not significantly improved on children's television.

The research of Barcus and others who have monitored the frequency of presentation of blacks and other minorities on children's television is important. However, the issue is more than proportional representation of blacks on television. Television serves to perpetuate myths and to shape children's images of the world and the good life. When dealing with race, television operates at a symbolic level as well. Yet

studies of the symbolic nature of television content with respect to race
are rare.

Analysis of the symbolic and latent messages surrounding the portrayals of blacks on television tend to be written by blacks with artistic
and humanistic training. Collier (1974) argues that shows featuring
blacks are not black shows but are shows created for whites, conceived,
written, and directed by whites. Thus, she argues that television is a
potent weapon for keeping blacks "lulled, deceived, and impotent
[p. 209]." She adds, "the task of the writer is to look beyond surface reality and bare the complexities that comprise human experience [p. 214]."

In research designed to examine the influence of television content
on minority children, content analysis must move in the direction of
interpretative analysis (Geertz, 1973). This entails assessing the meaning of the content to children of different ages in relation to their personal and cultural experiences. Pierce et al. (1977) suggested that the
perception of the same stimulus could have a highly positive
psychological value for one viewer but the opposite value for another.
Unfortunately, there are few researchers who are as well trained and as
prepared to conduct interpretative analysis as are critics, artists (see, for
example, Bentzen & Brown, 1977–1978), and anthropologists.

These analyses must be informed by a knowledge of black history,
culture, and the nature of institutional racism. One study (one of many)
can serve as an example of how lack of this knowledge can lead to
faulty hypotheses and interpretations of the findings. An investigation
of tokenism and negative stereotyping of blacks in television drama
and comedy during 1973 found that blacks were shown significantly
more often than whites in bit parts and minor roles, supporting the
hypothesis of tokenism in the portrayal of blacks (Hinton et al., 1974).
However, these researchers argued that the hypothesis of negative
stereotyping was not supported: Blacks, in fact, were treated very well
in television comedies and drama programs. "They were portrayed as
industrious, competent, and law abiding [p. 431]." More specifically,
Hinton et al. (1974) found that white males were portrayed significantly more often than black males as violent and hostile. Whites were
also portrayed as illegal and immoral significantly more often than
were blacks. These findings could be alternatively interpreted as media
images to keep blacks in their place as nonthreatening to whites, particularly white males. This alternative interpretation of the findings
serves as an example of the critical importance of linking coding
categories for television content to the historical, social, political, and
economic structures of American society (Level I of the conceptual
framework).

A study that supported the findings of Hinton *et al.* (1974), but which attempted to link the results to social conditions, was conducted by Donagher, Poulos, Liebert, and Davidson (1975). The focus of their analysis was on character portrayals of black and white females and males in interracial television entertainment. Donagher *et al.* (1975) found that white males were presented as being capable of persisting at tasks and at delaying gratification. They were more likely than other groups to display intent, threat of, or actual physical harm to others. They were not shown, however, as resisting temptation to the rules of society or as acting to repair physical or psychological damage they caused to others. Donagher and her associates suggest that the character portrayal of the white male is one who is "a powerful, forceful, rule-breaking, independent, and rather callous individual [p. 1032]."

In contrast, the portrayal of the black male attests to an individual who is neither forceful nor powerful in the society. The black male was portrayed as a "good" person, outdoing all other groups in reparation for bad behavior. He was represented as engaging in altruistic acts of helping, sharing, and cooperating, as persisting at tasks and as delaying gratification, and as attempting to make up for his harmful actions to others.

White females were presented as "virtuous gate-keepers of societal rules and, on the other hand, as lacking in the necessary persistence to accomplish a task [p. 1032]." They engaged in altruistic acts more than other groups and more often repaired damage they caused to other people. They were portrayed as able to resist temptation but unable to delay gratification. Black females were portrayed as high in resistance to temptation and low in delay of gratification and in task persistence. Although they were not shown as aggressive, altruistic, or making up for bad behavior, they were highly engaged in explaining feelings to increase understanding, resolve strife, and reassure others. Donagher and her associates (1975) interpreted these findings in terms of television's role in maintaining and fostering stereotypes. They observed that even though blacks are being cast in major roles in television, character portrayals within these roles may still convey and support stereotypes.

In summary, television serves as a socializing agent not only by the frequency of its presentation of blacks and other minorities, but even more potently through the multiple images it transmits about the values and appropriate roles for individuals of different ethnic groups. In order to study the impact of television on ethnic identity, content analysis must move toward interpretative analyses of content. A certain problematic feature of this direction is that adults do not view the messages of television in the same way as do children of different ages

(Greenberg, 1965; Meyer, 1976). Thus, research must also focus on how children with different characteristics interpret the messages transmitted on television, as well as the equally difficult questions of whether and how these messages may affect ethnic identity.

Level III: The Viewer—The Minority Child

Television content exerts its potential influence on the viewer, in this case the minority child. The conceptualization of the role of the viewer is crucial for future research. In most studies based on traditional social learning theory, the child is considered a passive recipient of television's transmissions. An alternative view of the child, consistent with reconceptualizations in social learning theory itself (Mischel, 1973), as well as with socialization theory (Richards, 1974), sees the child as an active participant, mediating the content and hence the influence of television. Within this perspective, who the child is (age and developmental status, ethnicity, sex, social status, individual differences, attitudes, geographical residence, etc.) and how the child, given these characteristics, interprets the content are important. In short, in order to understand how television influences the child, we must understand how the child understands the content of television programming.

AGE

Age is a moderating variable in research on the influence of television on young children, particularly as age is related to perceptual, cognitive, and social development. Age is also a variable for consideration because of age-related changes in ethnic identification (Goodman, 1952).

Television viewing begins very early in life, and children's choices of programs change over time (National Science Foundation, 1977). The early school years are ones in which the children change in the ways they react to the medium; this is related to developmental changes. Collins (1970) demonstrated age-related changes in the learning of the media content. Lyle and Hoffman (1972) found that nearly one-half of all first-graders believed that adults on television were "just like" or "pretty much like" adults the children knew. More than one-half believed that children on television were like themselves or their friends. While in the first grade, children understand little of the motivation and consequences of program content, but this changes by the beginning of adolescence (Leifer & Roberts, 1972).

Children ascribe less reality to television as they grow older (Greenberg & Gordon, 1972) and become more skillful in evaluating advertising. Ward (1971) found a growing awareness of the intent of commercials with age. By the second grade, children are aware that commercials are trying to sell them things, and by fourth grade they are likely to have developed critical and skeptical attitudes toward advertisements.

Lyle and Hoffman (1972) found that although black children in the first and sixth grades were more likely to see television portrayals as real to life than were white children, by the tenth grade both groups were nearly equal in their evaluation of the realism of television. In some instances, black children in the tenth grade were more critical of television portrayals than were white children. Yet we know little about the factors involved in these developmental changes. How do minority children decide when portrayals are relevant to them? How are changes in children's perception of television related to developmental changes in ethnic identity?

Research on the effects of advertising on black children indicate that there is a tendency for awareness of racial cues to increase with age (National Science Foundation, 1977). Preschool children appear to be little affected by racial differences in endorsers. However, the effects of black and white endorsers of products are complicated by the child's age. In the 10- to 12-year-old group, two studies found no significant same-race endorsement effects. However, Hyams, Tanner, and Rossiter found strong own-race effects for this age group, particularly for the black children who were in an intergrated school setting (cited in National Science Foundation, 1977). In another study, Atkin found a significant cross-race effect for this age group, but none for the white children (1975, cited in National Science Foundation, 1977). The National Science Foundation report (1977) concluded that the observed effects depend on the prior socialization experiences of the children with regard to race (e.g., interracial or segregated schools). Whereas older children have been found to be more affected by racial cues, *how* they are affected appears to depend on their prior experiences.

SOCIAL CLASS

The data on social class differences are mixed because of the use of different samples and because of historical changes. The existing studies confound ethnicity and social class, that is, the comparisons tend to be between lower-class blacks and middle- and/or upper-class whites.

There appear to be social class differences in the way in which children use television as a medium. Greenberg and Gordon (1972) found that black, fifth-grade, lower-class boys perceived less violence than did middle-class white boys shown the same segment of videotapes. The black boys also found the violence more acceptable and liked watching it more than did the white boys. In a replication study with children aged 14, however, lower-class blacks did not differ significantly from the middle-class whites in perceiving violence.

Williams (1969) reported that children from different social class groups talk about television differently. However, he did not report results by race even though his sample was composed of black and white children from both lower-class and middle-class backgrounds.

Social class is a gross indicator of family and community variables that may mediate television's impact on the child (Comer & Pouissant, 1975; Leifer, Gordon, & Graves, 1974). Comer and Pouissant (1975), for example, suggest a number of strategies by which parents can mediate the potentially deleterious effects of television on identity formation in their children.

LEARNING PROCESS

Salmon (1976) has suggested that processes governing learning through the medium of television are different from learning through other media. He has demonstrated this through his research on the learning of cognitive material. Television may shape ethnic identity, but if so, it does this by processes that are not yet understood. Related questions include: How do children learn about people of other ethnic identities from television? What aspects or features of minority group individuals do children attend to? Graves (1975, cited in Leifer et al., 1974) has demonstrated experimentally that children's positive and negative attitudes toward their own and other races can be influenced by the specific ways in which characters of different ethnic groups are portrayed. The learning of ethnic group behavior and attitudes will also be influenced by developmental factors. If we hope to assess television's influence on ethnic identity, future research will have to focus on learning about ethnicity through the medium of television.

The influence of television is also mediated by other socializing agents during viewing periods. Ethnographic data on peer, sibling, and family interaction during television viewing could enhance our knowledge of how the content is perceived and reinterpreted by all participants.

MODELING

Studies of modeling in experimental situations indicate that the race of the model, per se, does not necessarily lead to imitation (Sattler, 1973). Although children are more likely to imitate a model who is similar to them, studies indicate they do not necessarily imitate people who are similar in sex, age, or race (Akamatsu & Thelen, 1974; Bandura, 1969; Kunce & Thelen, 1972; Thelen & Freyeer, 1971).

A number of studies examining children's perceptions of black models support the findings of the modeling literature. Clark (1972) found that black adolescents had more positive attitudes toward a black television character who conformed to societal norms than they did toward a black militant. These findings led Clark to suggest that the portrayal of blacks in middle-class roles is a form of social control and co-option rather than a source of ethnic identity and value.

The complexities involved in studying the effect of black models on black children is illustrated by Meyer's (1976) study on the impact of *All in the Family* on 6- to 10-year-old children. Of relevance to this discussion, black low-income and white high-income children were interviewed regarding their character preferences after viewing an episode in which Archie Bunker tried to make a deal with a black auditor at the local Internal Revenue Service office. The results indicated an absence of a strong like or dislike of the major black character in relation to the child's race. Meyer concluded: "Despite the favorable portrayal of the IRS man, black children were no more inclined to identify with him than were white children [p. 28]." Black and white children did have distinct character preferences, but these preferences were not related to the child's race.

The small number of studies makes it impossible to draw conclusions at the present time. However, the findings do suggest that the effects of black characters as models are very complex. Teplin (1977) points out that minority children may use different criteria in their racial preferences. For example, they may have different perceptions of their situations and consequently base their choices on different criteria. In Meyer's (1976) study, the black girls chose Gloria as their favorite *All in the Family* character, citing reasons such as, "she's pretty . . . she has nice hair [p. 30]." Teplin (1977) also suggested that although children may use the criterion of similarity, it is *perceived similarity* that may govern the actual choices. An additional problem in using a modeling approach is that even though choice and preference data are indicators of children's attention to and feelings about characters, they are related to actual behavior in complex ways.

In summary, a conceptualization of the child as an important mediator in research on the influence of television on ethnic identity is needed. Furthermore, a more systematic sampling of children's characteristics is needed. A number of studies support Meyer's (1976) conclusions: "Different types of children bringing different beliefs, attitudes, and values to the viewing of the show as a result of different socialization processes, are affected in distinctly different ways [p. 32]."

Level IV: "Outcome"—Ethnic Identification

At this level, we face conceptual and measurement problems in determining how television influences the ethnic identity of the black child (Nobles, 1972). But ethnic identification is not characterized here solely as a dependent variable. The existing ethnic identification of children can affect how television influences their feelings about their ethnic group.

The research on ethnic identity is based primarily on white and black samples. Similar research on Asian-American, Native American, and Hispanic and other Spanish-speaking populations is sparse. For more extensive descriptions of the literature, the reader is referred to several excellent review articles (Brand, Ruiz, & Padilla, 1974; Katz, 1976; Proshansky, 1966; Sowder, 1972; Williams & Morland, 1976).

Research on ethnic identity has been basically descriptive and atheoretical. However, three "traditions" of research in the area can be identified. The first and most commonly used approach comes from psychology, best represented in the doll preference and interview studies of Clark and Clark (1950). A second approach, cultural anthropology, is represented by the Goodman (1952), whose research focused on the developmental progression in ethnic identity and intergroup attitudes. A third approach can be called psychoanalytic and psychiatric, as in the work of Coles (1964), who focuses on the intensive study of individual children. Workers in the psychoanalytic tradition stress both the resiliency and adaptiveness of black children as well as the self-hatred, denial, and anger that racism, discrimination, and poverty cultivate (Hauser, 1971; Spurlock, 1973).

METHODOLOGICAL ISSUES

The nature of the research, particularly the contradictory findings, necessitates an examination of the methods by which ethnic identification and preference are measured and of the variables influencing the respondent's choice (Brand et al., 1974). Findings vary with the instrumentation and method used. In research conducted with children, a variety of procedures are used, including the doll preference task, the picture preference task, interviews, projective techniques, social distance scales, behavioral measures, and learning, memory, and perceptual indices (Katz, 1976). Each of these methods has been thoroughly critiqued by Brand et al. (1974). For the purposes of this overview, the methods most commonly used with children will be examined.

Doll Preference Task

Most researchers studying ethnic awareness and preference have used sets of dolls identical except for skin and hair color and asked children to select the doll according to specific verbal requests: "Give me the doll that you like to play with." "Give me the doll that is a nice doll." "Give me the doll that looks bad." "Give me the doll that is a nice color." "Give me the doll that looks like a Negro child." "Give me the doll that looks like you."

The doll preference procedure has come under scrutiny in recent years. It is suggested that children's preferences for the white doll may not necessarily be related to the black child's actual ethnic identification, and therefore, that research findings based on this method must be viewed with caution. Measurement is particularly problematic when children are asked to verbalize their feelings in such a sensitive area as their ethnicity.

Several investigators have suggested that the dolls may not represent reality for children. Brand et al. (1974) note that, until recently, black dolls were uncommon and question whether the black and white dolls were equivalent stimuli. Black children, they suggest, may have rejected the black dolls due to their unfamiliarity rather than the ethnicity they represented.

In addition, the features of the doll in terms of the actual skin coloring and eye and hair color may influence children's preferences. In most of the doll studies, the facial characteristics have been those of white dolls. Black children might choose black dolls if they were conceived as black in facial structures, hair texture, and color. Furthermore, in most studies, the dolls have differed in eye and hair color as well as skin color. Katz and Zalk (1974) reported that when hair and eye color were held constant, no preference for the doll's skin color was found. Kircher and Furby (1973) found that both skin color and hair type could significantly determine the young children's preferences. Greenwald and Oppenheim (1968) found that the inclusion of a doll of intermediate color ("mulatto") significantly reduced black children's "mis-identification." The intensity of skin color of the dolls has seldom been considered. Brand et al. (1974) recommend that in future studies the physiogonomy and color of the dolls should be selected for familiarity, representativeness, and attractiveness.

Studies on the reliability and validity of the doll procedure are rare. Hraba (1972) studied item variability of Clark and Clark's (1950) questions using scalogram analysis and reported that greater variety of racial preference among questions reduced racial ethnocentricism. Ward and Braun (1972) validated the doll tests as measures of self-concept related to ethnic identification. Construct validation of ethnic preference tasks is virtually nonexistent.

Preference for Photographs or Line Drawings

Other studies have used pictoral stimuli, such as line drawings. Brand, et al. (1974) point out that in studies with young children, the subjects' ability to discriminate the ethnicity of the stimuli must be secured before measuring preference for ethnic stimuli. There is still the need for concurrent validity of the drawings with other measures of ethnic identification. Finally, since standards of attractiveness may differ among ethnic groups, the relative appeal of the pictures should be controlled.

Direct Interview

Another commonly used technique is the direct interview in which children are asked to verbalize their preferences and attitudes. The method is fraught with response and cultural bias and with problems involved with forced selection (Brand et al., 1974). Interviews and questionnaires often reflect a white, middle-class bias in language (Proshansky & Newton, 1968). Blakeley & Somerville (1970) found differences between white and black children in their preferences for racial terms.

Brand et al. (1974) identified nine variables related to patterns of ethnic preference. Of these, the examiner's ethnicity will be discussed here because it is of particular relevance to ethnic identification among young children. The remaining factors will be discussed in the context of research findings on ethnic identification. The effect of the examiner's ethnicity is inconsistent across the ethnic identification studies. Apparently, the ethnicity of the examiner interacts with a number of variables, including the subject's age, sex, and the task (Sattler, 1973).

Brand et al. (1974) suggest that examiner variables are more important when the testing situation is of high threat. In studies with children, examiner ethnicity may be minimally threatening in situations in which the subjects are acquainted with individuals of different ethnic groups, such as in integrated settings (Hraba & Grant, 1970). Thus, examiner ethnicity may be significant if the children have had minimal contact with individuals of other ethnic groups and if the questions are perceived to be highly personal.

The major problem with existing methods used in studying ethnic identification is that they are projectively based and nonbehavioral in orientation. Teplin (1977) investigated the relationship between children's racial preferences as exhibited in projective or imaginary situations versus real-life interaction patterns. She found that the inference of behavior from projective-test date (choice of photographs) is problematic. The relationship between children's racial preferences as determined by projective methods as opposed to actual behavior is neither simple nor direct. The discrepancies between projective choice and actual behavior differ based on the sex, ethnicity, and prior socialization experiences of the group.

Teplin concluded that children's racial preferences are neither indicative nor predictive of prejudicial behaviors. This conclusion raises the issue of the validity of methods used to determine children's ethnic identity outside the testing situation. Given the methodological problems already cited, this question is a reasonable one.

DEVELOPMENT OF ETHNIC IDENTITY

Current research indicates that racial awareness is learned and that it begins to develop during the preschool years for both white and black children. Our knowledge is based on samples of children at different age levels. There are currently no longitudinal studies and none conducted with children below the age of 3. Factors contributing to racial awareness presumably operate before the age of 3, but little is known about them.

Racial awareness is viewed as part of the human task of establishing a sense of self-identity (Goodman, 1952). Using the doll-play and other projective techniques, a number of investigators have supported the early findings of Clark and Clark (1950) in black, white, and Chicano groups (Sowder, 1972). A majority of black and white children express a preference for white dolls. Black children are also observed to express denial and ambivalence over choosing the black doll and to attribute negative characteristics to it.

Most studies on ethnic identification and preference have not controlled for the social class background of the child. Where studies have controlled for the social class variable, results are mixed. Landreth and Johnson (1953) found that socioeconomic class was as significant as race in the selection of skin color in a sample of black and white children. Asher and Allen (1969) found no differences between middle- and lower-class children in racial attitudes and social distance scores, but the lower-class black children expressed significantly less preference for white dolls than did their middle-class counterparts.

Porter (1971) found that welfare and working-class white children chose white dolls more often than middle-class white children did. The finding was reversed for black children. The rejection of the black doll was higher among middle-class than among lower-class black children. The latter group expressed hostility toward the white doll. Porter related these class differences to the position of blacks in American society. She observed that the black middle class has a marginal status, and its children orient more toward white society. Working-class blacks, although economically dependent on white employers, have few social contacts with whites and are more involved in black community institutions.

In their review of the literature, Brand et al. (1974) concluded that many studies indicate that minority children of lower SES tend to be more accepting of their own ethnicity than are children of middle and upper SES (see, however, Spurlock, 1973). These findings may be explained by noting that lower-class groups develop their own cultural patterns and values, rejecting dominant definitions of success. This hypothesis has yet to be tested.

Membership in ethnic minority groups appears to be a factor in the early development of ethnic awareness. Black children appear to be more concerned with color differences and racial cues than are their white peers (Katz, 1976). However, these findings differ in the northern and southern regions of the United States. Powell (1973) found that southern black teenagers (12–15 years of age) in an urban area had a stronger self-concept than did whites due to the presence of a cohesive black community. In a northern city, she found that there were no significant differences in self-concept between white and black teenagers. Similar findings were reported by McAdoo (1970), who compared children in a northern, urban, integrated community and in a southern, rural, all-black community. Brand et al. (1974) note that geographical residence of the sample is an important factor in interpreting ethnic identification studies.

Studies on nonblack minority groups are scarce. Werner and Evans (1968) assessed skin color discrimination and preference among Chicano children. The children were more likely to attribute "good" qualities to a white doll and "bad" ones to a black doll. Elementary-school-age Chicano children were more likely to identify with the white doll than were preschool children. This study is flawed in an important aspect since black dolls were used to represent Chicanos and this group tends to have a wide range of skin color.

Rice, Ruiz, and Padilla (1974) examined the relationship between ethnic awareness, self-identification, and ethnic preferences in white, black, and Chicano preschool and third-grade children (9–11 years). The preschool children were enrolled in a Head Start program in an elementary school in Kansas City, Missouri, whereas the third-graders were students at the same school. All children came from lower socioeconomic backgrounds.

Children were shown color photographs of white, black, and Chicano adult males by white female experimenters. All third-graders were able to make correct ethnic group identifications, but the preschool children had trouble differentiating between the white and Chicano adult males. Data on ethnic group preferences indicated that neither the black nor the chicano children expressed a significant preference for their group. In response to one indicator of preference—"Show me the one you would like to grow up to be like"—both the black and chicano children selected the white male. Only the Chicano third-graders expressed a preference for their own group, suggesting the development of ethnic pride for this sample.

The results indicated that young children were able to differentiate between photographs of white and black males. However, the distinction between white and Chicano may either have been too fine a distinction to be made by preschool children or the term *Chicano* was not understood by the children.

It remains unclear what impact the Civil Rights and ethnic militancy movements of the 1960s have had on children's ethnic identification. Most of the studies in the late 1960s and early 1970s reported that black children still preferred to play with a white rather than a mulatto or dark brown doll (Asher & Allen, 1969; Gitter, Mostosky, & Satow, 1972; Greenward & Oppenheim, 1968; Morland, 1966; Sowder, 1972; Taylor, 1966), but other studies suggest that social changes may be influencing black children's preferences for the brown dolls (Datcher, Savage, & Checkosky, 1973; Fox & Jordan, 1973; Hraba & Grant, 1970; Katz & Zalk, 1974; Ward & Braun, 1972). These contradictory findings may be a matter of regional differences (Powell, 1973), as positive attitudes tend to be found in large urban centers (Fox & Jordan, 1973; Hraba & Grant, 1970). A number of measurement problems reviewed earlier may also be a source of mixed findings (Brand et al., 1974; Katz, 1976).

Spurlock's (1973) psychiatric work with black children also suggests that the impact of the 1960s should be viewed with caution. She found that although black children clearly indicate black awareness in their drawings and shout, "Black is beautiful," these same children reveal negative feelings about their identity. She notes that her findings suggest that reaction formation occurs for some black children, while for others, "Black is beautiful" has provided feelings of unity, self-acceptance, and "protection against the onslaught of a hostile world [Spurlock, 1973, p. 158]."

It appears that the enduring racism of American social institutions continues to have an influence on the racial awareness and ethnic identity of minority children. There has been some change, and black children are more ready to assert their blackness (Weinberg, 1977), but the changes do not appear to be pervasive. As the country slides back on its commitments to racial equality, it can reasonably be predicted that minority children will be negatively affected.

One area that has been totally neglected by psychologists is children's awareness and concepts of racism as it affects individual and group behavior. Often, findings are not conceptually linked to sociocultural contexts. We know very little about children's understandings of institutional racism, a concept that challenges the idea that the problems of minorities are solely personal and interpersonal. Ignorance of racism can create confusion and self-hatred in minority children and encourages distortion of reality in white children. It is in this area that Coles (1964) and Cottle (1974), using the intensive interview method, have made significant contributions. In these interviews, children reveal an understanding of their world that is in direct opposition to educational programs for fostering better intergroup attitudes (Takanishi & Jordan-Marsh, 1976). For example, one of the major policy goals of educational programs for low-income children is to provide equal opportunity. But some minority children question whether this goal can be achieved through educational strategies alone. There is an awareness of class structure and of the relationship between race and occupation which Adrien Keller (age 11) painfully noted when Cottle told her she could be a lawyer: "Rich folks like you are lawyers and poor folks like me go into the army [Cottle, 1974, p. 136]."

In summary, the problems of conceptualizing and measuring the major varible of interest—ethnic identification—are critical to future research regarding television's influence on ethnic identity. We must proceed with caution until some of these important measurement problems are attacked.

FUTURE DIRECTIONS FOR RESEARCH

Our review of the research on ethnic identity indicates that important conceptual and measurement problems exist for investigators seeking to determine the influence of television on the ethnic identity of minority group children. Future research should focus on these problems as an important priority, particularly since knowledge of ethnic identity and its formation is important in its own right. Longitudinal studies involving interdisciplinary teams of investigators are especially important if we are to understand the interrelationship of personal and social factors in the development of ethnic identification. Since ethnic identity is a sensitive area, the involvement of clinically trained individuals is highly desirable.

The importance of television as a factor in ethnic identity formation needs further research attention since questions are being raised about this medium's role as a socializing agent in American society (National Science Foundation, 1977). Research should be conducted on a national, representative sample of children to determine the relative importance of and interaction among various socializing agents in the development of ethnic identification.

Research is also needed on how children of different characteristics perceive representative samples of actual programs that portray minority group characters on both children's and adult's television shows. Research should focus in particular on the *child's* interpretation of the television material and on how these interpretations change with age and developmental status and vary with the sex, ethnicity, social class, and related socialization experiences of the child. Research should be continued on the processes involved in children's social role learning and on their role as minority group members, in particular. Children might be assisted to develop more critical appraisals of existing television content by their families (e.g. Kaye, 1974) and by the schools (Bentzen & Brown, 1977–1978; Berry, 1977), and how social reform can provide conditions in which positive ethnic identity can develop.

As a potential socializing agent in the lives of children television reflects the dominant social structure and its values. Despite the limited victories of activist consumer groups in changing programming content and advertising, the television industry is not likely to alter its programming in ways that significantly challenge or question existing societal arrangements. These observations, which are supported by a number of social analysts (Mankiewicz & Swerdlow, 1978; Melody, 1973), raise questions about research on television's influence that does not attend to why the present state of affairs exists.

REFERENCES

Akamatsu, T.J., & Thelen, M.H. A review of the literature on observer characteristics and imitation. *Developmental Psychology*, 1974, *10*, 38–47.

Asher, S.R., & Allen, V.L. Racial preference and social comparison processes. *Journal of Social Issues*, 1969, *25*, 157–166.

Ball, S. Methodological problems in assessing the impact of television programs. *Journal of Social Issues*, 1976, *32*(4), 8–17.

Bandura, A. *Principles of behavior modification*. New York: Holt, 1969.

Barcus, F. *Saturday children's television: A report of TV programming and advertising on Boston commercial television*. Boston: Action for Children's Television, 1971.

Barcus, F. *Children's television: An analysis of programming and advertising*. New York: Praeger, 1977.

Bentzen, M.M., & Brown, J.A. (Eds.). Media and education. *UCLA Educator*, 1977–1978, *20*.

Berry, G.L. Television and the urban child: Some educational policy implications. *Education and Urban Society*, 1977, *10*, 31–54.

Blakely, K.B., & Somerville, A.W. An investigation of preference for racial identification terms among Negro and Caucasian children. *Journal of Negro Education*, 1970, *39*, 314–319.

Bond, J.C. The media image of black women. *Freedomways*, 1975, *15*, 34–37.

Blu, K.I. Varieties of ethnic identity: Anglo-Saxons, blacks, Indians and Jews in a southern county. *Ethnicity*, 1977, *4*, 263–286.

Brand, E.S., Ruiz, A., & Padilla, A.M. Ethnic identification and preference: A review. *Psychological Bulletin*, 1974, *81*(11), 860–890.

Bush, R.F., Solomon, P.J., & Hair, J.F., Jr. There are more blacks in TV commercials. *Journal of Advertising Research*, 1977, *17*, 21–25.

Clark, C.C. Television and social controls: Some observations on the portrayals of ethnic minorities. *Television Quarterly*, 1969, *8*(2), 18–22.

Clark, C.C. Race, identification, and television violence. In G.A. Comstock, E.A. Rubinstein, & J.P. Murray (Eds.), *Television and social behavior* (Vol. 5). *Television effects: Further exploration*. Washington, D.C.: US Govt. Printing Office, 1972.

Clark, K.B., & Clark, M.P. Emotional factors in racial identification and preference in Negro children. *Journal of Negro Education*, 1950, *19*, 341–350.

Coles, R. *Children of crisis: A study in courage and fear*. Boston, Massachusetts: Little, Brown, 1964.

Collier, E. "Black" shows for white viewers. *Freedomways*, 1974, *14*, 209–217.

Collins, W.A. Learning of media content: A developmental study. *Child Development*, 1970, *41*, 1133–1142.

Comer, J.P., & Pouissant, A.F. *Black child care*. New York: Simon & Schuster, 1974.

Comstock, G. *Television and human behavior: The key studies*. Santa Monica, California, Rand Corporation, 1975.

Cottle, T.J. *Black children, white dreams.* New York: Dell, 1974.

Dashefsky, A. (Ed.). *Ethnic identity in society.* Chicago, Illinois: College Publishing, 1976.

Datcher, E., Savage, J., & Checkosky, S. School type, grade, sex, and race of experimenter as determinants of racial preference and awareness in black and white children. *Proceedings of the 81st Annual Convention of the American Psychological Association,* 1973, *8,* 223–224.

DeFleur, M.L., & DeFleur, L.B. The relative contribution of television as a learning source for children's occupational knowledge. *American Sociological Review,* 1967, *32,* 777–789.

Dominick, J., & Greenberg, B. Three seasons of blacks on television. *Journal of Advertising Research,* 1970, *10,* 21–27.

Donagher, P.C., Poulos, R.W., Liebert, R.M., & Davidson, E.S. Race, sex and social example: An analysis of character portrayals on inter-racial television entertainments. *Psychological Reports,* 1975, *37,* 1023–1034.

Eslien, E.B. Television and the Mexican American. *Public Telecommunications Review,* 1974, *2*(1), 13–18.

Fox, D.J., & Jordan, V.B. Racial preference and identification of black, American-Chinese, and white children. *Genetic Psychology Monographs,* 1973, *88,* 229–286.

Geertz, G. *The interpretation of cultures.* New York: Basic Books, 1973.

Gitter, A.G., Mostosky, D.I., & Satow, Y. The effect of skin color and physiognomy on racial misidentification. *Journal of Social Psychology,* 1972, *88,* 139–143.

Goodman, M.E. *Race awareness in young children.* Cambridge, Massachusetts: Addison-Wesley, 1952.

Greenberg, B.S. Television for children: Dimensions of communication and audience perceptions. *AV Communications Review,* 1965, *13,* 385–396.

Greenberg, B.S. Children's reactions to T.V. blacks. *Journalism Quarterly,* 1972, *49*(1), 5–14.

Greenberg, B.S., & Dervin, B. Mass communications among the urban poor. *Public Opinion Quarterly,* 1970, *34,* 224–235.

Greenberg, B.S., & Dominick, J. Television behavior among disadvantaged children. In B.S. Greenberg & B. Dervin (Eds.), *Use of the mass media by the urban poor.* New York: Praeger, 1970.

Greenberg, B.S., & Gordon, T.F. Perceptions of violence in television programs: Critics and the public. In E.A. Rubinstein, G.A. Comstock, & J.P. Murray (Eds.), *Television and social behavior* (Vol. 4). *Television in day-to-day life: Patterns of use.* Washington, D.C.: US Govt. Printing Office, 1972.

Greenberg, B.S., & Mazingo, S.L. Racial issues in mass media institutions. In P.A. Katz (Ed.), *Toward the elimination of racism.* New York: Pergamon, 1976.

Greenberg, B.S., & Reeves, B. Children and the perceived reality of television. *Journal of Social Issues,* 1976, *32* 86–97.

Greenwald, H., & Oppenheim, D. Reported magnitude of self-misidentification among Negro children—Artifact? *Journal of Personality and Social Psychology,* 1968, *8,* 49–52.

Gregor, A.J., & McPherson, D.A. Racial attitudes toward white and Negro children in a deep South standard metropolitan area. *Journal of Social Psychology,* 1966, *68* 95–106.

Halpern, F. Self-perceptions of black children and the Civil Rights movement. *American Journal of Orthopsychiatry,* 1970, *40,* 520–526.

Hauser, S.T. *Black and white identity formation.* New York: Wiley, 1971.

Hinton, J.L., Seggar, J.F., Northcott, H.C., & Fontes, B.F. Tokenism and improving imagery of blacks in TV drama and comedy: 1973. *Journal of Broadcasting*, 1974, *18* 423–432.

Hraba, J. Doll technique: A measure of racial ethnocentrism? *Social Forces*, 1972, *50*, 522–527.

Hraba, J., & Grant, J. Black is beautiful: A reexamination of racial preference and identification. *Journal of Personality and Social Psychology*, 1970, *16*, 398–402.

Katz, P.A. The acquisition of racial attitudes in children. In P.A. Katz (Ed.), *Toward the elimination of racism*. New York: Pergamon, 1976.

Katz, P., & Zalk, S. Doll preferences: An index of racial attitudes. *Journal of Educational Psychology*, 1974, *66*, 663–668.

Kaye, E. *The family guide to children's television*. New York: Pantheon, 1974.

Kircher, M., & Furby, L. Racial preference in young children. *Child Development*, 1973, *42*, 2076–2078.

Kunce, J.T., & Thelen, M.H. Modeled standards of self-reward and observer performance. *Developmental Psychology*, 1972, *7*, 153–156.

Landreth, C., & Johnson, B.C. Young children's responses to a picture and inset test designed to reveal reactions to persons of different skin color. *Child Development*, 1953, *24*, 63–79.

Leifer, A.D., Gordon, N.J., & Graves, S.B. Children's television: More than mere entertainment. *Harvard Educational Review*, 1974, *44*(22), 213–245.

Leifer, A.D., & Roberts, D.F. Children's responses to television violence. In J.P. Murray, E.A. Rubinstein, & G.A. Comstock (Eds.), *Television and social behavior* (Vol. 2). Washington, D.C.: US Govt. Printing Office, 1972.

Liebert, R.M., & Schwartzberg, N.S. Effects of mass media. *Annual Review of Psychology*, 1977, *28*, 141–172.

Lyle, J., & Hoffman, H. Children's use of television and other media. In E.A. Rubinstein, G.A. Comstock, & J.P. Murray (Eds.), *Television and social behavior* (Vol. 4). *Television in day-to-day life: Patterns of use*. Washington, D.C.: US Govt. Printing Office, 1972.

McAdoo, J. An experimental study of racial attitude change in black preschool children. Ann Arbor: Univ. of Michigan, 1970. (ERIC Document Reproduction Service, No ED 062497).

Mankiewicz, F., & Swerdlow, J. *Remote control: Television and the manipulation of American life*. New York: Time Books, 1978.

Melody, W.H. *Children's television: The economics of exploitation*. New Haven, Connecticut: Yale Univ. Press, 1973.

Mendelsohn, G., & Young, M. *Network children's programming: A content analysis of black and minority treatment on children's television*. Boston, Massachusetts: Action for Children's Television, 1972.

Meyer, T.P. Impact of *All in the Family* on children. *Journal of Broadcasting*, 1976, *20*, 23–33.

Mischel, W. Toward a cognitive social learning reconceptualization of personality. *Psychological Review*, 1973, *80*, 252–283.

Morland, J.K. A comparison of race awareness in northern and southern children. *American Journal of Orthopsychiatry*, 1966, *36*, 22–31.

National Science Foundation. *Research on the effects of television advertising on children*. Washington, D.C.: US Govt. Printing Office, 1977.

Nobles, W.W. Psychological research and the black self-concept: A critical review. *Journal of Social Issues*, 1972, *29*, 11–31.

Ormiston, L.H., & Williams, S. *Saturday children's programming in San Francisco, California: An analysis of the presentation of racial and cultural groups on three affiliated San Francisco television stations.* San Francisco, California: Committee on Children's Television, 1973.

Pierce, C.M., Carew, J.V., Pierce-Gonzalez, D., & Willis, D. An experiment in racism: Television commercials. *Education and Urban Society,* 1977, *10,* 61–87.

Porter, J. *Black child, white child.* Cambridge, Massachusetts: Harvard Univ. Press, 1971.

Powell, G.J. Self-concept in white and black children. In C.V. Willie, B.M. Kramer, & B.S. Brown (Eds.), *Racism and mental health.* Pittsburgh, Pennsylvania: Univ. of Pittsburgh Press, 1973.

Proshansky, H.M. The development of inter-group attitudes. In L.W. Hoffman & M.L. Hoffman (Eds.), *Review of child development research.* New York: Russell Sage Foundation, 1966.

Proshansky, H.M., & Newton, P. The nature and meaning of Negro self-identity. In M. Deutsch, I. Katz, & A.R. Jensen (Eds.), *Social class, race and psychological development.* New York: Holt, 1968.

Rice, A.S., Ruiz, R.A., & Padilla, A.M. Person perception, self-identity, and ethnic group preference in Anglo, black and Chicano preschool and third-grade children. *Journal of Cross-Cultural Psychology,* 1974, *5,* 100–108.

Richards, M.P.M. (Ed.). *The integration of a child into a social world.* London and New York: Cambridge Univ. Press, 1974.

Rutstein, N. *Go watch TV!* New York: Sheed & Ward, 1974.

Salmon, G. Cognitive effects of visual media. In R.F. Riegel & J.A. Meacham (Eds.), *The developing individual in a changing world* (Vol. 2). Chicago, Illinois: Aldine, 1976.

Sattler, J.M. Racial experimenter effects. In K.S. Miller & R.M. Dreger (Eds.), *Comparative studies of blacks and whites in the United States.* New York: Seminar Press, 1973.

Seggar, J.F. Television's portrayal of minorities and women, 1971–75. *Journal of Broadcasting,* 1977, *24,* 435–445.

Seggar, J.F., & Wheeler, P. World of work on television: Ethnic and sex representation in TV drama. *Journal of Broadcasting,* 1973, *17,* 201–214.

Sowder, B. *Socialization determinants in the development and modification of intergroup and intragroup attitudes and behaviors.* Washington, D.C.: Social Science Research Group, 1972.

Spurlock, J. Some consequences of racism for children. In C.V. Willie, B.M. Kramer, & B.S. Brown (Eds.), *Racism and mental health.* Pittsburgh, Pennsylvania: Univ. of Pittsburgh Press, 1973.

Takanishi, R., & Jordan-Marsh, M. Children's views and minority education: Some discrepancies. *UCLA Educator,* 1976, *19,* 17–24.

Taylor, R.G. Racial stereotypes in young children. *Journal of Psychology,* 1966, *64,* 137–142.

Teplin, L.A. Preference versus prejudice: A multimethod analysis of children's discrepant racial choices. *Social Science Quarterly,* 1977, *58,* 390–406.

Thelen, M.H., & Fryer, J.L. Effects of observer and model race on the imitation of standards of self-reward. *Developmental Psychology,* 1971, *5,* 133–135.

Ward, L.S. Effects of television advertising on children and adolescents. In E.A. Rubinstein, G.A. Comstock, & J.P. Murray (Eds.), *Television and social behavior* (Vol. 4). Washington, D.C.: US Govt. Printing Office, 1971.

Ward, S.H., & Braun, J. Self-esteem and racial preference in black children. *American Journal of Orthopsychiatry,* 1972, *42,* 644–647.

Weinberg, M. *Minority students: A research appraisal.* Washington, D.C.: US Govt. Printing Office, 1977.

Werner, N.E., & Evans, I.M. Perception of prejudice in Mexican-American preschool children. *Perceptual and Motor Skills,* 1968, *27,* 1039–1046.

Williams, F. Social class differences in how children talk about television. *Journal of Broadcasting,* 1969, *13,* 345–355.

Williams, J.E., & Morland, J.K. *Race, color, and the young child.* Chapel Hill: Univ. of North Carolina Press, 1976.

Gloria Johnson Powell

The Impact of Television on the Self-Concept Development of Minority Group Children

Self-concept is the growing child's most basic structure of who he or she is. It is the foundation on which children base their actions, thoughts, and the direction of their lives. Because of the psychological and humanistic essence of the self-concept, the theory about its etiology, significance, and growth has become central to the psychology of the self. Although space does not permit a comprehensive discourse on the subject, in this chapter the development of self-concept in the child as well as the most significant theories of self-concept that highlight the complexities of this cognitive, affective, and social development process will be reviewed. The relationship of self-concept to mental health is presented to initiate an understanding of the development of ethnic and racial awareness in minority group children, and television has become a vital part of that awareness process.

Since one of the major effects of television on the self-concept of minority group children involves the projection of racial stereotypes, it seems important that the reader understand the nature of stereotypes and their uses. Then, because it is always difficult to understand the complex social psychological process of prejudice, the subject is discussed not only from the standpoint of the victim, but also from the standpoint of the perpetrator.

105

TELEVISION AND
THE SOCIALIZATION OF THE MINORITY CHILD

In order to understand the effects of television on minority group children (and in most instances we will be referring to the Afro-American child), one must understand several aspects of the children's developmental process as well as the milieu in which that development occurs. It is basic to understanding the self-percept of children to know how children come to know themselves and the world in which they live, and what they think and feel about themselves. Cognitions and emotions about the self do not evolve in a vacuum. The context within which concepts of self emerge influences not only the content of what a child learns about himself, but also how he is perceived. The self-concept of minority-group children is so entwined with the racism and bigotry within our country that one discussion is incomplete without the other.

Finally, television is another reflected appraisal of how the larger society perceives the minority-group person. The images are changing, but new ones are still needed. We need to understand how these images are perceived by the child and in what way they are being molded into his self-system and into his understanding of his relationship to the world in which he lives.

THE DEVELOPMENT OF
SELF-CONCEPT IN THE CHILD

After an earlier review of the literature, Wylie (1961) concluded that there were no longitudinal studies on which to base a description of the development of the self-concept. In many respects, Fitts (1971) concurred, stating that the self-concept does not exist at birth, yet noting that the paucity of literature of such studies is a result of the little work in developmental psychology which has been generated by self-concept theory. There have been studies of influences on the individual's self-concept (Clark & Clark, 1947; Coopersmith, 1967; Erikson, 1956; Morland, 1963; Proshansky & Newton, 1968). Most theories of self-concept development, however, share the premise that the ideas and attitudes that make a self aware of its own existence take shape in early childhood, with varying degrees of understanding at different points in time.

The development of the self involves a process of differentiation between the self and other objects, both animate and inanimate. Sometime during the first 6–8 months of life, infants discover themselves and begin to separate the boundaries of their bodily selves from those of their mothers'. This is the first stage of selfhood; Taylor (1953) feels it begins to occur at about 6 or 7 months of age. The process becomes accelerated with the development of language, which enables children to make sharp distinctions between themselves and the rest of the world and to symbolize their experience.

Allport (1963) was the first to describe the stages of selfhood, that is, the self as felt and known, or self-concept development. These stages include:

1. Sense of bodily self
2. Sense of continuing self-identity
3. Self-esteem, pride
4. The extension of self
5. The self-image
6. The self as a rational coper
7. The self as a propriate striver

The first three aspects of self-awareness—the sense of bodily self, the sense of continuing self-identity, and self-esteem or pride—gradually evolve during the first 3 years of life and coincide with the cognitive stages of sensorimotor development and preoperational thought proposed by Piaget (Piaget & Inhelder, 1969). During Stages 4 and 5, that is, the extension of self and self-image, children enter Stage 4 at 4 years of age and complete Stage 5 by 6 years. According to Piaget, this is still part of the period of preparation for and organization of concrete operations of cognitive development. During Stage 6, self-concept development, children come to know themselves as thinkers with reflective, conscious, rational ability. Stage 6 begins when children are in the Piagetian concrete operations stage of cognitive development, which involves primarily semiotic and symbolic functions. By Stage 7 children emerge into abstract, hypothetico-deductive reasoning. This is the beginning of long-range purposes and propriate strivings. Self-concept is a cognitive process and as such is vitally related to children's process of cognitive development and vice versa. Self-concept development is also a crucial part of the psychosocial and sexual development of children. Consequently, affective, social, and sexual development effect self-concept development, and vice versa. It is clear, then, that only when self-concept is viewed in its developmental context can its importance to the total development of the child be understood.

After the early differentiation of self from the animate and inanimate worlds, the process of self-concept development becomes more social in nature. It begins to involve identification with others, introjection from others, and expansion into interpersonal relationships. Children begin to appraise themselves based on other peoples' appraisals of them. The approval of others who are significant to the children's lives plants the seeds of self-approval. The significant others in a child's life vary according to the child's age. Very early in life the most significant person is the primary caretaker; second are other members of the child's family, who provide the earliest and most permanent self-definition or basic concepts of self. The family provides the earliest experiences with feelings of adequacy and acceptance, as well as opportunities for identification, goals, and behavior models. It is from their families that individuals learn the values they attach to their perceptions of themselves.

Although parents and immediate family may be crucial to the initial development of self-concept, continuing development and changes in self-perceptions are mediated by many other people and processes, as we shall see in the case of minority group children. A part of self-differentiation occurs when children are able to compare themselves to their peers, at which time they also begin to form clearer conceptions of their families' SES or social class. Social groups, physical appearance, group membership, achievement, and acceptance all play a part in self-definition. Consequently, what people think and feel about themselves is largely determined by how they perceive other people's thoughts and feelings about them.

Within a given society, an individual's self-perception is influenced by status and by role; these are acquired or are assigned to the individual by the dominant members of that society. Children's views of themselves, then, are shaped by everything that affects the entire scope of their development, from their genetic make-up to the social and cultural influences of the society in which they live. Healthy personality development is dependent on a preponderance of favorable judgments about various aspects of the self. What others think of a child may differ in its importance to and effect on the child in determining his or her total self-esteem.

A REVIEW OF SELF-CONCEPT THEORIES

Self-concept is a diverse phenomenon, and Rosenberg's (1979) comprehensive review abstracts the essence of the prevailing major principles regarding self-concept formation. Sullivan (1953) views the self as made up of a collection of self-appraisals; Rosenberg (1979) summarized this reflected appraisal principle as follows:

> Specifically, these are the principles of (1) direct reflections, (2) perceived selves and (3) the generalized other. The first refers to how particular others

view us, the second to how we believe they view us, and the third to the attitudes of the community as a whole; these are internalized in the "me" and serve as a perspective for viewing the self [p. 63].

The major difficulty arising from the reflected appraisal perspective, in Rosenberg's view, is that there may be a vast discordance between one's self-view and the view others hold of one, and such a disparity may generate considerable difficulty. It stands to reason that some consistency is needed between how others view us and how we view ourselves.

The second theory reviewed by Rosenberg is that of social comparison, of which Pettigrew (1967, cited in Rosenberg, 1979) is the main proponent. In essence, it states that people learn about themselves by comparing themselves to others. Such a process, however, may result in positive, negative, or neutral self-perceptions, according to the standards employed for comparison.

The third review undertaken by Rosenberg is the self-attribution theory of Bem (1967, cited in Rosenberg, 1979). According to Bem, the definition of *attribution* includes the process of infering or perceiving the dispositional properties of entities in the environment. From these processes of attribution the bases from which people draw conclusions about their own motives or underlying characteristics and how they go about verifying their tentative conclusions are established and formulated.

The fourth theory advanced about self-concept in Rosenberg's (1979) review is the theory of psychological centrality. According to this theory, the self-concept is an organization of components that are hierarchically interrelated in complex ways: "What the principle of psychological centrality calls to attention, however, is that to the extent that individuals focus their sense of worth on different self-components, the success of one person is not necessarily achieved at the expense of the other [Rosenberg, 1979, p. 74]." One of the outstanding proponents of this view is Fitts (1970, 1971, 1972). His theory is important to elucidate more fully inasmuch as he is the author of the most widely used self-concept scale for most age groups. Extensive use has been made of his scale in research and in clinical settings. Fitts represents those few theorists who have been able to operationalize their constructs to the actual measurement of self-esteem. His theory of the self concentrates on and defines the internal dimensions of the self, but it also includes descriptions and processes of the external dimensions of self. His view (Fitts, 1971) proposes, as do other theories of psychological centrality, that "the self-concept blends together into a dynamic whole whose parts or subselves interact freely yet cohesively with each other [p. 14]." In Fitts's conceptualization there are three principal internal parts, or subselves: (a) self as object, or the *Identity Self*, (b) self as doer, or the *Behavioral Self*, and (c) self as observer or judge, or *Judging Self*. Other theorists have other definitions of the internal dimensions of the self that they consider to be more central to the phenomenological self (Sarbin, 1952).

Fitts's proposal of the self as object, or the Identity Self, is a crucial contribution because of the confusion in the self-concept literature among identity, self-concept, and self-esteem, all of which will be dealt with subsequently. For Fitts, the Identity Self is the most basic aspect of the self-concept, the "Who am I?" feature to which labels and symbols are attached to establish identification.

Before the complexities of self-description emerge, young children are what they are doing or how they are feeling. Thus, the source of the Identity Self is shaped early in life by the Behavioral Self. It is also important to note that very early in childhood, as later in life, the Behavioral Self is mediated by how an individual is feeling. Thus, affective development becomes an important part of self-concept development and has particular ramifications in the self-concept of minority group children (Powell, in press). The interrelatedness of the Identity Self and the Behavioral Self is aptly summarized by Fitts (1971): "[The child] does whatever he is prompted to do by internal and external stimuli. The consequences of his behavior influence their continuation or extinction; they also determine whether new behaviors are abstracted, symbolized, and incorporated into his Identity Self [p. 16]."

Psychoanalysis focuses on human identity vis-à-vis its definitions, distortions, and evolution. Erikson alternately uses identity as the core of inner unification or as ego, that part of the personality structure that serves a mediating function between the self and the environment. Erikson's astute observations and conceptualizations of the process of identity among black children have been reviewed elsewhere, and the reader is referred to the bibliography that follows (Erikson, 1964; Powell, 1979).

The third subself described by Fitts is the Judging Self—the evaluator and the mediator between the other two selves. For Fitts, the evaluative capacity of the self is perhaps the most important aspect of self-perception, for it provides the very sustenance and core of self-esteem, an aspect of self-concept that has been of primary concern for many researchers (Coopersmith, 1967). Self-esteem, according to Coombs and Snygg (1959), is significantly dependent on self-enhancement. Whatever is self-enhancing will foster self-esteem, which greatly influences the maintenance of the self-concept. Whatever factors put self-esteem at risk threaten the maintenance and continued integration of the other two internal dimensions of the self-concept, that is, the Behavioral Self and the Identity Self. Self-esteem is derived from two main sources: the self and others. Initially, the values and standards are learned from others, and one's self-esteem is dependent on their judgments. Much later, if the self-concept development process goes well, self-esteem will emanate from one's own needs, standards, values, and goals.

The Judging Self is the link to self-esteem, and self-esteem is the key to the humanistic psychological concepts of Maslow's (1959) theory of self-actualization, to Rogers's (1961) view of the fully functioning person, to Seeman's (1959) system on personality integration, as well as to Fitts's (1970) proposition on interpersonal competence. To a child psychiatrist and clinician like myself, psychological theories have no relevancy unless they have some practical implications for optimum psychological adjustment and function as well as for the optimal development of children's innate potentialities and mental health. The next section of this chapter will relate the process of self-concept and ultimate self-actualization to the field of mental health. As we review these developmental processes, we may well wonder how minority group children in a racist society can emerge with a self-concept that will help them realize self-actualization and some measure of psychological well-being and mental health. The degree to which socioeconomic, political, and educational factors and the media operate to interfere with these necessary developmental processes will become more evident as we discuss the nature of prejudice and the development and perpetuation of racial stereotypes.

SELF-CONCEPT, SELF-ACTUALIZATION, AND MENTAL HEALTH

Since the days of William James (1890), self and self-concept have been topics of concern to sociologists, educators, anthropologists, and psychiatrists as well as to theologians and philosophers. Indeed, a whole theoretical school or system-of-self theory has emerged. The term *self-concept* is used most often and is preferred because individuals may not always be cognizant of their absolute, complete selves. They may be aware only of their own cognitive concepts and the perceptions of themselves that are learned through experiences with other people and with the external world. The theory, nature, and dimensions of self-concept have been elucidated beyond James's initial view of the infant without a self at birth, and have expanded to include over 2000 publications in psychology and sociology. The renewal in self-concept as a phenomenological issue in the late 1940s has been credited with the resurgent interest of the social scientist in this issue (Gordon & Gergen, 1968).

Self-theory as evolved by Coombs and Snygg (1959), Fitts (1970), Lecky (1945), Rogers (1961), and Wylie (1961), holds that "man's behavior is always meaningful and that we could understand each person's behavior if we could perceive his phenomenal world as he does [Fitts, 1971]." The self-concept then becomes the process by which knowledge and the prediction of behavior are acquired and the frame of reference through which the self interacts with the world. This interactional process of self-concept is a powerful influence on human behavior.

Now a prominent construct in psychiatry and psychology, the self-concept is another way of understanding psychopathology, the rehabilitation process, and psychotherapy. Self-concept is a very important aspect of mental health, since it contributes to individuals' ability to participate as fully functioning persons and to actualize their own potentialities. As concepts and service programs have broadened, however, *rehabilitation* and *therapy* have become less adequate terms for humanistic psychology. *Self-actualization*, as Maslow terms it (1954, 1959), has seemed a more fitting description of the therapeutic process and of ongoing psychic growth. Indeed, Maslow's concept of self-actualization is the very core of humanistic psychology, which stresses the importance of the maximal development of human potential, that is, individuals' basic need for and drive toward becoming and being all that they are capable of being. Maslow postulates that the need for self-actualization can only be met by fulfilling all five basic groups of needs in order of priority. They are: (a) physiological needs, (b) safety or security needs, (c) needs for love, affection, and belonging, (d) esteem needs, and (e) the need for self-actualization (Maslow, 1959, p. 206).

It is clear that when the basic physiological needs for food, drink, rest, sleep, and relief from pain are unmet, these concerns will dominate a person's behavior. When the need for safety is dominant, it will preoccupy the individual's efforts and behavior. Threats to security and safety may take many forms beside physical danger, including the psychological dangers of cruelty, rejection, ridicule, discrimination, injustice, and exclusion. One of the most poignant reminders of the psychological dangers for minority group people and of a deterrent to self-actualization has been eloquently expressed by Pierce (1969):

> Now a minority-group person, of course, has many difficulties from a psychological viewpoint. The one which is probably the most oppressing is the fact that I don't believe that many blacks can live a total hour of their conscious life without recognizing the fact of their blackness and being reminded of it in all sorts of ways. This takes a great deal of energy and a great deal of concern and it depletes a further resource that might possibly contribute more to the nation because every black has to be hung up on these kinds of issues.

Maslow's (1959) criteria are very basic to the needs of all children: All children want to be loved and to receive affection, to have friends and to belong to and be part of a group. In fact, the need to have friends and belong to a group is one of the crucial landmarks of normal psychologic development from 5- or 6-years-old, and onward into adolescence. The preschooler goes from parallel play at 2 years of age, to collateral play at 3, to cooperative play at 4, and then onward to group play thereafter. Interference with this crucial developmental process can have serious consequences for the child. Powell (1973) found that black adolescent girls in newly desegregated schools in the South have very low self-concept scores because of a lack of friendships and of a sense of belonging. It was concluded that "black is not beautiful" in a previously all-white school where the stereotypes of black girls as "ugly" and "dirty" still prevail.

The esteem needs in the Maslow schema are to be valued as a way of comprehending the concept of psychological well-being. At first these needs may be experienced as desires to be met by others, for example, parents, peers, teachers. As one begins to realize self-actualization, however, self-esteem becomes more important than esteem from others. Finally, the need for self-actualization only reaches full potency when individuals are assured of the continued satisfaction of their other basic physiological and psychological needs.

In summary, the essence of the need for self-actualization is the need to be, fully and freely, what one is and wants to become; it is the motivating force in one's behavior and the prime priority in one's life. "What a man can be, he must be [Maslow, 1959, p. 38]."

Thus, through the adequate development of self-concept, one can realize self-actualization and the total integration of one's personality. One can not help but ask how a minority group person can achieve an integrated personality, a phenomenologic self-concept with self-actualization, in hostile environs that bombard the self with negative distortions from birth to death. That many minority group children do survive needs to be documented more frequently (Lawrence, 1975).

THE DEVELOPMENT OF ETHNIC AND RACIAL AWARENESS IN MINORITY GROUP CHILDREN

The issue of ethnic and racial identity is crucial to the sum total of the self-percept of minority group children, for the way in which children assimilate and accommodate these images will determine the course of their psychosocial development. The period from 3 to 7 years of age is the time during which children not only make self-differentiations but also become increasingly aware of racial and ethnic differences. They begin to learn social attitudes toward various racial and ethnic groups, including their own. The development of racial and ethnic identification is an integral part of minority group children's total development of self. The self-differentiation process occurs "in a continuing context of social interactions in which others both distinguish and evaluate him by means of his racial category and label him in affectively-laden terms which refer to his race [Proshansky & Newton, 1968, p. 184]." According to Proshansky and Newton, there are two basic processes involved in the development of racial identity. The first, racial conception, is the process by which children learn to make racial distinctions at a conceptual level. The second, racial evaluation, is the process by which children evaluate their own racial group.

Studies on racial identity in preschool children indicate that black children come to identify themselves in a negative way between the ages of 3 and 5. It is important to note, however, that the racial identity process and self-concept development are dependent on the social setting to which the black child is exposed. For instance, black children have higher self-esteem in totally black schools as compared with desegregated schools (Powell, 1973; Rosenberg & Simmons, 1975).

The child learns to distinguish differences in skin color and other physical characteristics by age 3. By 6 or 7, all children are able to make such distinctions; the most crucial period is from age 4 to 5. It is important to note that the awareness of religious and national ethnic groups also occurs during early childhood, but that it comes later than racial awareness; it, too, increases with age.

Although membership in an ethnic minority is critical to the early development of ethnic awareness, the social environment in which

children live may be equally important. If children live in neighborhoods that are composed primarily of their own ethnic group, their
exposure to the negative attitudes and behavior of ethnocentric groups
is delayed. There is some evidence to support the view that very early
exposure to negative ethnic attitudes regarding the children's group
can be difficult for young children whose self-esteem and pride are not
developed sufficiently to buffer such assaults (Powell, 1978). It is often
difficult to separate ethnic from racial identity. I shall focus only on
those aspects of ethnic identity that will help to elucidate particular
components of the self-concept process and prejudice; see Chapter 5,
this volume, for a more detailed discussion of ethnic identity.

Ethnic identity is generally acquired at birth and thus appears to be
fixed and unchangeable. Some group identities are lost by assimilation,
however, that is to say, by the process of the erasure of the boundary
between one group and another. Among racial minorities in the United
States, this kind of assimilation has been characteristic of Hispanics; to
some extent, of American Indians; and among biracial Afro-Americans
who do not have the typical physiognomy of the Negroid race. Of course,
the phenomenon of "passing" among Afro-Americans has occurred because of generations of miscegenation; it is not unique to only this group.
Among Asian Americans, group identity is eroded by intermarriage (Kim,
1974; National Institute of Mental Health, 1971; Tan, 1973). The loss of
group identity may occur by amalgamation, a process by which two or
more groups form a new, larger group which is different from any of the
component groups, for example, the Pacific/Asian minority group. The
boundary change among ethnic groups is dependent on the criteria of
identity on which judgments of collective likeness and unlikeness are
made. It is also dependent on the operational criteria of identity that, in
turn, are determined by the ready judgments on which individual
membership are made. Horowitz (1975) has noted that in the United
States even a small degree of known Negroid ancestry identifies a person as Afro-American, and that this knowledge alone is the sole criterion of membership. The more critical indices are color, physiognomy,
and so on, but no one, or even all, of these are anthropologically deter-
minative of the question of ancestry.

Ethnic identity becomes particularly confusing for American Indian
children. First, they may have a tribal identity that has become extinct;
second, their identity has become an amalgamation of races and
nationalities. Among American Indian children, the ethnic identity
confusion is evident in the way they partition themselves when they
describe who they are—for example, as one-third American Indian,
one-fourth Irish, one-eighth Spanish. For Hispanic children, for whom

many geographically, culturally, and racially (and even linguistically and historically) different groups have been subsumed under one name, the submergence of the unique differences of each subgroup becomes problematic. The merger of Asian and Pacific Island groups of people into one classification, as the Pacific/Asian group, has some political expediencies. The amalgamation, however, is only artificial; it has blurred the major differences and has not addressed the disparate needs of the individual groups that are subsumed into this category. This kind of blurring of ethnic identity confuses youth. The confusion of ethnic identity for minority group youth is intensified by the fact that the symbols employed to differentiate group from group may be widely divergent characteristics at different levels of identity. In this respect, Horowitz (1975) observed that "an overarching identity may be indicated by language, while a lesser one may be evidenced by a behavioral trait and a still lesser one by a visual one [pp. 120–121]." It is clear that the psychic energy youngsters must use to sort out the complexity of an ethnic or racial identity because of the importance it may play in their acceptance or rejection by their peers may take its toll in other important areas of their development.

Research data indicate that there is a direct relation between problems in the development of the self and the degree to which children's ethnic or racial group is socially unacceptable and exposed to discrimination and deprivation. The early studies of Clark and Clark (1947), Goodman (1952), Radke and Trager (1950) and Seward (1956), show that as the self-awareness of minority group children evolves, it does so in a race-conscious, ethnocentric sociocultural milieu that assigns negative values to the perception of any color other than white or to mores and norms that are non-European, more specifically, non-Western. The child does not learn about racial and ethnic differences in an affectless, value-free milieu. Although the evaluation process of racial awareness in American society has been reported by many investigators, it can be summed up most succinctly by a childhood ditty:

> If you're white, you're all right.
> If you're brown, you can hang around.
> If you're black, step way back.

THE DEVELOPMENT OF
RACIAL STEREOTYPES

At this juncture it seems worthwhile to pause in the discussion of self-concept of minority group children to review some of the literature of stereotypes and racial attitudes; it will help us to better understand the relationship between television and the self-esteem of minority group children. One of the most noted social psychologists in the area of race relations and attitudes, Allport (1954), defines stereotypes as "primarily images within a category invoked by the individual to justify either love-prejudice or hate-prejudice [p. 189]." Allport further elucidates certain other aspects of stereotypes that may add insight to our discussion: A stereotype (a) may sometimes grow in defiance of all evidence; (b) may be totally unsupported by facts; (c) may develop from a sharpening and overgeneralization of facts; (d) acts both as a justificatory device for categorical acceptance or rejection of a group and to simplify perception and thinking, making both processes less complex; (e) is sustained by selective perception and selective forgettings; and (f) changes in time.

This last characteristic of stereotypes is especially interesting and, of course, invites the immediate question of whether negative stereotypes of a minority group people are decreasing over time. Gilbert's (1951) study showed a "fading effect" of stereotypes for 10 national and ethnic groups between 1932 and 1950. In *Racial Discrimination in the United States*, Pettigrew (1975) notes that longitudinal research on the subject is not as prevalent as in other areas of social science research and that "nowhere is this fact more conspicuous than in research on racial attitudes, a domain that virtually begs for over-time studies [p. 22]." The most noteworthy studies in this area are those by Hyman and Sheatsley (1956, 1964) and Greeley and Sheatsley (1971). They found, for instance, that negative racial attitudes prevalent between 1950 and 1960 had changed in a significantly positive way even by 1956 (Hyman and Sheatsley, 1956). The Greeley and Sheatsley studies of 1964 and 1971 noted other improvements as well (Greeley & Sheatsley, 1964 and 1971). In the middle and late 1960s, shifting black attitudes about race relations were also noted (Pettigrew, 1975). Campbell (1971) found that positive attitudes of whites toward blacks had reached their highest recorded levels in the late 1960s and early 1970s and that black attitudes in the aggregate were definitely pro-integrationist (see Pettigrew, 1975, p. 31).

A cautious note must be included: An 18-survey series of racial attitudes contained one Gallup question designed to discover if people believe the "push for integration" is too fast, too slow, or about right. In a follow-up to this question in 1971, there was a noted shifting of black and white responses that were related to then-current sociopolitical and institutional changes (Pettigrew, Riley, & Rose, 1975). Pettigrew (1975) has called attention to the empirical link between change at the individual and societal levels. This supports findings from other related research about the influence of institutional alterations on personal changes in attitudes.

Wyatt, Bass, and Powell (1981) reported that American society is experiencing shifts in racial attitudes different from those reported by Campbell (1971). They are impressed with the increase of hostility of whites toward blacks and with the reciprocation hostility of blacks toward whites. There are still many studies that show that among higher socioeconomic classes and college educated people, class is a more important basis for discrimination than is race.

The reported changes in racial attitudes over the past 20–30 years toward a more tolerant and positive point of view overall do not mean that all is well in racial America. The 1980 riots in Miami are the harbingers of continued unrest and intolerance of minority group people toward white racism. In an article entitled "White Racism: Its Root, Form, and Function," Comer (1969) concluded that without a significant reduction in white racism, the response among blacks would only become more intense, eventually forming a basis for widespread and malignant black racism. Allport (1954) notes that:

> Heterogeneity and the urge toward upward mobility thus make for ferments in society and are likely to bring ethnic prejudice in their wake. But the process seems to be speeded up in times of crisis. . . .
>
> Whenever anxiety increases, accompanied by a loss of predictability in life, people tend to define their deteriorated situation in terms of scapegoats [p. 224].

As the domestic economy of the 1980s becomes more chaotic, one hears more negative references to "those Iranians," "those Vietnamese boat people and who is going to take care of them," "those illegal wetbacks," "those Cubans," "those Haitians," and, of course, "those blacks who think we owe them everything."

A recent study (Wyatt et al., 1981) showed that respondents were able to decrease the social distance between themselves and other ethnic groups. Increased social distance for Afro-Americans and Hispanics were significantly desired for marriage and as next-door neighbors but with less significance for other areas of social contact. A review of studies using the Bogardus Social Distance Scale reveals some striking commonalities in results (Allport, 1954). Similar patterns of preference in studies by Wyatt et al. (1981) have been found across the country, and these patterns vary little with respondents' income, region, education, occupation, or ethnic group. The English and Canadians are almost universally acceptable as citizens, neighbors, social equals, and kinsmen. In short, these ethnic groups have the least social distance. However, Hindus, Turks, and Afro-Americans (in that order) most consistently are at the other extreme, with the most social distance from them desired by other ethnic and national groups.

To a considerable degree, all minority groups in America suffer from the same state of marginality, according to Allport (1954). Afro-American marginality is always there and changes little over a period of time as compared with other minority groups. The marginality for the minority group person has, says Allport, "its haunting consequences of insecurities, conflict, and irritation [p. 241]." Especially for the Afro-American, efforts to achieve relatedness are almost always likely to be rebuffed. Blacks are never, ever, really part of the in-group. The stereotypes do not always become more extensive, but they do become more sophisticated and elaborate, for example, "Jensen-ism" and the stereotype of low academic achievement.

We have noted that the stereotypes become more sophisticated in form and less direct in intent. Kilson (1975) takes note of collusion between the media and national political process in shaping the racial attitudes process. In his astute analysis, "Blacks and Neo-Ethnicity in American Political Life (1975)," Kilson discusses Richard Nixon's 1968 election and subsequent developments that set the stage for a new definition of the federal government's relationship to black ethnocentric revitalization. Kilson says, "The 'war on poverty' was killed outright [p. 239]." His (1975) analysis shows that the Nixon administration established policies that attacked violence and riots regardless of their social causes and their roots in the racist patterns of black–white relations:

> Thus, in the eyes of millions of whites—perhaps a majority—such goals of black militants as cessation of police brutality, community control of police, prison reform, expanded welfare coverage, government responsibility for reducing [black] unemployment, and so on, were no longer to be treated as legitimate political issues deserving action by political decision makers. Instead, these goals became in some sense intrinsically [black] goals, hence, un-American. Through them millions [of blacks] sought to continue a life of crime, avoid apprehension by officers of the law, freeload on welfare agencies, and evade honest labor—or in Nixon's term, shirk responsibility to the work ethic. Thus through a process that might be called ethnicization of racial perceptions, the Nixon administration has helped attach to Afro-Americans a variant of an ethnic label—albeit negative in character [p. 239].

The role that the media played in the projection of the negative ethnicization of these racial perceptions, although not part of a process of individual racism, was that of a participant in the process of institutional racism. (Pettigrew, 1975). This is only one example of the way in which television helped national politics perpetuate and create racial stereotypes.

A BRIEF REVIEW OF
THE NATURE OF PREJUDICE

There have been many treatises on the psychology of prejudice. Time and space do not allow a comprehensive recapitulation of the many studies and theories about prejudice here, but Bettelheim and Janowitz (1964) have offered a thorough review of the subject that encompasses the causal problems within the perpetrator, as well as the consequences for the victim. Because it deals also with the self-concept of the perpetrator of prejudice and stereotypes, their theory is particularly important to the understanding of the effects of racist stereotypes depicted on television on the self-concept and identity of the minority group child.

When Erikson first came to this country, he was impressed with the prevailing problem of identity among Americans and he elaborated his concerns in *Childhood and Society* (1950). as well as in *Identity and the Life Cycle* (1959). Erikson (1959) has written that: "Whoever has not yet reached a secure personal identity of his own is threatened by self-doubt, by confusion about who he is, a nagging anxiety that he may be a nobody. This fear he tries to silence by telling himself, 'At least I am not a Negro, or a Jew; and this makes me at least something more than a nobody [p. 92].' " America is made up of a heterogeneous mixture of people from all over the world. It has often been described as a melting pot, but the amalgamation has never been complete. It remains, instead, an admixture of many social, racial, ethnic national, religious, and political groups, all searching for the American core identity within the sometimes elusive American dream.

According to Bettelheim and Janowitz (1950), ethnic hostility is a symptom of the individual's effort to maintain a balance in his psychic economy, and the expression of prejudice helps protect his individuality. The same authors also note (1964) that "as a person develops his need for securing his identity, this need may feed ethnic hostility and prejudice [p. 57]." In *Social Change and Prejudice* (Bettelheim & Janowitz, 1964), the thesis is elaborated:

> The search for identity, and with it the search for ego strength and personal control, might very well involve as a detour the desire to find one's identity or to strengthen it through prejudice. And those who fail to achieve an effective personal identity might temporarily or permanently come to use this devious method to establish some kind of identity. Prejudice then might be likened to

the tumultous solutions triggered by the adolescent's search for a personal identity, a search that often continues after the age of adolescence. As many persons seem to get stuck permanently in adolescence because they fail to establish their identity so many get stuck in prejudice in our society where . . . finding one's identity is very difficult. . . . Thus . . . reasons persist which tempt a person to seek to secure his identity (or in its absence, at least a feeling of identity) in various ways, including the devious ways of prejudice [p. 57].

In noting the pervasive problems of identity among his American patients, Erikson paid special attention to the danger of identity diffusion. He (1959) quotes the son, Biff, from Arthur Miller's play "Death of a Salesman": "I just can't take hold, Mom. I can't take hold of some kind of life." Erikson goes on to observe that when identity diffusion coexists with uncertainties about one's ethnic, social, personal, or sexual identity, then prejudice may be the readily available psychological outcome.

Dustin Hoffman, in his acceptance speech for his 1980 Oscar for Best Actor, referred to the precarious status of actors and writers in the television and movie industries in this country. The number of unemployed actors and writers is incredibly high, and the problems of personal identity that are created have been noted by many of us in clinical psychiatry and psychology. Rejection and deprivation do not breed secure identities for writers or the performers. Very often something is written or performed just for the money or to get one's foot in the door. Black actors and actresses have talked about the difficulty of maintaining high standards and a sense of racial pride despite the pressure to work. Television feeds on the insecurities of its professionals. There is a need to examine to what extent this promotes the portrayal of stereotypes, by leading to the suspension of one's social responsibility in situations regarding racial issues because of one's own sense of personal or professional insecurity (Writers' War Board, 1945, cited in Allport, 1954).

In their earlier work on stereotyping the minority, Bettelheim and Janowitz (1950) found that when there were two or more ethnic minorities, there was a tendency for the prejudiced person to separate the stereotypes into two sets and to assign each of them to one minority group. In their study of prejudice toward Afro-Americans and Jews in the Army, they found that the intolerant soldier selected the Jew for projection of those characteristics rejected by the superego and the black for those id desires that represented greater irrationality. They also found (1950) that when the two minority groups diffused in physical characteristics such as skin color, the minority group having the greater physical difference was used for projecting anxieties about dirt and sexual desires, whereas the minority group with more physical similarities was a target for the anxieties about overpowering control: "Ethnic hostility is a projection of unacceptable inner strivings onto a minority group. . . . Any survey of those characteristics to which the members of the in-group object in members of the out-group is frequently a list of all those characteristics which they fear in themselves [p. 146]."

A comparison of the patterns and stereotypes used to characterize Afro-Americans and Jews in the 1950 study uncovered several important differences in the structure of group hostilities. The five most frequent stereotypes about Jewish people were that (a) they are clannish and help one another, (b) they have money, (c) they control everything, (d) they use underhanded business methods, (e) they do not work and do not do manual labor. For Afro-Americans, the five most frequent stereotypes are that (a) they are sloppy and dirty, (b) they depreciate property, (c) they are taking over and forcing out the whites, (d) they are lazy and slackers in work, and (e) they are immoral. The tendency for there to be a preponderance of id stereotypes about blacks, Chicanos, and other dark-skinned people still persists, as the preceding review of stereotypes and ethnocentrism demonstrated.

THE EFFECTS OF TELEVISION ON THE SELF-CONCEPT OF MINORITY GROUP CHILDREN

Television and motion pictures have expanded the world of American children beyond their backyards and local community to expose them to the broader context of American society, and indeed the world. That larger world to which the child is exposed is primarily an adult world, struggling with the vicissitudes of power politics, economic survival, crime, violence, sex, and the puzzling questions of atomic energy, war, and space. Information is more instantly available, making the evolution of childhood less gradual, for television bombards the child not only with information, but also with visual images. For those who would censor television, their critics would remind them that television only mirrors what actually exists in the real world and in our society.

Television communicates to the young information about social structure, and thus leads them to fashion attitudes about themselves, others, and the world at large. Symbolic lessons are offered about occupations, racial groups, sex, and violence, and they perpetrate a biased reflection of the world. Gerbner (1972) wrote:

Representation in the fictional world (of television) signifies social existence; absence means symbolic annihilation.... Values and forces come into play through characterizations: good is a certain type of attractiveness, evil is a personality defect, and right is the might that wins. The issue is rarely in doubt; the action is typically a game of personality, group identification, skill, and power. [p. 44]

In their critique of television content vis-à-vis stereotypes and social roles, Liebert, Neale, and Davidson (1973) state that the most powerful figure on television is the white American male and that more than half of all the leading television characters fall into this category. Schary (1970), firmly asserts that the behavior of the mass media (which includes television programming for entertainment as well as for news) has had and continues to have an impact on the control of prejudice and discrimination in our society. Schary suggests that media programmers may not always be as conscious as they should be of their role in this process.

Liebert, Neale, and Davidson (1973) review the misconceptions of national and ethnic groups fostered by television. They note that in the early studies (mostly of the late 1950s and early 1960s) minorities were more likely than whites to be law breakers. In an examination of the presentation of blacks on television, Clark (1972) found that in the 1950s, blacks were rarely represented at all. When they were, it was either as minor characters or as lovable but stereotyped buffoons.

A study of the Television Violence Commission staff in 1969 found that 5 million children under 12 years of age were watching television between 10:30 and 11:30 P.M. (cited in McIntyre & Teevan, 1972, p. 13). Children of lower SES watch more television than children of higher SES status (Liebert et al., 1973). Young children of different racial and ethnic backgrounds do not seem to have different viewing habits, but differences do emerge at older ages, with older minority group children watching longer than their SES peers. Also, children with lower IQ scores tend to watch more television than those with higher scores. However, since IQ is linked with SES, especially for minority group children, the significance of these data is linked more to social status factors than to innate cognitive abilities (Clark, 1972; Liebert et al., 1973). Still other studies indicate that minority group children believe that whatever they see on television is true, significantly more than white children (Gibner, 1972; Lyle & Hoffman, 1972).

The consequences for television programming may then be more crucial in regard to the self-concept development of minority group children than it is to that of white children. Although the effects of sex stereotypes, occupational roles, and violence are equally as important to minority group children as to other children, the focus of this chapter is on the racial and ethnic stereotypes depicted on television and the effects they have on the self-concept development of minority group children.

If television is only a reflection of our world, let us peer a little harder and look at the images that are reflected and what impact these images have on the growing child. A growing person's conception of his or her selfness comes into being through the reflected appraisal of others. What are the reflections of the appraisals of our race-conscious society that television mirrors or projects to the minority group child viewer?

In his interpretive history of blacks in American films, Bogle (1973) has described five typical stereotypes of blacks depicted over time in motion pictures: the Tom, the coon, the tragic mulatto, the mammy, and the brutal black buck. He (1973) describes the Tom as the acceptable "good Negro" character: "Always as [Toms] are chased, harassed, hounded, flogged, enslaved, and insulted, they keep the faith, n'er turn against their white massas, and remain hearty, submissive, stoic, generous, selfless, and oh-so-very kind. Thus they endear themselves to white audiences and emerge as heroes of sorts [p. 30]."

The second stereotype is that of the coon, the black buffoon and amusing clown. Usually, Bogle (1973) says, the coon was depicted as the child pickaninny, "a harmless little screwball creations whose eyes popped [and] whose hair stood on end with the least excitement [p. 7]." (The pickaninny of *The Little Rascals* can still be seen every afternoon on television.) The pickaninny becomes, in adulthood, "[one of those] no-account niggers, those unreliable crazy, lazy, sub-human creatures good for nothing more than eating watermelons, stealing chickens, shooting craps or butchering the English [Bogle, 1973, p. 8]."

The third stereotype is the tragic mulatto, "a victim of divided racial inheritance," a "cinnamon-colored gal" with Caucasian features, the only black woman who comes close to the white ideal and thus is allowed any sex appeal (Bogle, 1973, p. 10). According to Bogle, the reason why actresses such as Eartha Kitt and Lola Falana failed to emerge as important screen love goddesses was that they were too dark.

The fourth stereotype is the mammy, the female counterpart of the comic coon. She is usually big, fat, cantankerous, and fiercely independent. Much later in time she becomes the Aunt Jemima, less headstrong than the mammy—sweet, jolly, good-tempered.

And finally, the super black bucks are "always big baaad niggers, oversexed and savage, violent and frenzied [Bogle, 1973, p. 11]."

Perhaps the most important point that Bogle (1973) makes is that "because the guises are always changing, audiences are sometimes tricked into believing the depictions of the American [black] are altered [p. 22]." The stereotypes have nevertheless persisted under different guises over the years.

> Afterward during the 1920's, audiences saw their [Toms] and coons dressed in the guise of plantation jesters. In the 1930's the types were dressed in servant's uniforms. In the early 1940's and the 1950's, they donned the gear of troubled problem people. In the 1960's [and 1970's] they appeared as angry militants [Bogle, 1973, p. 23].

The stereotypes are there for television, too, only in more sophisticated guises. The Toms, coons, mulattos, mammies, and bucks are still there in *The Jeffersons, Good Times, Baby I'm Back, Sanford and Son,* and *What's Happening.*

The Jeffersons are a black family that has "made it," but George, the husband, is still the comic coon or buffoon whose business acumen is never displayed, but only his lack of it. The maid, Florence, is the headstrong, cantankerous mammy who challenges George as the head of the household and makes disparaging remarks about his abilities and character. In *Good Times,* J. J. has become the comic coon and buffoon very much like the pickaninny in *The Little Rascals,* and unfortunately he now dominates the show and obscures some of the poignant drama about a honest, poor black family struggling together in a ghetto environment. Sanford, too, is a stumbling buffoon who often makes no sense, and his son is close to being cast as the young, oversexed black buck.

It seems unbelievable that *Baby I'm Back* could ever have reached the screen. An Afro-American man deserts his family and then returns several years later to resume his role in the family. His departure from the family was for some self-serving reason, and so is his return. His mother-in-law is the domineering matriarch who makes his life and her daughter's complicated. That these stereotypes persist is incredible, given the post-Civil Rights and urban explosions of the 1960s.

The guises are there in *Starsky and Hutch, Kojak,* and *Baretta.* In these shows the pimps, prostitutes, informers are usually minorities who get bullied and frightened into "squealing." They are always there to remind us of the antisocial nature of minority group people. All of these are on prime time in every home, a knob's turn away on ABC, CBS, or NBC, in color or in black and white. They readily reinforce the negative reflected appraisals in the self-concept development of the Afro-American child and reinforce the stereotypes for the white child who will reiterate those negative images in turn to another Afro-American child.

Schary (1970) believes that, despite many hopeful signs, the media unwittingly may be nourishing prejudice. He gives two examples of this process. Because of the growing power of the black minority from the 1950s through the early 1970s, the media were compelled to pay attention to them. The dilemma of how to depict blacks presented itself and remained a problem for some time. The solution was to transform the qualities attributed to the blacks as described in Bogle's (1973) historical account of black stereotypes in the media. Suddenly the black depicted on television was transformed from everything whites despised (as described by Bettelheim & Janowitz, 1950, 1964) into all that whites admire. In short, if blacks had to be seen on television, then they would be presented in a light that reflected only white's life styles and values. Bill Cosby's *I Spy* and Diahann Carrol's *Julia* exemplified the new product, as did the young, clean-cut, successful blacks (as Schary [1970] describes them) who increasingly began to appear in commercials. They are the carbon copies of whites.

Schary (1970) indicates that a second way in which the media may unwittingly nourish prejudice is through their failure to recognize that times and culture have changed. Although they may have transcended the past in many other noteworthy ways, the media may be accommodating today's prejudice:

> So, for example, just as our society is nearly silent on the subject of Mexican Americans, Puerto Ricans, and American Indians, the media too are silent. By this silence, the media obviously do not intend to condone prejudice against these groups, but such of course, is the indirect result. For where prejudice is not directly engaged, it is in effect sustained [p. 105].

A look at some of the "family shows" aired on prime time reveals that they depict a homogeneous white society in spite of the cultural plurality that exists in America today. Is it possible that in the ABC production of *Family* not any of those five family members ever comes in contact with, relates to, or associates with a minority group person— ever? Like Dick and Jane, they live in an all-white world of affluence and material success that is devoid of minority group people. Minority group people are never depicted in their lives because a community of gracious houses with lawns and guest houses, a nonworking mother, a successful lawyer father, and a maid are unattainable to a minority group family. Minority group people are invisible, nonexistent, unacceptable in, and worse still, inaccessible to that world of affluence and leisure. The invisibility of minority group people was also evidenced for a long while in such longstanding shows as *The Waltons, The Brady Bunch, Happy Days, Bewitched, I Love Lucy,* and *Marcus Welby.*

They all depict a middle-class, white, mostly suburban life exclusive of minority-group people and any cultural diversity. The invisibility of the American Indian, Asian, and Hispanic is even more glaring, for it is rare that these minority groups are seen in commercials, let alone as minor characters in any major drama or special. Television has yet to produce a documentary or special on our treatment of American Indians, who are still depicted as stupid savages who lose every war with the whites. Most views of Pacific/Asians are that of the "Jap" enemy of World War II, a glimpse of Hawaiians with grass skirts on *Hawaii Five-O*, or Chinatown in some spy drama. The Chicano, who is seldom depicted at all, is presented in *Chico and the Man* as an illiterate laborer with broken English who clowns and tries to please his white boss. In all these instances, none of the other minority group people are presented as thinking, feeling, believable human beings with a viable cultural heritage. They are not allowed dignity.

In some respects, invisibility may be more destructive to minority group children's self-concept because it denies the importance of their existence and, as Schary (1970) pointed out, is symbolic of the annihilation they suffer as a result of racism. The annihilation is psychological and ultimately cultural, often leaving minority group children feeling fragmented and marginal because of the cultural conflict they begin to experience. The most serious problem that occurs for minority group children who try to live in a bicultural world is confusion and sometimes the loss of self-identification. Although America has ostensibly been proud of its heterogeneous population—"the hungry masses yearning to be free" (Statute of Liberty) the actual expectation is for cultural conformity. The concept of cultural plurality, the coexistence of numerous separate cultures living in cooperative harmony, has never been a reality and is, in fact, only a conceptualization for those who strive for harmony in race relations. Most Americans expect cultural conformity, especially to the white, western European norms. For any cultural ethnic group whose language, color, or way of life differs from those majority norms, there is persistent pressure to acculturate and assimilate. For children it begins in school with teachers discounting and degrading their language and their cultural values (Powell, 1979).

In my travels all over the country to schools with diverse cultural groups, some segregated and some integrated, and in my many years as a child psychiatrist who has treated many minority group children, I have come to agree with the poignant commentary of D'Arch McNickle, a Native American social scientist. It characterizes the self-concept problems and resultant conflict and turmoil that minority group chil-

dren experience as they encounter racism in every facet of their lives—
the schools, the social institutions, the media. I have often quoted
McNickle because what he says is true not only for American Indian
children but for all minority group children (Powell, 1979, in press). To
the quotation one might add the words Afro-American, Chicano, Hispanic, Pacific/Asian and any other racial groups, in which the word
Indian appears:

> The problem of being Indian, and being obliged to function at two levels of
> consciousness, for many individuals reduces itself to this: they are aware that
> their community, their people, their kinsmen are Indians and held in low
> esteem by the general society. The young people, especially, recognize them-
> selves as Indians, but they do not want the low-status equivalent. They look
> for some way in which they can share in the status ascribed to middle-class
> Americans without ceasing to be Indian [McNickle, 1968, p. 2153].

The record is not all bad; more accurately, it is mixed. I would agree
with Schary (1970) in acknowledging that television has seized the
crusading spirit at some important moments and has provided "some
of the most eloquent testimonies to brotherhood and good will that we
have known in our time [p. 24]." Such portraits have been particularly
outstanding; they include *Nothing but a Man* and *One Potato, Two
Potato.* The airing of *Roots* and *Sojourner Truth* have been historical
landmarks and have accented the "Black is beautiful" theme that has
been significant in changing the self-esteem patterns of black children
(Powell, 1973). Indeed, more recently some of the older shows have
incorporated sensitive moving episodes involving minority groups.
The *Waltons* is a case in point where there have been several shows in
which minority group people, primarily blacks, have been depicted in
a sensitive, real human way. *Little House on the Prairie* has also had
their share of some sensitive dramas depicting minority groups.
Whenever and wherever such programs occur, it is appreciated,
needed, and applauded, and should be continued.

Schary (1970) presents the issues in the debate that continues to rage
in the mass-media industry regarding entertainment and public service. That there is such a continuing debate gives this author at least
some reason for optimism. I remember attending a conference 20 years
ago at which a television executive told a group of social scientists that
television was not interested in messages, that delivering messages was
the task of Western Union. We have come a long way from that con-
stricted opinion, but there is still a long journey ahead. My dream is
that within my lifetime television will present the concept of American
cultural plurality in which people of various ethnic, racial, or religious

backgrounds interact in a drama together, that there will be a series depicting a Puerto Rican family in New York, a Chicano family in Texas, an American Indian community in New Mexico, a black family visiting Africa, or an Pacific/Asian American family in Los Angeles or Seattle or New York, and many more. Minority group people can be a part of the American dream and television can help make it so.

REFERENCES

Allport, G. *The nature of prejudice.* Reading, Massachusetts: Addison-Wesley, 1954.
Allport, G. *Pattern and growth in personality.* New York: Holt, 1963.
Bettelheim, B., & Janowitz, N. *Dynamics of prejudice.* New York: Harper & Row, 1950.
Bettelheim, B., & Janowitz, N. *Social change and prejudice.* New York: Free Press, 1964.
Bogle, D. *Toms, coons, mulattoes, mammies, and bucks.* New York: Viking, 1973.
Campbell, A. *White attitudes toward black people.* Ann Arbor, Michigan: Inst. for Social Research, 1971.
Clark, C.C. Race, identification, and television violence. In E. Rubenstein & J. Murray (Eds.), *Television and social behavior* (Vol. 5). Washington, D.C.: US Govt. Printing Office, 1972.
Clark, K.B., & Clark, M.P. Racial identification and preference in Negro children. In T. Newcomb & E. Hartley (Eds.), *Readings in social psychology.* New York: Holt, 1947.
Comer, J.P. White racism: Its root, form, and function. *American Journal of Psychiatry,* 1969, *1266,* 803–806.
Coombs, A., & Syngg, D. *Individual behavior* (rev. ed.). New York: Harper, 1959.
Coopersmith, S. *The antecedents of self-esteem.* San Francisco, California: Freeman, 1967.
Erikson, E.H. *Childhood and society.* New York: Norton, 1950.
Erikson, E.H. The problem of ego-identity. *Journal of the American Psycho-Analytic Association,* 1956, *4,* 56–121.
Erikson, E.H. *Identity and the life cycle: Selected papers.* New York: International Universities Press, 1959.
Erickson, E.H. Memorandum on identity and Negro youth. *Journal of Social Issues,* 1964, *20,* 29–42.
Fitts, W. *The self concept and performance.* Nashville, Tennessee: Dede Wallace Center, Monograph V, Counselor Recordings and Tests, 1972.
Fitts, W. *Interpersonal competence: The wheel model.* Nashville, Tennessee: Dede Wallace Center, Monograph II, Counselor Recordings and Tests, 1970.
Fitts, W. *The self concept and self-actualization.* Nashville, Tennessee: Dede Wallace Center, Monograph III, Counselor Recordings and Tests, 1971.
Gerbner, G. Violence in television drama: Trends and symbolic function. In G. Comstock & E. Rubenstein (Eds.), *Television and social behavior* (Vol. 1). Washington, D.C.: US Govt. Printing Office, 1972.
Gilbert, W.M. Stereotype persistence and change among college students. *Journal of Abnormal and Social Psychology,* 1951, *46,* 245–254.
Goodman, M. *Race awareness in young children.* Reading, Massachusetts: Addison-Wesley, 1952.
Gordon, C., & Gergen, K. (Eds.). *The self in social interaction.* New York: Wiley, 1968.

Greenley, A., & Sheatsley, P. Attitudes on racial integration. *Scientific American*, 1971, *225*, 13–19.

Horowitz, D. Ethnic identity. In N. Glazer & D. Moynihan (Eds.), *Ethnicity*. Cambridge, Massachusetts: Harvard Univ. Press, 1975.

Hyman, H., & Sheatsley, P. Attitudes on desegregation. *Scientific American*, 1956, *195*, 35–41.

Hyman, H., & Sheatsley, P. Attitudes on desegregation. *Scientific American*, 1964, *211*, 16–23.

James, W. *The principles of psychology* (2 vol.). New York: Henry Hold, 1890.

Kilson, M. Blacks and neo-ethnicity in American political life. In N. Glazer & D. Moyniham (Eds.), *Ethnicity*. Cambridge, Massachusetts: Harvard Univ. Press, 1975.

Kim, H. Some aspects of social demography of Korean Americans. *International Migration Review*, 1974, *8*, 23–42.

Lawrence, M. *Young inner city families: Development of ego strength under stress*. New York: Behavioral Publications, 1975.

Lecky, P. *Self consistency*. New York: N.Y. Island Press, 1945.

Liebert, R., Neale, J., & Davidson, E. *The early window: The effects of television on children and youth*. New York: Pergamon, 1973.

Lyle, J., & Hoffman, H. Childrens' use of television and other media. In T. Newcomb & E. Hartley (Eds.), *Readings in social psychology*. New York: Holt, 1972.

McIntyre, J., & Teevan, J., Jr. Television and deviant behavior. In G. Comstock & E. Rubenstein (Eds.), *Television and social behavior* (Vol. 3). Washington, D.C.: US Govt. Printing Office, 1972.

McNickle, D. Hearing before U.S. Senate Subcommittee on Indian Education (Part 5), 1968, 2153.

Maslow, A. *New knowledge in human values*. New York: Harper & Row, 1959.

Mead, G. *Mind, self, and society*. Chicago, Illinois: Univ. of Chicago Press, 1934.

Morland, J. Racial self-identification: A study of nursery school children. *American Catholic Sociological Review*, 1963, *24*, 231–242.

National Institute of Mental Health. *1st National Conference on Pacific Island Peoples and Asian American Mental Health* (DHEW Monograph No. 74-46). Washington, D.C.: US Govt. Printing Office, 1971.

Piaget, J., & Inhelder, B. *The psychology of the child*. New York: Basic Books, 1969.

Pettigrew, T. (Ed.). *Racial discrimination in the United States*. New York: Harper & Row, 1975.

Pettigrew, T., Riley, R., & Rose, J. *Understanding racial change*. Cambridge, Massachusetts: Harvard Univ. Press, 1975.

Pierce, C. *The effects of racism*. Paper presented at the AMA 15th Annual Conference of State Mental Health Representatives, Chicago, Illinois, Mar. 14–15th, 1969.

Powell, G. *Black Monday's children: A study of the psychological effects of school desegregation on southern school children*. New York: Appleton, 1973.

Powell, G. *Self-concept, academic achievement, and school desegregation among Afro-American children*. Paper presented at the annual meeting of American Educational Research Association, San Francisco, California, April 1978.

Powell, G. Growing up black and female. In C. Kopp & M. Kirkpatrick (Eds.), *Becoming female*. New York: Plenum, 1979.

Powell, G. The social and emotional problems of minority-group children. In D. Cantwell & P. Tanguay (Eds.), *Clinical child psychiatry*. New York: Spectrum, in press.

Powell, G. The psychosocial development of Afro-American children. In G. Powell, J. Yamamoto, A. Morales, & A. Romero (Eds.), *The psychosocial development of minority-group children*. New York: Brunner/Mazel, in press.

Proshansky, H., & Newton, P. The nature and meaning of the Negro self-identity. In M. Deutsch, I. Katz, & A. Jensen (Eds.), *Social class, race, and psychological development*. New York: Holt, 1968.

Radke, M., & Trager, H. Children's perceptions of the social roles of Negroes and Whites. *Journal of Psychology*, 1950, *29*, 3–33.

Rogers, C. *On becoming a person*. Boston, Massachusetts: Houghton, 1961.

Rosenberg, M. *Concerning the self*. New York: Basic Books, 1979.

Rosenberg, F., & Simmons, R. Sex differences in the self-concept in adolescence. *Sex Roles: A Journal of Research*, 1975, *1*, 147–159.

Sarbin, T. A preface to a psychological analysis of the self. *Psychological Review*, 1952, *59*, 11–22.

Schary, D. The mass media and prejudice. In C. Glock & E. Siegelman (Eds.), *Prejudice USA*. New York: Praeger, 1970.

Seeman, J. Toward a concept of personality integration. *American Psychologist*, 1959, *14*, 633–637.

Seward, G.H. *Psychotherapy and culture conflict*. New York: Ronald, 1956.

Sullivan, H. *The interpersonal theory of psychiatry*. New York: Norton, 1953.

Tan, M. *The Chinese in the United States: Social mobility and assimilation*. Taipei: Orient Cultural Service, 1973.

Taylor, D. *Consistency of the self-concept*. (Doctoral dissertation, Vanderbilt University, 1953). (University Microfilms No. 70-10, 915).

Wyatt, G., Bass, B., & Powell, G. Mental health professionals' attitudes toward Afro-Americans. In B. Bass, G. Wyatt, & G.J. Powell (Eds.), *The Afro-American family: Assessment, treatment, and research issues*. New York: Grune Stratton, 1981.

Wylie, R. *The self-concept: A critical survey of pertinent research literature*. Lincoln: Univ. of Nebraska Press, 1961.

TELEVISION, SOCIALIZATION, AND SELECTED CONCERNS ABOUT SPECIFIC MINORITY GROUPS

Molefi K. Asante

Television and the Language Socialization of Black Children

Most of the literature on television's impact on children has dealt with agression and violence. Since the late 1950s a considerable corpus of research has issued forth, like some massive wave, in an unending effort to link the behavior of children to television's influence, but research on television and the black child has been a vast wasteland. Almost none of the hundreds of experimental studies has tested hypotheses derived from communication theories or dealt with black children. Moreover, although there is general psychological interest in the developmental socialization problems of black youth and the works of Brody (1964), Erikson (1964), Hauser (1971), Pettigrew (1964), and Taylor (1976) have added to the psychosocial development literature on black children, no substantial data exist on how black children are affected in their language socialization by television.

It is the purpose of this chapter to propose heuristics for the study of television's influence on the language socialization of black children. I will discuss my assumptions, the implications of those assumptions, and research on prosocial effects.

TELEVISION AND
THE SOCIALIZATION OF THE MINORITY CHILD

ASSUMPTIONS

Essentially, three assumptions support my inquiry into the nature of television's influence on the language socialization of black children:

Assumptions

1. The strongest unit of linguistic control for an individual is the reinforcing speech community.
2. Television serves as an influence mediator for black children.
3. The impact of television on black children's language socialization is compounded by cultural–environmental factors.

The Speech Community

A person's speech community constitutes his or her principal reinforcing agency. Such a community supports the accepted and demonstrates the acceptable rules of language usage. Since it is comprised of siblings, parents, and peers, the reinforcing speech community may exist within the general speech community and yet be touched by that community in only insignificant ways. Parents are the primary models for infants and young children; they represent the standards of communication and social conduct. Normally, what passes for acceptability among members of the speech community strongly influences the young child.

Children are members of at least two speech communities, that is the immediate speech community and the general speech community. When the immediate speech community and the general speech community conform, uniformity results, but diverse speech communities produce critical tension. Awareness alone, that is, recognition of differences, introduces this critical tension, and a sort of bilingualism emerges. It is the most persistent speech community that constitutes the main social agency for language reinforcement.

It is the speech community that demonstrates most effectively the critical difference between black and white communication behaviors. Kochman (1972) and Smith (1973) have shown that blacks and whites tend to have perceptual variances because of cultural factors. Kochman has also explored the area of cultural dissimilarity of the signification *guilt–innocence* among blacks and whites. Erikson's (1964) microanalysis reveals that blacks and whites tend to be out of synchronization when speaking to each other, but in excellent synchronization when communicating within their own group. The work of Smith (1973) and of Taylor and Ferguson (1975) has served to establish the cultural differences that emerge in interracial interactions. Daniel (1972), Rich (1974), and many other scholars have advanced reasons for difference as well as ways to achieve better interracial communication.

The language of speech communities contains two elements: (a) structure, and (b) meaning. Structure refers to the basic syntactical and grammatical principles of the language; meaning is the intent or purpose denoted by a unit of language. Structure and meaning become, for intercultural scholars, elements of language to be analyzed in any intercultural meeting.

Television, as a political as well as a technical achievement, combines consciousness-raising with structuring of audience territories (Asante, 1976). It highlights differences in communities and promotes the imperialism of image.

There are many misunderstandings about the code-switching abilities of Asian-American, black, or Chicano children because they exist within two language communities. Perhaps the first assumption posited should be considered in light of semantic and structural switching.

When some black people say, *Ain't got no money*, you cannot translate that to "I do not have any money." To do so would be to obtund the expression by obliterating a whole history, personal and collective, of deprivation. *Ain't got no money* means *I ain't got none now, ain't had none, and if I get some I won't have none because it's gone before I get it*. It is too easy to infer from the common translation "I do not have any money" that I may have some one day. This is to miss the language. Code switching cannot always be a one-to-one relationship. Young black children who say *I'm fixner go* know precisely what they mean, and it is not "I am getting ready to go." *Fixner* implies that you are already ready and that you indeed are on your way.

Greenberg and Dominick (1969) show that Chicanos in the sixth and tenth grades watch more television than their white peers. The same researchers have shown that low-income black teenagers watch over 6 hr of television a day, while low-income white teenagers watched only 4½ hr. Liebert, Neale, and Davidson (1973) suggest that such differences exist regardless of economic background. Given this information, we can assume that television constitutes a larger window on the world for Chicanos and blacks than for whites. One might propose that, through television, these minority teenagers are more likely to have greater exposure to world affairs and domestic affairs than their white peers, regardless of the shows they watch. This being likely, the data gathered by Greenberg and Dominick (1969) have a significance far greater than as a mere record of use: It is possible that the sociopolitical maturity of minority children is greater than that of white children. Gerbner (1975) asserted that anyone not viewing at least 4 hr of television per day is out of touch with society. We may, in fact, have crossed the threshold into visual literacy, with minority children outdistancing their white counterparts in television analysis. The impact of television viewing on language development, however, would have occurred much before the high school years. Despite the racial difference in viewing data at the teenage level, there appear to be no clear differences in terms of television use at earlier ages. Preteenaged children seem to view about the same amount of television regardless of race, so the critical difference in the rate of language development for preteens is most probably the immediate family.

The contention that the speech community is the strongest reinforcing agency has definite implications for research into television's impact on the black child. If this is so, television's influence on the language socialization patterns of black children is a secondary rather than a primary influence. What influence does a sibling, parent, or peer have on a child? Listening to and watching television may have some influence, as we shall see, but television reinforced by parents probably has more impact on language socialization than does television unreinforced by the primary speech community. There is no evidence to suggest this with any strength at this time; the point is made here as an alternative answer to the influence question. One may raise some interesting hypotheses in this regard.

Television's Role

Television's role as influence mediator for black children has not been studied in any great detail. In 1961 Schramm, Lyle, and Parker wrote *Television in the Lives of Our Children,* in which they explained a demonstration project called Teletown and Radiotown. The efficacy of an audiovideo program was demonstrated when children who were regular television watchers scored higher on a standard vocabulary test.

Depending upon whose data you analyze, it is possible to get almost any interpretation about television's impact on children. The work by Gerbner (1975), Greenberg and Dominick (1969) and Klapper (1960) has been concentrated primarily on patterns of television use. Greenberg and Dervin (1970) have dealt extensively with use of television by what they call the disadvantaged or urban poor. That few of the studies of television's influence are rooted in hypotheses derived from communication does not minimize the value of the works mentioned, but it does point to a serious flaw. The lack of emphasis on black children, combined with the absence of hypotheses derived from communication theory, indicates that studies of television's influence on black children's language socialization are nearly nonexistent.

The *creation*, *presentation* and *reception* of symbols constitute the core of the communication process. The nexus of presentation and reception becomes an historical event, an event that possesses the markers to identify the communicative situation as *influential*, *persuasive*, *entertaining*, or *informative*. Combinations of these purposes exist within most communicative situations. I view all communicative acts as persuasively designed to modify beliefs, attitudes, values, and behaviors; I am convinced that any communicative event designed to entertain or inform transforms its audience in some way. Measuring the extent of the transformation has been the subject of a large part of our communication research.

Television represents the most potent symbol-creating and presenting device yet developed for mass audiences; in its symbol production and symbol manipulation roles, it manages to create its own audiences. Perception, visual discrimination, color sensitivity, and listening skills are integral factors of audience appreciation of televised messages.

The function of television as mediator of symbolic messages is more significant to social development than is its McLuhanesque technological contribution to society. In one sense, the technological device has taken its place alongside the 10 billion other artifacts of our natural and technical environment. One cannot minimize the instrumental importance of the machine, but what it *does* apart from its technical existence is more significant for persuasion. This concept can be likened to the story of the son who received a telegram that read "Mother is better." Because his mother had been seriously ill and he had awaited word from his sister, when the telegram finally arrived, he framed it and hung it over the mantle. The telegram as instrument appeared to loom larger in his mind than the actual fact of the recovery of his mother. As an instrument for message delivery, the telegram's primary importance lies in its rapid long-distance transmission. In a similar manner, the television is an *instrument* for transmission of symbols. Yet it is in its production and presentation of those symbols that television assumes its real significance. It is, in fact, one of two contemporary architechtonic devices; the other is the computer.

A considerable bibliography exists on television as a technical instrument. For example, research on use, rate of viewing, number of sets per household, relationship between use and economic status is concerned with work characteristics of the instrument's impact rather than characteristics of communication message. Although there is research dealing with messages, the hypotheses have not been adquately formed to suggest generalizable conclusions about the language acquisition of minority children.

The situation of American society with regard to television sets is such that black children have about equal access with white children to the symbols of television. Virtually all black children have some access to television. In addition to our data on how much and what kind of use is made of television by black children, we need to know what linguistic acquisitions or modifications take place.

The assumption that television's impact on black children's language is primarily linguistic is logical, given the nature of the communication process. Television socializes through action as well as speech, however, and minute displays of emotion such as affection, pride, guilt, and anxiety (rather than the words used, the meanings intended, or the philosophy implied) transmit to children the outlines of what really counts in their world (Erikson, 1964). Emotional expressions, with or without accompanying language, serve to influence children's socialization and are a form of social influence that provides a cognitive reservoir for expression at some later time.

Whether specifically linguistic or more generally symbolic, television's role in the socialization process appears to be persuasive. Bogatz and Ball (1972) have shown that black and white children's vocabularies have benefitted from Sesame Street, a show that also influenced behavior, attitudes toward school, and attitudes toward people of other races. By providing meaningful warrants for actions, television deals with the basic needs of individuals.

The child's language behavior may be described in a functional sense as instrumental, ego-defensive, value-expressive, or knowledge-seeking. According to Katz (1960), these four categories represent the individual needs of human beings. To influence the socialization of children it is necessary, in a strict functionalist view, to change the motivational and personality needs of the children. If we accept these classifying criteria for human language behavior, then it is clear that any of the categories may represent the black child's response to television at any given time.

The instrumental function of attitude is served, for example, when children who regularly view television maximize their ability to secure parental favors by repeating that "Nationwide is on your side." The ego-defensive language mechanisms may be influenced by televised statements such as "express yourself." This encourages the ventilation of one's internal feelings and helps in the discharge of inhibited influences, effecting a change in ego-defense attitudes.

The value-expressive function is served when a child seeks to enhance self-identity and self-image. Television may conceivably produce identity confusion in black children. For example, a black child who identifies with the characters or personalities of a television program may be induced to adopt the language patterns of the characters, and when the characters are unrepresentative of the child's actual self, physical and psychological, a dissonance is created. The kind of banter that typifies most black children's interactions is generally not heard on television. Consider the following dialogue I overheard between two of my cousins:

> Git out the way ole fat girl.
> Don't say nothin' to me.
> You goin' do something about it?
> You can't make me.

Or the statement, If you had asked me before I might of could but I'm tore up now, as the refusal of a drink. Television dialogue at no time approaches the authenticity of such interchanges. Writers for television, both black and white, often miss the richness and dignity of this dialogue. Value-expression, then, may be achieved more through peer relationships than through television influence. Children learn which language cues and communication behaviors are representative of the speech community; an elongated vowel as in long train or ugly boy is more likely to come from parents, siblings, and playmates than from Sesame Street.

Because it serves as the frame of reference that gives meaning to a child's ambiguities and complexities, the knowledge-seeking function of behavior is inextricably joined to value-expression. Who we are and what we will become can be clarified by the restatement of messages associated with our previous histories. In this way, an ambiguity created for a child by new knowledge acquired outside the home can be reinforced or not reinforced by television. A friend of mine who teaches at Howard University told me that she had to take her son to Maryland and Virginia periodically because at 8 years of age he had begun to think that the whole world was black. Living in Washington, D.C., even watching Washington, D.C. television, you can get a distorted view of America. Thus, cues have to be reinstated and concepts have to restated in order to maintain a consistent defense against crippling ambiguity.

Cultural-Environmental Factors

My third assumption is that the impact of television on black children's language is compounded by other factors. This may account for lagging research on television's affect on black children's language. The impact of black language on television has not been calculated. All of the irony, much of the syntax, and most popular expressions from the black community tend to become victims of television's rapacity. The intertwining of the black influence on television writers with the influence of television on American society complicates the process of assessing to what extent television is responsible for black language socialization. Although the televised dialogue may not assume the exact characteristics of its source, there appears to be enough borrowing for one to recognize its root within the black community. "Polishing" the authentic black word becomes a part of television.

In order to measure the impact of television on black children's language development, it would be necessary to control all extraneous factors. This is clearly not possible, we cannot totally isolate children from their environment. Nevertheless it is possible to hypothesize about the impact of particular television programs on black children language. Lasswell's (1948) classic statement regarding communication was

> who
> says what
> to whom
> on what channel
> with what effect [p.37]?

Although I have assumed that measuring the effect of television on the language socialization of black youth is not feasible, I have attempted to answer some of the fundamental questions regarding black children's perception by asking for their responses to five communication-based statements.

The results and implications of my recent survey with black youth in Buffalo, New York, provide direction for an heuristic. Greenberg and Dominick (1969) reported three projects involving the use of media by the poor. Although none of these studies was meant to deal with language socialization, one was concerned with the functions television performed for disadvantaged children. In this study, Greenberg and Dominick asked black and white youngsters whether or not they perceived some similarity between the world portrayed on television and their world. Five disagree–agree statements were used. Typical of the statements were

Families I see on television are like my family.
The programs I see on television tell about life the way it really is.

Race and income differences among the youngsters were apparent; however, blacks were said to perceive television as more realistic than whites. Among the conclusions one can draw from this project is that black children are more inclined to view the language of television as realistic as well. At least, such a conclusion is possible if one argues that children are influenced by the physical symbols as well as the verbal symbols that are transmitted by television. What children hear becomes equivalent to what they see. For children, the ability to separate language from other cultural aspects of life does not develop, in any analytical sense, until early adolescence. Differentiation occurs as children grow older.

In the Buffalo survey five communication-oriented statements of the agree–disagree variety were used to test whether black elementary school children from an inner-city school perceived any similarity between the language spoken by television characters and their own communication patterns. Statements employed in the study were

1. The way people talk on television sounds funny.
2. The way people talk on television is the way I try to talk.
3. Television news reporters talk like my mother and father.
4. Programs on television remind me of the way my friends talk.
5. I like the way people talk on television.

The subjects were 65 girls and 35 boys from the fourth grade of the Buffalo Build Academy, a predominantly black elementary school in the inner city. The age range was 8–10 years. All subjects were black. The subjects were given questionnaires during regular class time.

The questionnaires were administered by the researcher. Each student was allowed as much time as necessary to complete the questionnaire. The longest completion time was 5 min. Each child indicated that a television set was available in the home. This project was concerned only with perceived language reality. Students were told that they should be as thoughtful as possible in their answers and were asked to indicate which television programs they watched the most.

Response scores to the five items were computed in strict percentages in order to provide an indication of survey results.

	Yes (%)	Don't know (%)	No (%)
Statement 1	63	7	30
Statement 2	29	11	60
Statement 3	52	0	48
Statement 4	38	12	50
Statement 5	51	0	49

Rather this preliminary survey cannot be considered conclusive, it can be seen as an indication that black children at this particular school do not see television language as their reality. The cumulative index of perceived language reality indicates that black children do not perceive the language of television as real. Such results imply that the finding by Greenberg and Dominick (1969) that black children perceived television to be more real than white children may be misleading. There exists no single television reality; many factors constitute the "real" for television viewers and listeners. Language reality could conceivably be isolated from overall television reality. Furthermore, what has been considered the perceived reality of television may have more to do with images, symbols, and ideas than the spoken language of television characters and personalities. Another implication of this study is that television's impact on black children's language may be more idiomatic than structural. A child may employ idioms, colloquials, expressions from children's programs, cartoons, and commercials but not be impressed by the structural linguistic content of regular adult programming. Indeed, the idiomatic expressions may only appear in the child's language for a brief period of time, corresponding with the popularity of *Dr. Who, Wonder Woman, The Electric Company, Sesame Street,* or *Fat Albert and the Cosby Kids.*

IMPLICATIONS

The implications of this discussion are enormous for any theoretical heuristic device. How do minority children make sense out of the television symbols and signals they receive? Such a question assumes that syntax is achieved through external reinforcement. People make sense out of the world for children. An equally plausible belief is that the knowledge of making sense with sentences comes from deep inside children. If this is the case, then phylogeny announces ontogeny as much as ontogeny recapitulates phylogeny.

Behaviorist Implications

According to the behaviorist perspective, language is a learned phenomenon and can be acquired in the same manner as anything else is learned. Children are presumed to be tabulae rasae at the initial stages of language acquisition, without an inherent "something" making them more capable of language development. The principles of learning are universal and can be applied to all experiences of raw data. Children choose the principles that give them results; they are rewarded for conformity and penalized for aberrations. In a behaviorist's perspective then, imitation becomes significant. The questions raised in the Greenberg and Dominick (1969) study address issues of imitation, but the evidence on imitation is difficult to interpret. Wardhaugh (1976, p.143) argues that children do not repeat all the utterances they hear; they are not very good imitators, if perfect reproduction is used as a criterion, and they produce in imitation only the forms they would say in spontaneous speech. In Wardhaugh's judgment, if children are asked to use sentence structure they are not familiar with, they fail badly (*the boy the book it was crying* is imitated as *boy the book was crying*), or they change what they hear to conform to what they can say. Consequently, imitation does not appear to be grammatically progressive. It is used only to practice what has already been learned and not to try out new forms. Acceptance of this view would mean that television could only provide a child with opportunities for practice. What the child does in response to the language transmission of television can be predicted, according to this view, by analyzing the child's prior language capacity. "Practice makes perfect" only insofar as children are capable of repeating what they hear.

The behaviorist view, with its heavy reliance on imitation, is an important perspective for developing a heuristic. In fact, the importance of environment, the significance of data gathering, and the access that a child has to the language enrich the learning experience, but cannot explain all of the issues in language acquisition. It is possible, then, that the perception of language reality in television is of no consequence to the developmental question for the black child. Only in the sense that television provides a considerable number of words to be imitated can it be considered contributive to learning. Not all verbal statements are religiously repeated or imitated by children, black or white. In fact, there appears to be a cultural mechanism that inhibits black children from using *gee whiz, golly,* or *Jesus,* as interjections.

Nativist Implications

In this view, children are specifically endowed with an innate ability to acquire generative-transformational grammar. Without this ability, children would not be able to convert degenerate stimuli from the environment into meaningful sentences. According to the nativist perspective, perception, categorization, and the capacity for transformation are biologically given. This view is diametrically opposed to the behaviorist perspective. B. F. Skinner, a leading proponent of the behaviorist school (Skinner, 1957), has been attacked by scholars of the nativist position. From the nativist view, the influence of television is seriously questioned since the innate mechanism for language acquisition operates without regard to environmental conditions.

RESEARCH ON PROSOCIAL EFFECTS

In several studies (Ball & Bogatz, 1970; Fowles, 1971; see, especially, Bogatz & Ball, 1972), the relation of children's programs on educational television to learning has been examined. *Sesame Street* and *The Electric Company* have become alternatives to the violence and mayhem that continue to appear on commercial television programs geared to children. These public television programs have benefited from planning, monitoring, and ongoing evaluations.

Sesame Street grew out of the combined efforts of public and private agencies to establish the Children's Television Workshop. In 1969, the program was first aired; its concentrated planning and development helped to make it an instant success. *The Electric Company* was also a Children's Television Workshop project; it was aimed primarily at improving reading ability. In *Sesame Street* and *Electric Company*, educators participated in identifying curriculum strategies, evaluating effectiveness, and assessing basic instructional procedures.

Research based on *Sesame Street* and *The Electric Company* seems to indicate that programs on educational television do improve children's ability to recognize the alphabet, write their names, and develop reading skills. (Liebert et al., 1973, pp. 106–107). How much of this difference can be attributed to normal maturation is not known; what has been established is that children who watch *Sesame Street* and *The Electric Company* tend to achieve higher scores on alphabet recitation and the writing of their names. The effect of television in this case tells us that it can serve as a conduit for a deliberate pedagogical endeavor.

To the credit of commercial television, CBS has established an on-going committee under the direction of Gordon Berry to assess the educational value of *Fat Albert and the Cosby Kids*. This example is not often repeated among commercial networks. Public television, not commercial television, has provided our most comprehensive rationale for studying the impact of television on language socialization of minority children.

In as much as any heuristic device must be grounded in some theory, it is necessary to understand how communication as a process under-scores our search for implications. In the classic Berlo (1960) source–message–channel receiver (SMCR) model, a source encodes and sends a message through a channel to a receiver. The children who receive a message decode it before acting on it. If the message is a recitation of the alphabet, children must decode that message before they are able to understand it. This does not mean that the message is unrepeatable, only that unless the children decode it, they will not know what they are repeating. All of us have had experiences with young children who seem to know so much for their age. Children can imitate their parents or television speakers; in many cases, the language is "over their heads" but can be repeated by children who have mastered the appro-priate phonemes.

Normal children who are exposed to language will begin to talk. In fact, "no special teaching is necessary for the emergence of language [Lenneberg, 1967, pp. 135–137]." Environment seems to influence lan-guage development; that is to say, a deprived environment leads to poor language development and an enriched environment leads to im-proved language development. We must be careful, however, not to equate deprivation with minority or enrichment with white. The fact is that different experiences at home, whether the media or parental teaching, appear to influence vocabulary growth (Smart & Smart, 1972, p. 265). The National Institute of Mental Health's volume, *Cognitive and Mental Development in the First Five Years of Life* (1970) mentions home environment, parental attitude, the child's exposure to the wider world, and the quality of the child–parent relationship as factors in the early cognitive development of the child. If all these factors, in addition to the child's own innate patterns for languaging, influence linguistic development, then it is, as I have assumed, quite impossible to isolate television's impact. What we do see and respond to are the children's visible and vocal communication cues.

My heuristic assumes (a) the strongest unit of linguistic control for a child is the reinforcing speech community, (b) television serves as an influence mediator, and (c) the impact of television on black children's language socialization is compounded by other cultural–environmental factors. Furthermore, the theoretical base of all research in communication theory must emphasize principles of information dissemination and reception, audience analysis, and message presentation and purpose.

The continuing presence of numerous uncontrollable cultural–environmental variables makes it extremely difficult to obtain significant and practical results at a level commensurate with the research investment of time and energy. Results will always seem to be highly specific to the situation, group, or television program. I believe that this is one reason we have not had the kind of substantial data necessary for productive theory generation. We work within the very few generalizations that have been ventured, knowing full well that ingredients for an all powerful, architectonic theory of television's impact on minority children are still being assembled.

REFERENCES

Asante, M. Television and black consciousness. *Journal of Communication*, 1976, 26, 137–141.
Ball, S., & Bogatz, G. A. *The first year of* Sesame Street: *An evaluation.* Princeton, New Jersey: Educational Testing Service, 1970.
Berlo, D. *The process of communication.* New York: Holt, 1960.
Bogatz, G. A., & Ball, S. *The second year of* Sesame Street: *A continuing evaluation.* Princeton, New Jersey: Educational Testing Service, 1972.
Brody, E. B. Color and identity conflict in young boys. *Archives of General Psychiatry,* 1974 10, 354–360.
Daniel, J. *Black communication.* New York: Speech Communication Association, 1972.
Erikson, E. Memorandum on identity and Negro youth. *Journal of Social Issues,* 1964, 20, 30.
Fowles, B. Building a curriculum for *The Electric Company.* In The Electric Company: *An introduction to the new television program designed to help teach reading to children.* New York: Children's Television Workshop, 1971.
Gerbner, G. Institutional forces and the mass media. In M. Cassata & M. K. Asante (Eds.), *The social uses of mass communication.* Buffalo, New York: Communication Research Center, 1975.
Greenberg, B., & Dervin, B. *Use of the mass media by the urban poor.* New York: Praeger, 1970.
Greenberg, B., & Dominick, J. Racial and social class differences in teenages' use of television. *Journal of Broadcasting,* 1969, 13, 331–334.
Hauser, S. T. *Black and white identity formation.* New York: Wiley, 1971.
Katz, D. The functional approach to the study of attitudes. *Public Opinion Quarterly,* 1960, 24, 163–204.
Klapper, J. *The effects of mass communication.* New York: Free Press, 1960.
Kochman, T. *Rappin' and stylin' out.* Chicago: Univ. of Illinois Press, 1972.

Lasswell, H. D. The structure and function of communication in society. In L. Bryson (Ed.), *The communication of ideas*. New York: Harper & Row, 1948.

Lenneberg, E. H. *Biological foundations of language*. New York: Wiley, 1967.

Liebert, R. M., Neale, J., & Davidson, E. *The early window: Effects of television on children and youth*. New York: Pergamon, 1973.

National Institute of Mental Health. *Cognitive and mental development in the first five years of life*. Washington, D.C.: U.S. Government Printing Office, 1970.

Pettigrew, T. F. Negro American personality: Why isn't it more known? *Journal of Social Issues*, 1964, *20*, 4–23.

Rich, A. *Interracial communication*. New York: Harper & Row, 1974.

Schramm, W., Lyle, J., & Parker, E. B. *Television in the lives of our children*. Stanford, California: Stanford Univ. Press, 1961.

Skinner, B. F. *Verbal behavior*. New York: Appleton, 1957.

Smart, M., & Smart, R. *Children: Development and relationships*. New York: Macmillan, 1972.

Smith, A. L. *Transracial communication*. Englewood Cliffs, New Jersey: Prentice-Hall, 1973.

Taylor, O., & Ferguson, D. A study of cross cultural communication between blacks and whites in the U.S. Army. *Linguistic Reporter*, 1975, *17*(3), 8, 11.

Taylor, R. L. Black youth and psychosocial development: A conceptual framework. *Journal of Black Studies*, 1976, *6*, 353–372.

Wardhaugh, R. *The context of language*. Rowley, Mass.: Newbury House Publishers, 1976.

Patti Iiyama
Harry H. L. Kitano

Asian Americans and the Media

MEDIA STEREOTYPES OF ASIAN AMERICANS

Asian Americans are seldom seen, seldom heard, seldom felt on American television. Like many racial minorities, they remain invisible on the screen and seem to gain public attention only when they stage a protest. They were seen in Los Angeles in June, 1980 protesting the return of Charlie Chan to the movie screen in *Charlie Chan and the Curse of the Dragon Queen* by carrying signs that said: "We Don't Talk in Fortune Cookie Language," "Anglos in Yellow Face Insult the Asian Pacific-American Community," "Charlie Chan Still White," "Peter Ustinov Chinese?"

For those unacquainted with the experience of Asians in the movies and on television, there was an air of incongruity, for Asians were protesting one of the few films dealing with Asians. However, as Victor Huey, spokesperson for the group, said: "When I was growing up, old Charlie Chan movies were something to be laughed at. Now, however, we have come to realize how derogatory they are; how they don't depict Asian people as constructive members of society but as bunglers and stupid [Grant, 1980]."

TELEVISION AND
THE SOCIALIZATION OF THE MINORITY CHILD

To many Asians, Charlie Chan is a white man's stereotype of Asians: "Played by white actors pretending to be Chinese with an inscrutable attitude, phoney accent, hands folded in subservient bow and taped eyes.... Each revival of Charlie Chan points out Hollywood's lack of imagination and refusal to develop contemporary Asian/Pacific American characters with realistic, human qualities [Grant, 1980]."

The Asian American picket lines have not been the first, nor will they be the last, because Hollywood in the past has dealt with Asians through stereotypes and their current response reflects no great change of heart. For example, Peter Ustinov, who plays the role of Charlie Chan in the movie "Charlie Chan and the Dragon Queen," could not understand the reasons behind the protest and responded to the pickets by questioning the availability and qualifications of Asian American actors. But for Asians there were a number of unanswered questions: Why are there so few roles for Asians on television? Why, in the few vehicles for Asians, do white actors and actresses get the leading roles? And in the few presentations about Asians, why is there so much stereotyping?

Before exploring the problems of Asians and the media, it might be helpful to define the term *stereotype*. Walter Lippmann (1922) was among the first to define stereotypes; his characterization of a stereotype is that it is: (a) a way of organizing images, (b) a fixed, simplified impression, and (c) salient features chosen to represent the whole. Lippmann also describes stereotypes as fundamentally negative and unfavorable, as well as incorrect, inaccurate, and with no objective basis in fact. In contrast, others hold the view that a stereotype may also include valid judgments (Ogawa, 1971). The definition we favor embraces both points of view: It recognizes that a stereotype may be supported by facts or be false; it may be favorable or perjorative; and it shows the characteristics usually agreed on—it is a simplified, generalized, rigid image of a social group that glosses over the differences among the members of that group. According to Farquhar and Doi (1978),

> The chief problem with stereotypes of ethnic groups is that one character (e.g., Uncle Tom or Fu Manchu) is allowed to stand for a whole diverse collection of human beings. Mass media may never stray far from the symbolic realm, but by moving away from simplistic representations of people toward a more subtle and pluralistic set of images, they can become more humanistic in the best sense of the term [p. 24].

Stereotypes are potentially highly damaging to isolated groups such as the Asian Americans, whose geographic distribution is primarily along the West Coast and Hawaii, with a high degree of segregation, since there are limited opportunities for equal-status interaction with the dominant group. Under such conditions, the image on television may be the primary source of information, so that the picture becomes the reality. People are more inclined to accept a photograph, motion picture, or television show as real than words on a printed page.

The history of Asians on television begins with their appearance in old Hollywood movies. Prior to 1955, Hollywood had tried to compete with television by refusing to release their old films. After losing an antitrust suit, RKO, followed by other major Hollywood studios, began to release old films to distributors for use in television. The old movies soon became a television staple because they were an inexpensive way to program. Although these old movies presented a view of American life and culture that was already dated, they continued to have an impact on younger generations and reinforced old prejudices and images through their dissemination on television.

The basic images of Asians developed by American cinema have been continued in the stereotypes of Asians projected by the smaller but even more influential television screen. The Hollywood movies, from the first feature films at the beginning of the century through the present, have consistently presented stereotypes of Asians that have varied depending on the social, political, and economic context of the times. International relations have had an important impact on how Asians have been portrayed on film; for instance, the war with Japan in World War II cut off the use of the positive stereotype of the brilliant, though humble, super-sleuth, Mr. Moto, and shifted to the image of the fanatical kamikaze "Jap" who brutally tortured, raped, and pillaged his way across the screen (e.g., *Bataan*, 1943; *Behind the Rising Sun*, 1943; *Objective Burma*, 1945; *Back to Bataan*, 1945). This theme of the inhumanity of the Asian was part of the wartime propaganda drive that conditioned Americans to accept the extermination of the non-white enemy with the atomic bomb at Hiroshima and Nagasaki and has since been utilized successively against the Chinese, Koreans, and Vietnamese as reinforcement of American foreign policy. These stereotypes were also convenient in the justification of the internment of over 110,000 Japanese Americans, most of whom were United States citizens, in concentration camps without benefit of trial.

But no matter what the stereotype in vogue at any particular time, two conclusions have always prevailed:

1. The way that Asians gain power in the white world is through their mastery of mysterious Eastern knowledge of drugs and diabolical tortures—that is, as Fu Manchu villains attempting to conquer the world. In their more modern guise, they use their mastery of technological and psychological knowledge to bring about their victory (Chinese

Communist brainwashers, sadistic Vietnamese guards). Of course, the bad guys can never win in the movies, so the fundamental lesson is that the Asians can never really have power in the white world.

2. The way that Asians can be accepted in American society is to become passive, dependent, and Americanized. Asian women, in particular, since they are stereotyped as helpless, dependent, and servile, have found greater acceptance on the American screen. Asian women have been pictured in two stereotypes: they are either "docile, submissive, and sexless" or "exotic, sexy, and diabolical" (Asian Americans for a Fair Media, 1974, p. 27). Miyoshi Umeki in *Sayonara* (1957) played the humble wife role to perfection, while Nancy Kwan in *The World of Suzie Wong* (1961) perpetuated the myth of the Asian woman as sex object. The greater acceptance of the Asian woman can be seen in the relaxation of the miscegenation taboo for love affairs between Asian women and white men in the 1950s, although it is still applied to Asian men. The Hays Office censorship guide of the motion picture industry (Moley, 1945) strictly forbade miscegenation on the screen between whites and Asians, and the taboo was not broken until *Sayonara* in 1957. The new wave of films that began after *Sayonara* with the theme of white men breaking the miscegenation taboo with Asian women reflected the social reality of American society; many white G.I.'s stationed in Japan after World War II brought home Japanese war-brides.

Asian men have not been able to break the miscegenation barrier on screen. They are still where they were in 1916: Leading Asian male roles are usually played by white men in "yellow face." In fact, the three most famous stereotypes of the Asian male were played by white men: Dr. Fu Manchu was played by actors such as Warner Oland, Boris Karloff, Henry Brandon, and Christopher Lee. Charlie Chan was played by Asians in the first two movies (George Kuwa and Kamiyama Sojin), but after the detective became popular, he was played by Caucasians—E. L. Park, Warner Oland, Sidney Toler, and Roland Winters. Mr. Moto was played by Peter Lorre in the eight films made between 1937 and 1939. Even in 1980, two resurrections of the old stereotypes are being played by Caucasian actors in "yellow face"—Peter Sellers portrayed Dr. Fu Manchu in *The Fiendish Plot of Dr. Fu Manchu* and Peter Ustinov portrayed Charlie Chan in *Charlie Chan and the Curse of the Dragon Queen*.

The more Americanized and assimilated they are, *the less negative their portrayal.* The ultimate Americanization is for the Asians to be played by whites made up to look like Asians; this makes them even more acceptable as positive images. The "positive" stereotypes of Asians that have developed have emphasized Americanization, from the superintelligent yet self-effacing Charlie Chans and Mr. Motos to the powerless, self-effacing minor characters today whose nationality is often irrelevant (they could be played by anyone, they are so minor). These characters wear American clothes and follow American customs. As Irvin Paik (1971), wrote about Charlie Chan,

> How could Americans accept an Asian outwitting whites in forty-six feature films? Easy. Charlie Chan was not Asian, he was a white actor pretending to be Asian. So, anything good that Charlie did, the audience could attribute to the white actor. Any disparaging aspects of his character (eyes, accent, syntax) would be attributed to the Asian character he was playing [p. 32].

So the real message that comes across in American cinema is that the more Asian you look and act, the less acceptable you are and the more you are portrayed as a villain (for Asian ways are evil), whereas the more white American you look and act, the more acceptable you are and the more positively you are portrayed (for Western civilization is good). Asian inferiority to Western–white superiority is clearly defined.

IMAGES OF ASIANS ON TELEVISION

In the early days of television, stereotypic treatment of Asians was usual in their few appearances on the screen. Very few programs featuring Asians in leading roles were put on prime-time television prior to the 1970s. Until then, the major Asian stereotype was the Fu Manchu villain. Fu Manchu was actually resurrected in 1956 for what Isaacs (1958) described as "one of the corniest adventure shows ever seen on TV [p. 218]." It did not last out the season.

Not until the early 1970s, with the development of minority political aggressiveness and activity, were Asian characters visible in major television roles. A survey of trends, by race, in the representation of major characters on prime-time television from 1970 through 1976, indicated that major Asian roles began to increase in 1971 (from 0% to 1.2% of all major characters), stayed fairly constant for the next 2 years (1.4% in 1972, 1.0% in 1973), peaked in 1973–1975 (2.6%), and began a steady decline (.9% in 1975–1976, .6% in 1976) from 1975 on (Gerbner & Signorielli, 1979). Although these figures reveal that Asians are overrepresented relative to their percentage of the population, most of these Asian roles allowed no character development and were in short-lived series that lasted one season or less (e.g., Mr. T and Tina, a situation comedy about a Japanese businessman and his problems with a white governess, September 1976–October 1976). The perennial Charlie Chan was dusted off in 1971 with Ross Martin playing the pigeon-toed, bowing, inscrutable detective for a brief, unsuccessful season; Miyoshi Umeki played the shy, soft-spoken housekeeper, Mrs. Livingston, on the longer running *The Courtship of Eddie's Father,* 1969–1972. The only series focused on a major Asian character that ran for several seasons was the highly successful *Kung Fu,* where a half-breed Chinese martial arts master (played, naturally, by David Carradine, a Caucasian) roamed the Wild West single-handedly rescuing people while teaching them Eastern philosophy he learned as a "grasshopper" at the knees of a kindly Asian priest. *Kung Fu* lasted from 1972 to 1975 and is presently being re-run on local stations. The long-running television series, *Hawaii Five-O* (1968–1979), featured a stereotypical Asian villain based on the Fu Manchu image who periodically appeared as the nemesis of the head of the police department and finally was killed off in the last episode. He was a bald-headed, mustached Chinese Communist master spy who sadistically utilized the latest technological and psychological devices to torture as many people as possible for no reason whatsoever. It is an ironic note that the major characters on this show, which is set in the state with the highest percentage of Asian Americans, were mostly white, except for the villains.

The U.S. Commission on Civil Rights (1977) conducted a detailed study of the 1973 and 1974 seasons. In 1973, only 12.2% of all characters on prime time were nonwhite; in 1974, the percentage was still only 12.5%. The number of major roles (leading roles that are central to the story) was qualitatively smaller. In 1973, two Asian males were major characters; they were a priest and a mob leader in *Kung Fu.* No Asian women were given major roles that year (U.S. Commission on Civil Rights, 1977). In 1974, there was a slight increase—four major Asian male roles (Master, Sha-Lin Religious Order; two students, religious order, and one unknown) in *Kung Fu* and one major Asian female role, that of Helen Funai, a manager, in *Sanford and Son* (U.S. Commission on Civil Rights, 1977).

One of the few exceptions to the stereotypical Asian was the role played by Jack Soo on *Barney Miller* from 1975 until his death in 1978. This was the only situation comedy where there was an Asian presence and where the Asian was portrayed as a more well-rounded individual than is normally allowed on television. Another example is that of Robert Ito, who plays the coroner's assistant, Sam, on *Quincy* (1977 to present); his role began as a token one but has been expanded to become more rounded in some episodes, due to the high volume of fan mail he has received.

In children's programming (weekend daytime and weekday afternoons) the same trends are reflected but cannot be analyzed reliably because of the even smaller number of minority characters (Gerbner & Signorielli, 1979). In a survey of racial and cultural groups portrayed on Saturday children's programs on three network-affiliated television stations in San Francisco, California, (Ormiston & Williams, 1973), Asians appeared on only 1 of the 27 programs monitored; in contrast, whites appeared on 25 of the 27 programs. The program with Chinese characters was *The Amazing Chan and the Chan Clan*, a cartoon series about the famous detective, this time with nine children. Still, 81% of the Asians in this cartoon series had secondary roles, and 67% were followers rather than leaders. Although none of the Asians were villains, only one had a skill, and most of the characters acted stupidly more often than creatively (namely, the nine sons carrying on the tradition of the bumbling Chinese-American established in the 1930s Charlie Chan series). According to Ormiston and Williams (1973), "The fact that monitors found such a negligible number of character traits to score is as important a fact as that only three percent of all characters on a Saturday morning were Chinese [p. 8]."

Most of the increased visibility of Asians on television during the 1970s came from an increase in minor characters rather than major ones (Gerbner & Signorielli, 1979). Even these minor characters fell into stereotypical categories. The U.S. Commission on Civil Rights (1977) found certain patterns emerging about both the types of programs in which Asians appear and the ways in which they, as well as other ethnic minorities, were depicted. Over two-thirds of the action-adventure programs involved at least one nonwhite character; almost one-half the nonwhite characters on television appeared in this kind of show. In several shows, groups of characters from one ethnic background were all involved in the same occupation or activity, thus emphasizing them as a group rather than individuals. Thus, in one episode of *Hawaii Five-O* a prominent role was played by a prostitution ring managed by Hawaiian gangsters; 11 Asian Americans were affiliated with a religious order in one episode of *Kung Fu*. Whereas Asian males constituted 26.1% of the minor nonwhite characters in the 1973 sample and 25.7% of the minor nonwhite character sample for 1974, they were clustered in only a few shows: *Hawaii Five-O*, *Kung Fu*, and *MASH*.

In addition to being clustered, many nonwhite characters have token roles in action-adventure series, such as police officers hunting down other nonwhite criminals. In these token roles, their lines are confined to statements of fact: "Steve, take a look. Finished." Or, "The governor wants you." Or, "So far no trace anywhere." (*Hawaii Five-O*, cited by Paik, 1971, p. 30) and their participation in the plot is limited to drawing guns and kicking down doors. Another type of token role consists of Asian technicians feeding facts to whites; as George Takei, who plays Mr. Sulu in the television series and movie *Star Trek*, states, "It would be nice if Mr. Sulu could have a little more to say than 'Aye, Aye Captain.' [Kurtzman, 1980, p. 7]." Occasionally, the token will be advanced to center stage; in several episodes of *Quincy*, for instance, the plot revolves around the problems of the coroner's assistant, Sam, a Japanese American.

Several of the action–adventure programs and situation comedies are set in exotic locales where Asians can be part of the background scenery. Two episodes of *Hawaii Five-O* account for 18 Asian-American characters; of 22 minor Asian roles recorded in the 1973 television sample, 12 were from *Hawaii Five-O*. Korea, the setting for the situation comedy *MASH*, provides another plausible reason for the appearance of Asians.

The occupations that Asian characters have are also stereotyped. Asians are seen as priests and martial arts experts (*Kung Fu*), pimps, assassins, and mobsters (*Hawaii Five-O*), loyal supporters of police officers, coroners, or captains (*Police Story*, *Hawaii Five-O*, *Quincy*, *Star Trek*), coolies, cooks, laundrymen, or gardeners (*Bonanza*, *McHale's Navy*), and nurses or doctor's receptionists (*MASH*, *The Brian Keith Show*) (U.S. Commission on Civil Rights, 1977). These occupational stereotypes have been particularly strong for the minor parts that go to Asians, serving to reinforce the familiar pattern that reduces Asians to a few work categories and to a simplified human existence.

In addition to these perennial characterizations, most of the Asian characters, both major and minor, are male, not female, as indicated in the 1973 and 1974 television samples. The only major Asian woman character in 1973 and 1974 was the manager of her husband's business on *Sanford and Son*, and this role, like those of most minority women, was not a continuing character on the series. Thus, Asian women on television perform the same function that they do in the movies; they emphasize the helplessness, dependency, and weakness of the Asian in the Western world, and as such project an image acceptable to whites.

There have been a few "specials" or entertainment dramas on television about Asians in America that have tried to go beyond the familiar stereotypes, but by and large, they have not had a wide audience. *If Tomorrow Comes*, a 1971 ABC–TV movie putting the *Romeo and Juliet* story into a Japanese-American setting, was not popular. *Farewell to Manzanar*, a 1976 NBC–TV production about Japanese Americans in World War II concentration camps, was more widely viewed but, despite being based on a book by a Japanese American, and despite being played by outstanding Asian American actors in all the lead roles, it gave a deceptive picture of that time by leaving out the racist context in which the internment took place (see criticisms by Iiyama, 1976; Okamura, 1976). The only two dramas that have been successful in depicting Asians as complex human beings are two plays written by Asian Americans and performed by the "East/West Players," an all-Asian theater group, on public television (which limits their audience impact): *The Gold Watch* and *And the Soul Shall Dance*. The classic and familiar stereotypes therefore predominate on television, as well as in the movies.

The stereotypes on television, however, have been more on the positive than the negative side. Proportionately more nonwhite characters on television are perceived positively than is true for white characters; nonwhite women in particular are portrayed as good more often than any other group (U.S. Commission on Civil Rights, 1977). Thus,

> Even though women and most minority types are deprived of adequate representation and restricted in their scope of activities, they are not presented as evil or inept. In fact, they have more than their share of positive characterizations and less than their share of failure. Benign roles, limited but agreeable fate, and . . . diminished powers are the favored role characteristics of women and minorities on prime time television [Gerbner & Signorielli, 1979, p. 17].

However, the positive stereotype of the Asian American that has developed since World War II vividly reinforces the belief that the only way to become accepted in American society is to become assimilated as much as possible. The "highly Americanized" image indicates that social acceptance hinges on the Asian acting white, being sterilized of an alien, Asian identity, and imbued with American values and behavior patterns. This stereotype also serves to perpetuate the prejudice that Asian attributes are inferior and that white culture, language, and values are superior, since "assimilation" means acculturation to the white civilization. The stereotype of the Asian as the subordinate, reliable sidekick or technician thus functions as "(1) a justification that white America is non-racist; it demonstrates that the minority group can be accepted and become successful in the United States; and (2) a criterion for other minorities—Blacks in particular—to follow [Ogawa, 1971, p. 52]." The message is as clear as that of the movies: Asians are inferior to whites and the only way to gain acceptance in American society is to become as assimilated and "Americanized" as possible.

Little attention has been paid to Asians in the United States in terms of instructional programs. A few national documentaries have been shown on the Japanese-American concentration camps: *Nisei: The Pride and the Shame* (CBS–TV, 1965, Walter Cronkite narrating) and *Guilty By Reason of Race* (NBC–TV, 1972, Robert Northshield narrating) (Okamura, 1976). Segments of programs like *60 Minutes* have also covered the concentration camp experience and presented some analysis of present-day Asians in America (e.g., Chinatown gang wars or immigrant workers in the garment district of Chinatown). These documentaries do not, however, serve to counteract the stereotyped images of Asians because they are too few and far between to have a consistent impact.

One documentary that was supposed to explode the myths about Chinese Americans was *Bad Times on Gold Mountain,* a half-hour documentary that was aired on PBS several times in 1974. The all-black writer, director, narrator, producer, and crew from Washington, D.C. had only 2 weeks for production in San Francisco's Chinatown; they virtually ignored the advice of the only Asian associated with the project, associate producer Genevieve Lim, and came up with a superficial overview of Chinatown that perpetuated the Asian myths. According to Go and Wong (1974):

> "Bad Times on Gold Mountain" shows us nothing but external glimpses of Chinamen. Where does Batten say white racism has kept the Chinaman corralled along Grant Avenue? Where are we shown Chinamen who have felt the negative and positive impacts of cultural conflict that Batten so glibly foists upon our ears? [p. 26].

News coverage of Asian events, whether in the United States or in Asia, has also been inadequate. During a panel discussion between community and media spokespeople about media coverage of the Chinese community in San Francisco, it was pointed out that the mass media continue to portray the Chinese as foreigners who are peculiar, quaint, and mystifying. In addition, the media failed to cover specific community activities, such as the Asian Anti-War and Poverty demonstration in San Francisco's Chinatown on May 18, 1970. Sparse media coverage of community events was complemented by a lack of focus on the issues that the Chinese community felt were important, while most events that were reported were from the perspective of what mattered to others rather than to the Chinese community (Li, cited in Wu, 1972). In the past, the media were unresponsive to complaints about the accuracy and representativeness of coverage of the Asian American community. Now, while verbally acknowledging their limitations they have not improved their coverage significantly.

This ignorance of and lack of interest in the Asian American community by the news media is a reflection of ignorance about Asia in general. A startling example of this ethnocentrism was the coverage of then-President Nixon's first, historic trip to Peking in 1972, when networks did not assign even one specialist in Chinese language, culture, or history to the trip. As a result, television reporters were unable to provide much interpretation of the significance of events they witnessed, even having difficulty in identifying Chinese leaders. Apart from their ignorance of Chinese history, culture, politics, and language, the American reporters also revealed their racist attitudes. Walter Cronkite, perhaps the most respected reporter in the United States, compared acupuncture sets to voodooism and repeated the familiar cliché: "Everyone looks exactly alike ["China through the Boob Tube," 1972, p. 6]."

In terms of who reports the news on television, Asian women appear to have been accepted as on-camera reporters in California. Tritia Toyota and Connie Chung anchor news in Los Angeles; Wendy Tokuda anchors news, Jan Yanchiro hosts "feature stories," and Joanne Ishimoto reports news in San Francisco. In Hawaii, there was an Asian woman on camera.

Asian men, however, are still discriminated against in terms of on-camera jobs; there have been no long-term Asian male reporters on local or national news in any of the urban centers in the United States, although there is at present a Chinese male reporter for Channel 5 news in San Francisco. George Lum, one of the few Chinese American television directors in the United States, relates how he turned to directing when it became obvious that he would never get an on-the-air job: "Even as cosmopolitan as the San Francisco Bay Area seems to be, no radio or television station is going to hire an Oriental for on-the-air work [Lum, cited in Wu, 1972]." The image of the passive, dependent Asian male who is no threat to the white man might not hold up if the Asian man were allowed to have an authoritative position as reporter on-camera, although Asian women are still "cute" enough to pose no threat.

Interestingly, although the Asian image is utilized in television shows, it is more rare in advertisements and commercials. In fact, before the late 1960s and early 1970s, Asians, like other ethnic minorities, were very infrequently found in television commercials. Since advertising is a means of selecting and reinforcing certain values and needs within the consumer, the advertising industry probably feared that

> the use of Asians in advertisements would constitute negative effects in areas of the Southern Midwest and Eastern United States. They are in a business to sell and since selling and profit is the name of the game, they focus on the majority. It is known that you cannot please everyone and therefore, the majority is better than the minority [Harada & Hodoka, cited in Hayashi, 1975, p. 16].

Asians in commercials are usually associated with products that are representative of the stereotypes, such as the Chinese laundryman bewildered by stay-press Arrow shirts, the grass-skirted Hawaiian girl doing the hula on Chevron Island, and the Asian woman with Jade East cologne. A particularly harmful commercial for a popular insecticide shows the spray instantly eliminating a large swarm of menacing insects with slanted eyes and Asian faces (Kaku, 1973). Most of the advertisements are more innocuous, however:

> Sugar commercials continue the idea that the islands are covered with sugar cane and all the Hawaiians are farmers. The Chinese Communist is pictured as a fat politician who is astounded by Fruit of the Loom (with difficulty in saying "L"). Another group of Chinese Communists are astounded by a Volkswagen bus. These stereotypes are not obviously evil characterizations but are insidious in their innocence [Paik, 1971, p. 33].

Many of these stereotypes have been so popular in the media that Asian Americans have unconsciously accepted them and do not even realize the true extent of racism in the media. "So effective is the 'brainwashing' that Asian Americans have actually built up a tolerance for racist ads [Kaku, 1973, p. 40]."

Thus, the Asian image presented on the television screen has been consistently stereotyped. The basic message is that Asians are inferior to white Americans and that the only way to become accepted by white society is for Asians to become passive, dependent, and respectful— that is, to know their place. As the Chinese Media Committee wrote to Robert Wood, President of CBS; "Unless you were an Asian who had to live with these limiting, shallow and stereotyped categorizations you might not understand why these so-called 'positive' images are as offensive as the 'Step-'N-Fetchit' stereotype is to blacks in America [Fong, 1973, Appendix]."

Each of the major television networks maintains that it is its policy not to portray minorities in a derogatory way. ABC and NBC have written guidelines about avoiding misrepresentation, ridicule, promotion of stereotypes, or denigration of any group or race, and CBS is supposed to follow such a policy in practice, though they have no written guidelines (U.S. Commission on Civil Rights, 1977). The analysis just presented, however, indicates that they have not followed their own rules. Thomas Baldwin and Colby Lewis, in their interviews with industry people, suggest a partial explanation for this contradiction. The network censors are basically not concerned about the depiction of minorities and are insensitive to the guidelines for "special sensitivity" about minority portrayal on television. The censors' major concern is to assure the networks that the programs they broadcast are in the public interest and conform to the NAB Code, not to watch out for damaging or demeaning stereotyped characters (U.S. Commission on Civil Rights, 1977).

The other reason for the perpetuation of stereotypes is the lack of Asian Americans in decision-making positions in both the movie and television industries. Asian Americans are the only ones who have a real stake in seeing that myths about Asians are discontinued and in presenting a more realistic, well-rounded perspective on Asians. Only 2 Asian Americans belong to the Directors Guild of America (out of 951 members) and virtually no producers of movies are Asian. In 1975, most Asians employed in motion-picture production were concentrated in the professional and technical aspects (James, 1978). In 1976, when the major studios reported their employment statistics to the California Advisory Committee on the U.S. Commission on Civil Rights, Paramount, Universal, and MGM had no Asians as officials and managers (Walt Disney had 3 and Twentieth Century had 1), Paramount and MGM had no Asian professionals (Walt Disney had 13, Universal 2, Twentieth Century 12), Universal had no Asian technicians, and Paramount, Twentieth Century, and MGM had only one each (Walt Disney had 4). Most of the Asian women, like all women, were concentrated in the office and clerical division; Walt Disney had 7 women, Paramount 5 women and 2 men, Universal 24 women and 5 men, MGM 3 men and 7 women, and Twentieth Century 3 men and 17 women (James, 1978, p. 17).

In television, Asians are also not in a position to set broad policies or to exercise overall responsibility for administration of those policies. In a survey of 40 television stations, the U.S. Commission on Civil Rights (1977) found that in 1975 Asian men accounted for .79% and Asian women 1.16% of the professionals employed; on the three network-owned stations, they varied from .31% to 2.66%, whereas on affiliated stations and public stations they were under 1.0% of professional employees in 1975. The professional job titles reported by eight television stations in 1975 included five Asian women (no Asian men), 1.0% of their professional category: one producer, one associate producer, one newswriter, one chief accountant–chief cashier, and one senior acting clerk (U.S. Commission on Civil Rights, 1977). For officials and managers, the percentage drops, ranging from no Asian women at ABC, CBS, or NBC-owned stations to 1.35% for Asian men at ABC, 1.0% at CBS, .91% at affiliated stations (.61% for women), .41% for both men and women at public stations, and .73% for Asian men and .27% for Asian women at 40 stations in 1975. One Asian-American male was listed under the official and manager job titles reported by eight television stations, constituting .4% of the total; he was a production cost controller ranking below subsidiary officials and managers in the administration department (U.S. Commission on Civil Rights, 1977).

Even these figures for officials and managers are suspect. The U.S. Commission on Civil Rights (1977) found that minorities and women who do not hold policy-making positions were being misclassified as officials and managers. White males were found to predominate at the highest levels of station management and minorities and women at the lowest levels. Many of the job titles appeared to be clerical or administrative in nature rather than fitting the FCC's definition for official and manager positions.

Asians have begun to become more vocal about protesting these media stereotypes and have been able to exert a certain amount of influence. The Japanese American Citizens League was able to pressure ABC to cancel an *FBI* segment in 1971 that dealt with a Japanese spy ring and sabotage in the United States, and pressure (or lack of ratings) also led CBS to cancel the cartoon show *The Amazing Chan and the Chan Clan* in 1974. The picketing of new films like *The Fiendish Plot of Dr. Fu Manchu* and *Charlie Chan and the Dragon Queen* has received some publicity. These are important first steps in educating the media to refrain from utilizing Asian stereotypes and in educating the public about those stereotypes and the harm they cause. But not until Asian Americans are in a position to affect movie and television policy and to administer that policy will the image of Asians in the media change appreciably.

EFFECTS OF STEREOTYPES ON ASIAN AMERICAN CHILDREN

Although these stereotyped images of Asians have been widely disseminated through television, little is known of the effects of these images on Asian American children. In fact, few researchers have even studied the effects of television in general on minority adults, let alone minority children; only about 7% of the publicly available studies provide significant data on ethnic minorities or persons of lower SES (Comstock & Fisher, 1975). And, except for a small number of studies on Chicano children, minority groups other than blacks have been ignored. A comprehensive search of the published literature has uncovered virtually no empirical research about television use by Asian American children and about the effects of television on them.

The only survey on television use that includes a significant number of Asian American children, *Children's Time Study* (Medrich, 1977, 1979; Rubin, personal communication, 1981) will not be published until 1981 and has many limitations in terms of its data. It is focused primarily on children's use of time outside the school and is only secondarily concerned with children's use of television; the effects of television on minority children are not studied at all. Further limiting its significance as a cross-cultural study, is that only 9.2% of the sample population studied is Asian American (70 families and children out of a total of 764), so any generalizations about Asian American children are limited by the small numbers involved and Asian Americans are consequently often omitted from the detailed data tables and analyses. The "Asian American" category includes only Chinese and Japanese Americans, which are among the largest Asian populations in the United States. The burgeoning immigrant population—the Pilipinos, Koreans, and Pacific Islanders that have been arriving in the United States since 1965 and the Vietnamese and other Southeast Asian refugees that have been arriving since 1975—are excluded. The Asian American sample of 70 families is concentrated in the middle and high SES: In this study 15.2% Asian Americans studied are high SES, 14.4% are medium SES, and only .7% are low SES, which is an uneven distribution since they are 9.2% of the sample population as a whole. Although the Asian American families have an income distribution that closely approximates that of white families (concentrated in the two upper categories of $10,000–$19,000 [37.5%] and $20,000 and over per year [43.7%]), they also have 1½ times more families with two wage-earners than white families do (60.0% of Asian; 38.4% of white families). This larger proportion of two wage-earner families indicates that Asians probably earn less than whites as individuals but manage to achieve a relatively high income level for the family. This concentration of Asians in the middle and upper SES does not reflect the Asian American population as a whole, however; more recent immigrants are more likely to be in the low SES category, especially if they are from the Philippines, Korea, or China ("Asian American Facts and Figures," 1975; Division of Asian American Affairs, Office of Special Concerns, Dept. of Health, Education, and Welfare, 1977). Nevertheless, in spite of these limitations, we will be referring to this study as one of the few sources of factual data about the viewing habits of Asian American children.

Although research on Asian Americans has tended to characterize them as a homogenous entity, it is important to remember that the term encompasses a variety of ethnic groups and cultures—Chinese, Japanese, Pilipino, Korean, Vietnamese and other Southeast Asians, Samoan, Hawaiian, and other Pacific Islanders. As a number of writers have argued, this placement of different groups into a single category and set of stereotypes (such as "the model minority") distorts reality and results in their problems being concealed and ignored (Chun-Hoon, 1973; Kitano, 1974; Yee, 1973). Another factor that has received even less consideration is the differences in subculture and language *within* each ethnic group. Generalizations about Asian Americans, then, can be problematic; future empirical research on Asian Americans should include a sample population that is representative of this diversity of nationalities and cultures.

Before attempting to analyze some of the effects of television and of the Asian American image it presents on Asian American children, we will explore the patterns of television use by Asian American children. Patterns of television use are a fundamental indicator of its influence. Almost everyone in the United States today has access to at least one television set. The United States 1970 census estimated that 96% of all American households have a television set; later studies dealing primarily with households in which children or adolescents are present have reported 98–99% with television sets (cited in Lyle, 1972).

Most children watch television for at least 2 hr a day, although great individual variation occurs (Comstock, Chaffee, Katzman, McCombs, & Roberts, 1978). A comparison of the results of earlier surveys (Schramm, Lyle, & Parker, 1961) and more recent studies (Chaffee, McLeod, & Atkin, 1970; Greenberg & Dervin, 1970; Lyle & Hoffman, 1972a, 1972b) suggests an overall increase in children's viewing of television. Lyle and Hoffman (1972a) estimate that first- and sixth-graders are watching about 1 hr more per school day than they were in 1959. Television viewing among children varies by place and time of year as well; viewing time decreases during the summer months and is less in winter in San Francisco, which has a mild climate, than it is in the Rocky Mountains at the same time. This suggests that television is attractive in inverse proportion to the attractiveness of other available activities (Schramm *et al.*, 1961).

It is likely that Asian American children follow the general pattern of age differences in television viewing. Children begin watching television as early as 2 years of age; by the time they are 3, they are typically high viewers. Viewing time continues to increase, reaching a peak just before the child begins elementary school, and drops as school cuts into the child's available time. As children are allowed to stay up later, viewing time increases steadily to another peak around preadolescence (11- to 12-years-old), then declines during high school (Chaffee *et al.*, 1970; Chaffee & McLeod, 1972; Lehrer & Cissna, 1978; Lyle & Hoffman, 1971, 1972a, 1972b; McIntyre & Teevan, 1972; McLeod, Atkin, & Chaffee, 1972a, 1972b; Schramm *et al.*, 1961). Adolescents thus watch less television than elementary or junior high school students, presumably because of their more active social lives and greater mobility (Lyle,

1972; Murray, Cole, & Fedler, 1970; A.C. Nielson Company, cited in Comstock *et al.*, 1978; Robinson & Bachman, 1972).

Although many studies have found that SES is inversely related to the amount of children's television viewing (Greenberg & Dervin, 1970; Greenberg & Dominick, 1969; Lefkowitz, Eron, Walder, & Huesmann, 1972; McIntyre & Teevan, 1972; A.C. Nielson Company, cited in Comstock *et al.*, 1978; McLeod *et al.*, 1972a; Schramm *et al.*, 1961), the results of the Children's Time Study (Rubin, personal communication, 1981) indicate that Asian American ethnicity, similar to the other ethnic minorities, cuts across social class as a factor in television viewing time. Black children appear to be heavier watchers of television than white children (Greenberg & Dervin, 1970; Greenberg & Dominick, 1969; McIntyre & Teevan, 1972), as do Chicano girls (Lyle & Hoffman, 1972a). The data clearly indicate that this greater viewing by the black population as a whole is not ascribable to the predominance within this population of households of lower income and education (Bogart, 1972; Bower, 1973; Robinson, 1972b).

On the other hand, the data from the Children's Time Study (Rubin personal communication, 1981) indicate that Asian American parents exercise much more control over their children's use of and access to television than any of the other groups, minority or white. Therefore, television is less accessible to Asian American children than it is to white, black, or Chicano children in Medrich's sample. For instance, the Asian American households are considerably less likely to have the television set on in the afternoon and during dinner than are any of the other groups, although their viewing time in the evening is the same as everyone else's. Asian American families are also the least likely to have the television set on all day. In addition, the Asian American children are much more discriminating than any of the other groups in their choice of programs; blacks and other non-Asians are twice as likely as Asian Americans to give a nonselective response when asked about their choice of viewing programs. All of these factors combine to indicate that Asian Americans are different from all other groups, white and minority, in their use of television and to suggest that Asian American children are likely to watch less television in comparison with black children of the same age.

One reason for the difference in Asian American children's viewing time is probably related to the Asian American parents' greater overall control of their children's behavior. Although the term *Asian American* encompasses many different nationalities, languages, and cultures, the cultures appear to have a great deal in common in the area of child-rearing practices. In Chinese, Japanese, Pilipino, Korean, and other Asian cultures, the primary family unit is strong, typically exerting great control over its members. Obedience to parents and deference to parental authority are reinforced through verbal techniques accentuating feelings of guilt and shame; strong family ties are emphasized, as well as the traditional adherence of children to parental mores (see, for instance, Benedict, 1946; Cattell, 1962; Caudill & Frost, 1972; Caudill & Weinstein, 1969; DeVos & Abbott, 1966; Diamond, 1969; Fenz & Arkoff, 1962; Frost, 1970; Guthrie, 1961, 1966; Guthrie & Jacobs, 1966; Hsu, 1948, 1971a, 1971b; Kitano, 1969, 1974; Lee, 1960; Lind, 1967; Maykovitch, 1972; Su, 1922; Whiting, 1963; Wolf, 1968.) One manifestation of this greater control is in television viewing.

However, for more recently arrived immigrant Asian families, we would expect a different pattern to emerge, one of substantially more viewing time than for the population as a whole, similar to the heavier viewing exhibited by black children. A number of studies on the process of acculturation among Asian immigrants have stressed the importance of the role of television and other mass media (Kim, 1976; Nagata, 1969; Ryu, 1978). Television aids in the socialization of Asian immigrants, teaching them the English language, supplying information about daily life, social customs, and social activities in the United States, and giving an understanding of what Americans are like (Ryu, 1978). Ryu (1978) found that among Korean immigrants, the lower their proficiency in English, the greater their need to learn English through the mass media, particularly television. As their assimilation increases, there is a corresponding increase in their need for information gained through the mass media, and as the degree of assimilation increases, the immigrant's use of television to satisfy the need for integration in American society also increases.

Lampkin (1976) notes that Asian American adolescents, along with blacks, made significantly greater use of television as a source of information than whites or Chicanos. Lampkin ascribes this information-use pattern to the fact that many of the Asians in his sample are first-generation Americans or children of immigrants who look to television to provide them with models of socially acceptable behavior. These findings suggest that immigrant Asian families watch more television in order to hasten the process of acculturation, so their children would be more likely to be heavy television viewers as well. As such, television plays an important role in teaching American culture.

Asian American children as a whole probably have the same preferences as the general population in terms of program preference. Definite program preferences are expressed by children almost as soon as they begin to watch television. Program preference appears to be related to age (Dominick & Greenberg, 1972; Lyle & Hoffman, 1971, 1972a, 1972b; Murray, 1972; Schramm et al., 1961; Stein & Friedrich, 1972), although at least one study found no indications of a maturing pattern of program selection (Lehrer & Cissna, 1978). Preschool and first-grade children prefer cartoons, situation comedies, and noncartoon children's programs, usually in that order. As the children grow up, their tastes become increasingly diversified. Situation comedies begin to dominate by the first or second grade and continue to be popular well into adolescence. The end of the elementary school years marks the transition to "adult" entertainment programs, with action–adventure, music and variety, and various dramatic shows being cited as favorites. By the mid-teens, action–adventure shows, along with other "adult" programming, dominate their preference list (Lyle & Hoffman, 1971, 1972a; A. C. Nielson Co., cited in Comstock et al., 1978; Schramm et al., 1961).

Black and Chicano children seem to have different preferences in television programming. While differences are not apparent among first-graders (Lyle & Hoffman, 1971, 1972a), by the sixth grade there is a discernible differentiation in favorite programs between black and white children. Fletcher (1969) found that southern black students in grades 6 through 12 tend to prefer programs in which the central character has no mate, such as My Three Sons, whereas Surlin and Dominick (1970–1971) and Greenberg and Dervin (1970), analyzing data from a sample of tenth- and eleventh-graders in the North, found that blacks prefer watching a family-group show such as Bonanza over an entertainment show such as the Smothers' Brothers Show. In contrast, white teenagers of the same age prefer entertainment shows (comedies and general variety). Ethnic minority children also seem to prefer programming with performers of the same ethnicity (Greenberg, 1972; Greenberg & Dervin, 1970; Lyle, 1972; Lyle & Hoffman, 1971, 1972a) although, because of the lack of programs with Asian American performers, it would be difficult to apply this generalization to Asian American children. The Children's Time Study (Rubin, personal communication, 1981) found no differentiation among the ethnic groups in terms of program preferences; Kung Fu was rated the favorite program of the preadolescent sample taken in 1976, and the other preferred programs were also the same across all ethnic groups, although the ordering was slightly different.

We would, however, expect that the children of Asian immigrants would have a slightly different pattern of program preferences than the general population. Since English is their second (or perhaps even their third) language, they probably prefer shows that depend more on nonverbal communication for entertainment, such as cartoons and I Love Lucy. Cartoons, in particular, attract these viewers, regardless of age. According to Winick and Winick (1979), "Cartoons rely so heavily on motion that it becomes possible for even the very young child to observe the movement. On the basis of the observed movement, the child can note changes in a scene and begin to apply reasoning capacity[p. 177]." Thus, we would hypothesize that children of Asian immigrants probably watch more cartoons and situation comedies—regardless of their age—than do children in general, including other Asian American children.

An important factor in describing program selection by Asian American children is the growing number of households in the United States with more than one television set. In general, it appears that multiple television sets are as common in working-class and ethnic minority homes as in white-collar and white homes, but white-collar and white children have greater accessibility to color sets (Lyle & Hoffman, 1971, 1972a). It is therefore highly likely that Asian-American children have as great an access to multiple television sets as the general population. The one major effect of multiple sets is that of isolation and the discouragement of total family interaction.

Joint viewing decreases from 94% in a single-set home, to 80% in a two-set home, to 65% in a three- or four-set home (Bower, 1973). Among the general population of American children, television watching is still most frequently done within a social context, with siblings the most frequent companions while viewing (Lyle & Hoffman, 1972a, 1972b). Asian American children, however, appear to follow a different pattern, with more solitary viewing of television than the rest of the population. Medrich (Rubin, personal communication, 1981) found that Asian American children are only one-half as likely to watch television with parents and/or friends as any of the other groups studied. Although the small size of the sample precludes conclusive statements and the children do not appear to have been asked about siblings as companions while viewing, these data indicate that Asian American children may be more likely to view television alone and therefore may be more affected by the television programs they see without the moderating influence of significant others.

Another factor that can modify the effects of television on children is the degree of attention that is paid to television when the set is on. A number of studies suggest that children's attention to television varies considerably; television has frequently been found to be secondary to some other activity and, even when viewing is primary, there is often secondary activity (Anderson & Lorch, 1979; Bechtel, Achelpohl, & Akers, 1972; Lorch, Anderson, & Levin, 1979; Ward, Robertson, & Wackman, 1971; Ward & Wackman, 1973; Winick & Winick, 1979). The most popular activities for children watching television are eating, studying, and talking with other members of the family (Bechtel et al., 1972; Lyle & Hoffman, 1971, 1972a), although a wide variety of other activities observed includes such things as playing with a dog, playing with a toy or with a game or cards, singing along, leaving the room, patting the television screen, talking to characters on the screen or to people in the room, laughing, imitating actions on the screen, dancing, clapping, shuffling feet, singing, exercising, throwing paper airplanes, wrestling, and combing hair (Winick & Winick, 1979). Asian American children probably resemble the general population in their attentional behavior. Due to the cultural emphasis of Asians on the work ethic (e.g., Kitano, 1974), however, television as an exclusive activity is probably not encouraged in Asian American families, whereas secondary activity is probably encouraged. The resulting divided attention of the children may serve to lessen the impact of television.

Television's influence on children's behavior and attitudes is much more difficult to assess than the objective descriptions of how much television children watch, what they watch, or how they watch it. Probably the least disputed generalization about the effects of television on children, including Asian American children, is that they learn from the medium (Comstock et al., 1978). Educational programs on television have been demonstrated to have pedagogical effects in classrooms with a wide range of age groups (Chu & Schramm, 1967), in such children's programs as Sesame Street and The Electric Company for ethnic minorities as well as the general population (Ball & Bogatz, 1970, 1973; Ball, 1974; Bogatz & Ball, 1971; Yankelovich, Skelly and White, Inc., 1978), although there is controversy over the range of such effects (Cook, Appleton, Conner, Shaffer, Tamkin, & Weber, 1975; Lesser, 1977). Informational programs such as CBS's National Citizenship Test also have pedagogical effects on children (Alper & Leidy, 1970). News programs convey information about current events like the Vietnam War (Tolley, 1973) and Watergate (Hawkins, Pingree, & Roberts, 1975), weather patterns (Robinson, 1972b), and politics (Chaffee, Ward, & Tipton, 1970). Even on entertainment programs, incidental learning occurs among children in such areas as vocabulary (Parker, 1960), facts basic and incidental to the plot (Katzman, 1972), sequences of important events (Leifer, Collins, Gross, Taylor, Andrews, & Blackmer, 1971), and the motives and effects of portrayed behavior (Leifer & Roberts, 1972). It is highly likely that Asian American children's cognitive development is affected by television in the same manner.

The aspect of the effects of television on children that has attracted the most attention in research is the possible influence of television violence on aggressive behavior in real life. The importance of this question is evidenced by the fact that empirical studies in this area exceed studies in all other problem areas combined, by a ratio of more than 4:1 (Comstock et al., 1978). It is not within our purview to attempt to summarize this vast literature (see, for instance, Bandura, 1973; Comstock et al., 1978; Liebert, Neale, & Davidson, 1973; Surgeon General's Scientific Advisory Committee, 1972). Whatever the relationship between viewing of violence on television and aggression, we think it probable that, although Asian American children watch as much violence as the general population, they rarely react with violent or aggressive behavior because it is not culturally acceptable (see Kitano, 1974). Any research on Asian American children in this area would have to take the cultural factor into account, since it undoubtedly influences findings that could not be predicted from the patterns of the general population.

Children appear to imitate televised behavior more when the model is a peer with the same background and interests (Rosekrans, 1967). This finding is consistent with other studies that demonstrate the importance of race of the portrayed model, although the studies differ in their conclusions: One experiment indicates that blacks are more influenced by a black model (Nicholas, McCarter, & Heckel, 1971a) and another finds that black children prefer a white model, even when the white model is punished and the black one rewarded (Neely, Heckel, & Leichtman, 1973). More research is needed to determine the effects of the ethnicity of television role models on imitative behavior. The implications for Asian American children, however, are serious, for if Asian American children identify strongly with Asian models on television, they have only stereotyped characters to imitate (Fu Manchu, Charlie Chan, or silent, passive types if male; prostitutes or shy housewives if female). If, on the other hand, they identify with the white characters, then they will be repudiating their racial identity because of their perception of the racism of this society. Either way, Asian American children lose.

Television content also has a greater impact on children if they believe that the events and characters are real. Younger children think that television is real and that people actually live inside the set (Schramm et al., 1961; Winick & Winick, 1979), although a major increase in comprehension of the nature of television appears at ages 3–4 (Lyle & Hoffman, 1972b). The ability to discriminate reality increases with age and viewing experience (Brown, Skeen, & Keith, 1979; Harlan, 1972; Morison, McCarthy, & Gardner, 1979; Murphy, 1973; Reeves, 1979). Even by the first grade, children distinguish between television and real life, although they are more likely to accept child characters on television as being like themselves and their friends than to accept television adults as being like the adults they know (Lyle & Hoffman, 1971, 1972a, 1972b).

The minority children studied followed these same age-related patterns, but appeared to express a greater belief that television accurately portrays real life than did white children of the same age (Gans, 1968; Greenberg & Dervin, 1970; Greenberg & Dominick, 1969; Greenberg & Gordon, 1972, 1972b; Greenberg & Reeves, 1976; Lyle & Hoffman,

1972a). This greater tendency by lower-class and minority youth to accept television as an accurate depiction of life probably also applies to Asian American children, especially the children of immigrants. This higher acceptance of the reality of television, then, will tend to cut across Asian American children's growing awareness of the differentiation between television and real life, making Asian American children more susceptible to the messages about social values being broadcast on television. When the stereotyped images are seen as reality, behavior and attitudes in real life are guided by the expectations derived from those stereotypes.

Few investigations into the racial preferences and identification of Asian American children have been undertaken. Springer (1950, 1953) examined Chinese, Japanese, Korean, part-Asian, and white children in Hawaii and found that more than one-half the Asian American children select pictures of Asian American children as their playmate preference, but that Asian American children choose their own race significantly less across all test items than do white children. Furthermore, a higher proportion of white children choose same-race pictures as the ones they "like the best" than do Asian American children. These results are also borne out by the Fox and Jordan study (1973), which compared black, Chinese American, and white children in New York City; the Chinese American children manifested the lowest magnitude of same-race preference and identification, whereas the black children appeared to have increased significantly their same-race preference and identification compared to earlier studies, and the white children had the highest same-race preference of all three groups. The Chinese American pattern of being one-half same-race and one-half cross-race-oriented is not significantly different from chance, suggesting that perhaps the Chinese American children are ignoring racial differences. These data indicate that Asian American children might very well identify more with white characters on television rather than with Asian American ones.

Although a few studies on the effects of films about successful blacks on the racial self-concept of black children have been inconclusive (Price, 1970; Teahan & Podany, 1974), other research suggests that motion pictures and television do influence self-esteem among black children. Dimas (1970) found that the self-concept of black children viewing successful black role models is enhanced in comparison to black children viewing only white role models. The results of research by Tan and Tan (1979) suggest that heavy television viewing leads to low self-esteem for blacks but not whites, probably due to the nonexistent or negative portrayals of blacks on most television entertainment programs as opposed to the positive role images of whites on those programs. Asian American children are likely to have patterns similar to that of black children in terms of influence of television on their self-concept, since the Asian American image in the media, although different from the black image, is still negatively stereotyped.

Movies and television can affect children's self-concept; they can also be instrumental in changing people's racial attitudes. Peterson and Thurstone (1933) initiated an investigation into the effects of motion pictures on social attitudes when the movie industry was still young. They documented that viewing motion pictures can modify people's attitudes about capital punishment, prison reform, gambling, war, Prohibition, and race relations. For instance, whites became more racist after viewing D. W. Griffith's masterpiece, Birth of a Nation, which romanticizes and whitewashes the Ku Klux Klan. Peterson and Thurstone's longitudinal analysis indicates that these effects on attitudes persisted over 6 months. After viewing Don't Be a Sucker, a film directed against intergroup religious prejudice, high school students exhibited selective changes in attitude, each specific religious group accepting the message directed at that group, with the principal appeal of the film being to the enlightened self-interest of the spectator (Cooper & Dinerman, 1951). Students in Germany, when exposed to a counterstereotypical movie with a dark hero, improved their evaluations of dark actors in general (Scherer, 1970–1971).

Television, which is a primary source of information about blacks for suburban and rural white children, has been found to determine some aspects of racial beliefs. Hartmann and Husband (1974) conclude from their study of white children and their parents in Great Britain that television and other mass media play a significant role in characterizing for their white audience the nature and meaning of the "coloured" presence in Great Britain. Greenberg (1972) finds that for white children, television exposure to blacks contributes to identification with black characters and black-featured shows. His data even indicate that a large proportion of white children (40% of his sample) learn from television how black children talk, look, and dress, although black children do not learn about white children from television. Since Asian Americans are an even smaller percentage of the population of the United States than are blacks and are more concentrated in specific areas (the West Coast and New York City), it is likely that many white children and adults who have little or no personal contact with Asian Americans, form their impressions about Asian Americans from the stereotyped images that are prevalent on television. These images probably serve to reinforce the concept of the inferiority of Asian Americans.

Much of the research substantiates the classic view that television reflects traditional cultural assumptions and therefore reinforces, rather than shapes or changes, existing attitudes. For example, a ten-

dency to have rigid and stereotyped thinking, as assessed by a dog-
matism scale, appears to correlate with both a preference for predictable, stereotyped television programs and more hostile attitudes toward
black people (Hartmann & Husband, 1974). Hartmann and Husband
also noted that people's attitudes affect the way they interpret what
they see on television; people seem to notice and recall only information that is consistent with their existing attitudes.

These intervening audience mechanisms, such as selective exposure
and selective perception, account for the lack of direct change in attitudes attributable to television. For example, a series of studies on *All
in the Family, Sanford and Son,* and *The Jeffersons* document how
prejudiced people ignore messages constructed to change their prejudice: Highly authoritarian and highly prejudiced viewers are more in
agreement with Archie Bunker's and George Jefferson's bigotry than are
viewers scoring low on the authoritarian and prejudice measures; consequently, the shows may reinforce the prejudice and close-
mindedness of the viewers who identify with Archie Bunker's and
George Jefferson's views (Brigham & Giesbrecht, 1976; Leckenby & Surlin, 1976; Surlin, 1974; Surlin & Cooper, 1976; Surlin & Tate, 1976; Tate
& Surlin, 1976; Vidmar & Rokeach, 1974). This process of selective
perception and recall probably also applies to children, although their
attitudes are in formation and therefore are more susceptible to influence.

A number of studies, however, have documented changes in racial
attitudes brought about by television, particularly for children. Singer
(1973) suggests that through extensive coverage of riots in black communities and of militant black leaders, television has transformed black
attitudes and helped to forge a new black identity. Ethnocentrism, as
scored on the Adorno Scale of Ethnocentrism, was reduced after subjects viewed a realistic motion picture (Goldberg, 1956), and children's
ethnocentrism exhibited a dramatic decline after viewing the television
series *The Earth's a Big Blue Marble,* which is a half-hour show aimed
at fourth-, fifth-, and sixth-graders to encourage international awareness in children by showing them how children in other countries live,
play, grow up, and work (Roberts, Herold, Hornby, King, Sterne,
Whiteley, & Silverman, 1974). The series seems to encourage perception
of greater similarities between the children and people from other
countries and to influence children's perceptions of the positive aspects of life in other countries, thereby decreasing, somewhat, feelings
of superiority or a preference for the United States. Roberts *et al.*
(1974:49) point out:

> There is some evidence that the results . . . are more reflections of attitude for-
> mation than change. For example, many of the mean before-scores on various
> scales hovered quite near to a hypothetical scale mid-point; children were

neither strongly pro nor con on many of the items. This might well indicate
that they simply hadn't thought much about the dimensions we were attempting to measure—that they really didn't have any articulated opinions or well-
developed impressions of life in other countries. This possibility is certainly
supported by the many changes from before to after viewing found in this
research. Roberts (1971), for example, has argued elsewhere that it is much
easier to induce formation of a new attitude or belief than to change an existing one.

The implications of the Roberts *et al.* (1974) study are serious. If
television influences children in the development of their racial attitudes, the evidence is that Asian Americans will be either ignored as
irrelevant or treated as inferior, since those are the major images (or lack
of images) projected about Asian Americans on television.

Other researchers seem to bear out the findings of the Roberts *et al.*
study that children's attitudes about race can be formed or changed by
viewing television programs. Two years (not 1) of viewing *Sesame
Street* seems to produce somewhat more favorable attitudes toward
children of other races (Ball & Bogatz, 1970). When *Sesame Street*
segments with nonwhite children are shown to 3- to 5-year-old white
children in Canada, the children exhibit a strong preference for playing
with nonwhites, in sharp contrast with the preference for white playmates of the control group not exposed to those segments (Gorn,
Goldberg, & Kanungo, 1976). As noted previously, Greenberg (1972)
found that white children who have been exposed to black television
shows and characters identify significantly more than before with black
role models.

An interesting example of the effects of television programs in
changing people's racial attitudes is *Roots,* the 12-hr ABC production
dramatizing black history that was seen by a record audience in the
United States in January of 1977. Seven of the eight episodes ranked
among the top 10 in all-time television ratings with between 62% and
68% audience shares; 130 million Americans watched at least one episode, and 80 million saw the last episode (Gantz, 1978; Hur & Robinson, 1978). It was widely assumed that appreciation of the historical
plight of blacks would be enhanced by the large-scale viewing of the
program, leading to more sympathetic attitudes in other areas of race
relations. A number of studies have been conducted to determine what
impact *Roots* has had on racial attitudes. Seven surveys, including one
national and one international, were taken between 1 day and 4 weeks
after the showing of *Roots* on national television. In all of them, a
substantial portion of both blacks and whites (60–80%) indicated that
they believed that *Roots* provided a learning experience for them, that
it accurately depicted the black experience during slavery, and that it
increased their understanding of the psychology of black people (Ba-

lon, 1978; Gantz, 1978; Howard, Rothbart, & Sloan, 1978; Hur, 1978; Hur & Robinson, 1978; McAllister-Johnson, 1977; Surlin, 1978).

This informational and emotional impact, however, does not appear to be matched by attitudinal or behavioral changes. In Hur's (1978) study of black and white teenagers, 30% of the whites and 21% of the blacks remain unconvinced that black slavery was any worse than the experiences of white immigrants. Similarly, Surlin (1978) found very little attitude change detected, although whites were more likely to express a favorable opinion about blacks after viewing than vice versa. In a longitudinal study where people initially interviewed within 1 week of the broadcast of *Roots* were re-interviewed 1 year later to determine its long-term impact, the respondents' behavior, in terms of relations with people of other races, of an active search to discover their own roots, or in reading the book on which the series was based, did not match the positive attitudinal changes in interracial knowledge, understanding, and respect that were still attributed to the program.

In fact, several of the studies indicate that selective perception influenced the effect of the series on viewers. Hur (1978) suggests that in line with his data, possibly those already more sympathetic to the program's content are the ones who were mainly affected in perceiving the hardships of black slavery. In both the United States and Great Britain, *Roots* viewers were found to hold more liberal racial attitudes than nonviewers (Hur & Robinson, 1978). Similarly, in the national survey there is a tendency for conservatives who feel that the pace of racial change in this country is too fast to deny the contemporary meaning of *Roots*, whereas those who feel the pace is too slow find the program very relevant (Howard et al., 1978). So, those who were more open to the messages of *Roots* appear to have obtained more positive attitudes about race relations from the series than those who were not so prepared.

Another reason for the lack of basic attitudinal changes from the showing of *Roots* is suggested by Gantz (1978): The changes may have been minimized by network programming that returned to "normal" and did not prioritize altering interracial attitudes or behavior. A one-shot deal like the showing of *Roots* can have a positive effect for awhile, giving viewers a greater appreciation of the horrors of slavery and the history and culture of blacks. But unless the networks are willing to continue to finance programs of such a nature, which break through the usual stereotyped characters and situations, people's attitudes are reinforced by their daily diet of television.

The research on *Roots* has implications for the NBC showing of *Shōgun* in September, 1980. *Shōgun* drew an audience almost as large as that of *Roots* for its 12 hr spread out over 5 days; it is estimated that over 72 million people saw the last episode of this historical epic about the acculturation of an Englishman in sixteenth century Japan. Because of the large audience throughout the country, the show may be expected to have an impact on people's attitudes about Asia and about Asian Americans. Like *Roots*, the show, whatever its inaccuracies, probably served to raise the consciousness of viewers about respect for the culture and people of Japan. Like *Roots* also, selective perception and retention on the part of the viewers probably limited the impact of the program. *Shōgun*, however, as a drama taking place during only a few months in 1600, does not have the scope of *Roots* nor the contemporary relevance, so its influence on racial attitudes toward Asians may be less. Again, unless *Shōgun* is followed by programming that cuts across the stereotypes of Asians that are the typical television fare, its long-range impact will probably be minimal.

This discussion about *Roots* and *Shōgun* points to a key factor in changing the image of minorities on television: One or two token changes, no matter how spectacular, will not change the overall impact of television on the child who spends up to 6 hr a day, week after week, month after month, year after year, in front of the set. The long-term, less striking effects of the environment created by television must be taken into account if any changes are to be made.

The studies that have been done on children and television have many limitations. Most of the studies have been small-scale, conducted at different times of the year in various parts of the country and have used different age groups, different measurement procedures, and different bases for reporting estimates. No surveys that attempt to represent the population of children in the United States, let alone Asian American children or the children of other ethnic minorities, have been carried out, and the Nielson samples are small, with analyses limited to roughly defined age categories (Comstock *et al.*, 1978). Furthermore, despite evidence about the differential effects of age and cognitive development on children watching television, few studies have taken a developmental perspective. New means for measuring the total impact of television will have to be developed.

In conclusion, we would like to recommend the following in terms of improving the Asian American image on television and studying the effects of that image on Asian American children:

1. That the Asian American image on television be expanded beyond narrow stereotypes. Asian Americans should be portrayed as serving in all facets of American life—in politics, professions, businesses, trades; as senators, doctors, executives, shopkeepers, laborers, and unemployed workers—so that these portrayals of Asian Americans in a wide variety of fields and positions will reflect the current reality. Asian Americans are also not all the same psychologically and this diversity should be depicted on the screen.

2. That Asian Americans be cast in major roles. It may very well be that the initial effect of an Asian American lead will be disconcerting, but once an audience becomes familiar with such a character, the individual's talent will take over. For example, in the *Don Ho Show* in Hawaii, a young man from Japan called "Tokyo Joe" is introduced to an audience of middle-aged (and over) tourists from American's heartland. There are some raised eyebrows and snickering when Tokyo Joe begins to play "country fiddle" in a deadpan fashion, but once the initial incongruity passes, the audience reacts to the talent, rather than to the ethnicity. At the end of the act, the ladies are enjoying Joe's hugs and kisses as much as Don Ho's, a Hawaiian. Such roles are not normally associated with Asian males. Ethnicity means visibility and may thus serve as an initial barrier; it does not necessarily have to remain an insurmountable one. The popularity of Bruce Lee and Toshiro Mifune among Americans attests to this.

3. That Asian Americans be trained, hired, and given opportunities for advancement in the production and managerial end of television broadcasting. This will tend to affect the area of stereotypes and broaden the use of Asian Americans on the screen.

4. That research on the effect of television on children sample a larger group of Asian Americans. There should also be a sensitivity to the large number of Asian American groups (there are over 20 in Los Angeles), each with their own background, experiences, languages, and culture.

REFERENCES

Alper, S. W., & Leidy, T. R. The impact of information transmission through television. *Public Opinion Quarterly*, 1970, *33*(4), 556–562.

Anderson, D. R., & Lorch, E. P. *A theory of the active nature of young children's television viewing.* Paper presented at Biennial Meeting of the Society for Research in Child Development, San Francisco, California, March 1979.

Asian American facts and figures: A closer look at the 1970 census. *Bridge*, 1975, *3*(4), 34–38.

Asian Americans for a Fair Media. Asian images—A message to the media. *Bridge*, 1974, *3*(2), 25–30.

Ball, S. *Reading with television: A follow-up evaluation of "The Electric Company."* Princeton, New Jersey: Educational Testing Service, 1974.

Ball, S., & Bogatz, G. A. *The first year of "Sesame Street:" An evaluation.* Princeton, New Jersey: Educational Testing Service, 1970.

Ball, S., & Bogatz, G. A. *Reading with television: An evaluation of "The Electric Company."* Princeton, New Jersey: Educational Testing Service, 1973.

Balon, R. E. The impact of *Roots* on a racially heterogeneous southern community: An exploratory study. *Journal of Broadcasting*, 1978, *22*(3), 299–307.

Bandura, A. *Aggression: A social learning analysis.* Englewood Cliffs, New Jersey: Prentice-Hall, 1973.

Bechtel, R. B., Achelpohl, C., & Akers, R. Correlates between observed behavior and questionnaire responses on television viewing. In E. A. Rubenstein, G. A. Comstock, & J. P. Murray (Eds.), *Television and social behavior* (Vol. 4). *Television in day-to-day life: Patterns of use*. Washington, D.C.: US Govt. Printing Office, 1972.

Benedict, R. *The chrysanthemum and the sword*. Boston, Massachusetts: Houghton Mifflin, 1946.

Bogart, L. Negro and white media exposure: New evidence. *Journalism Quarterly*, 1972, *49*, 15–21.

Bogatz, G. A., & Ball, S. *The second year of "Sesame Street:" A continuing evaluation*. Princeton, New Jersey: Educational Testing Service, 1971.

Bower, R. T. *Television and the public*. New York: Holt, Rinehart, and Winston, 1973.

Brigham, J. C., & Giesbrecht, L. W. *All in the Family*: Racial attitudes. *Journal of Communication*, 1976, *26*(4), 69–74.

Brown, M. H., Skeen, P., & Osborn, D. K. Young children's perception of the reality of television. *Contemporary Education*, 1979, *50*(3), 129–133.

Cattell, S. H. *Health, welfare, and social organization in Chinatown, New York City*. Report prepared for the New York Department of Public Affairs, 1962.

Caudill, W., & Frost, L. A comparison of maternal care and infant behavior in Japanese-American, American, and Japanese families. In U. Bronfenbrenner (Ed.), *Influences on human development*. Hinsdale, Illinois: Dryden Press, 1972.

Caudill, W., & Weinstein, H. Maternal care and infant behavior in Japan and America. *Psychiatry*, 1969, *32*(1), 12–43.

Chaffee, S. H., & McLeod, J. M. Adolescent television use in the family context. In G. A. Comstock & E.A. Rubenstein (Eds.), *Television and social behavior* (Vol. 3). *Television and adolescent aggressiveness*. Washington, D.C.: US Govt. Printing Office, 1972.

Chaffee, S. H., McLeod, J. M., & Atkin, C. K. *Parent-child similarities in television use*. Paper presented at the Annual Meeting of the Association for Education in Journalism, Washington, D.C., August 1970.

Chaffee, S. H., Ward, L. S., & Tipton, L. P. Mass communication and political socialization. *Journalism Quarterly*, 1970, *47*(4), 647–659; 666.

China through the boob tube. *Bridge*, 1972, *1*(5), 5–6.

Chu, G.C., & Schramm, W. *Learning from television: What the research says*. Palo Alto, California: Stanford University, Institute for Communication Research, 1967.

Chun-Hoon, L. K. Y. Teaching the Asian-American experience. In J. A. Banks (Ed.), *Teaching ethnic studies: Concepts and strategies* (43rd Yearbook). Washington, D.C.: National Council for the Social Studies, 1973.

Comstock, G., Chaffee, S., Katzman, N., McCombs, M., & Roberts, D. *Television and human behavior*. New York: Columbia Univ. Press, 1978.

Comstock, G., & Fisher, M. *Television and human behavior: A guide to the pertinent scientific literature*. Santa Monica, California: Rand Corporation, 1975.

Cook, T. D., Appleton, H., Conner, R. F., Shaffer, A., Tamkin, G., & Weber, S. J. "*Sesame Street*" revisited. New York: Russell Sage Foundation, 1975.

Cooper, E., & Dinerman, H. Analysis of the film *Don't Be A Sucker*: A study in communication. *Public Opinion Quarterly*, 1951, *15*(2), 243–264.

DeVos, G., & Abbott, K. *The Chinese family in San Francisco*. Unpublished master's thesis, University of California, Berkeley, 1966.

Diamond, N. *K'un Shen*. New York: Holt, Rinehart & Winston, 1969.

Dimas, C. *The effect of motion pictures portraying black models on the self-concept of black elementary school children*. Unpublished doctoral dissertation, Syracuse University, 1970.

Division of Asian American Affairs, Office of Special Concerns, Assistant Secretary for Planning & Evaluation, Office of the Secretary, Department of Health, Education, and Welfare. *Asian American field survey: Summary of the data.* Washington, D.C.: US Govt. Printing Office, 1977.

Dominick, J. R., & Greenberg, B. S. Attitudes toward violence: The interaction of television exposure, family attitudes and social class. In G. A. Comstock & E. A. Rubenstein (Eds.), *Television and social behavior* (Vol. 3). *Television and adolescent aggressiveness.* Washington, D.C.: US Govt. Printing Office, 1972.

Farquhar, J., & Doi, M. L. Bruce Lee vs. Fu Manchu: Kung fu films and Asian American stereotypes in America. *Bridge*, 1978, 6(3), 13–50.

Fenz, W., & Arkoff, A. Comparative need patterns of five ancestry groups in Hawaii. *Journal of Social Psychology*, 1962, 58(1), 67–89.

Fletcher, A. D. Negro and white children's television programming preferences. *Journal of Broadcasting*, 1969, 13(4), 359–366.

Fong, K. M. FCC oral arguments of the Chinese Media Committee. Speech presented to the Federal Communications Commission's Hearings on Children's Television, Washington, D.C., January 1973.

Fox, D. J., & Jordan, V. B. Racial preference and identification of black, American Chinese and white children. *Genetic Psychology Monographs*, 1973, 88(2), 229–286.

Frost, L. *Childraising techniques as related to acculturation among Japanese Americans.* Unpublished master's thesis, Sacramento State College, 1968.

Gans, H. J. *The uses of TV and their educational implications: Preliminary findings from a survey of adult and adolescent New York television viewers.* New York: Center for Urban Education, 1968.

Gantz, W. *The routes not taken: A look at the long-term impact of "Roots."* Paper presented at the 61st Annual Meeting of the Association for Education in Journalism, Seattle, Washington, August 1978.

Gerbner, G., & Signorielli, N. *Women and minorities in television drama, 1969–1978.* Philadelphia, Pennsylvania: Univ. of Pennsylvania, Annenberg School of Communications, 1979.

Go, R., & Wong, G. H. *Bad Times on Gold Mountain: A review. Bridge*, 1974, 3(3), 22–27.

Goldberg, A. L. The effects of two types of sound motion pictures on the attitudes of adults toward minorities. *Journal of Educational Sociology*, 1956, 29(9), 386–391.

Gorn, G. J., Goldberg, M. E., & Kanungo, R. N. The role of educational television in changing the intergroup attitudes of children. *Child Development*, 1976, 47(1), 277–280.

Grant, L. *Chan* filming draws local pickets. *Los Angeles Times*, June 25, 1980, Part VI, 3.

Greenberg, B. S. Children's reactions to TV blacks. *Journalism Quarterly*, 1972, 49(1), 5–14.

Greenberg, B. S., & Dervin, B. *Use of the mass media by the urban poor.* New York: Praeger, 1970.

Greenberg, B. S., & Dominick, J. R. Racial and social class differences in teenagers' use of television. *Journal of Broadcasting*, 1969, 13(4), 331–344.

Greenberg, B. S., & Gordon, T. F. Social class and racial differences in children's perceptions of television violence. In G. A. Comstock, E. A. Rubenstein, & J. P. Murray (Eds.), *Television and Social Behavior* (Vol. 5). *Television's effects: Further explorations.* Washington, D.C.: US Govt. Printing Office, 1972.

Greenberg, B. S., & Reeves, B. Children and the perceived reality of television. *Journal of Social Issues*, 1976, 32(4), 86–97.

Guthrie, G. M. *The Filipino child and Philippine society.* Manila: Philippine Normal College Press, 1961.

Guthrie, G. M. Structure of maternal attitudes in two cultures. *Journal of Psychology,* 1966, *62*(1), 155–165.

Guthrie, G. M., & Jacobs, P. J. *Child rearing and personality development in the Philippines.* University Park: Pennsylvania State Univ. Press, 1966.

Harlan, T. A. *Viewing behavior and interpretive strategies of a photographic narrative as a function of variation in story title and subject age.* Unpublished master's thesis, University of Pennsylvania, Annenberg School of Communications, 1972.

Hartmann, P. G., & Husband, C. *Racism and the mass media: A study of the role of the mass media in the formation of white beliefs and attitudes in Britain.* London: Davis-Poynter, 1974.

Hawkins, R. P., Pingree, S., & Roberts, D. F. Watergate and political socialization: The inescapable event. *American Politics Quarterly,* 1975, *3*(4), 406–422.

Hayashi, C. N. An analysis of Asian stereotypes and images in the mass media. Unpublished paper for PASE independent study course, Prof. Robert Cole, University of Michigan, Ann Arbor, 1975.

Howard, J., Rothbart, G., & Sloan, L. The response to *Roots:* A national survey. *Journal of Broadcasting,* 1978, *22*(3), 279–287.

Hsu, F. L. K. *Under the ancestors' shadow.* New York: Columbia Univ. Press, 1948.

Hsu, F. L. K. *The challenge of the American dream: The Chinese in the United States.* Belmont, California: Wadsworth, 1971. (a)

Hsu, F. L. K. *Kinship and culture.* Chicago, Illinois: Aldine, 1971. (b)

Hur, K. K. Impact of *Roots* on black and white teenagers. *Journal of Broadcasting,* 1978, *22*(3), 289–298.

Hur, K. K. & Robinson, J. P. *Roots and Racial attitudes: A cross-national survey.* Paper presented at the 64th Annual Meeting of the Speech Communication Association, Minneapolis, Minnesota, November 1978.

Iiyama, P. In review: *Farewell to Manzanar. The Militant,* April 23, 1976, *40*(16), 28.

Isaacs, H. R. *Scratches on our minds: American images of China and India.* New York: John Day, 1958.

James, S. E. *Behind the scenes: Equal employment opportunity in the motion picture industry.* Los Angeles, California: California Advisory Committee to the U.S. Commission on Civil Rights, 1978.

Kaku, M. Asian Americans for a fair media. *Bridge,* 1973, *2*(6), 40–42.

Katzman, N. I. Violence and color television: What children of different ages learn. In G. A. Comstock, E. A. Rubenstein, & J. P. Murray (Eds.), *Television and social behavior* (Vol. 5). *Television's effects: Further explorations.* Washington, D.C.: US Govt. Printing Office, 1972.

Kim, Y. Y. *A causal model of communication patterns of foreign immigrants in the process of acculturation.* Paper presented at the 62nd Annual Meeting of the Speech Communication Association, San Francisco, California, December 1976.

Kitano, H. H. L. *Japanese-Americans.* Englewood Cliffs, New Jersey: Prentice-Hall, 1969.

Kitano, H. H. L. *Race relations.* Englewood Cliffs, New Jersey: Prentice-Hall, 1974.

Kurtzman, C. R. From hyper-space to rapid transit: George Takei has a new enterprise. *UCLA Summer Bruin,* July 16, 1980, 6–7.

Lampkin, E. C. *Adolescent television use as a possible socialization agent: A cross-cultural comparison.* Unpublished doctoral dissertation, Stanford University, 1976.

Leckenby, J. D., & Surlin, S. H. Incidental social learning and viewer race: *All in the Family* and *Sanford and Son. Journal of Broadcasting,* 1976, *20*(4), 481–494.

Lee, R. H. *The Chinese in the United States of America.* Hong Kong: Hong Kong Univ. Press, 1960.

Lefkowitz, M. M., Eron, L. D., Walder, L. O., & Huesmann, L. R. Television violence and child aggression: A follow-up study. In G. A. Comstock & E. A. Rubenstein (Eds.),

Television and social behavior (Vol.3). *Television and Adolescent Aggressiveness.* Washington, D.C.: US Govt. Printing Office, 1972.

Lehrer, S. G., & Cissna, K. N. L. *Television viewing of selected sixth, seventh, and eighth grade students.* Paper presented at Annual Meeting of International Communication Association, Chicago, Illinois, April 1978.

Leifer, A. D., Collins, W. A., Gross, B. M., Taylor, P. H., Andrews, L., & Blackmer, E. R. Developmental aspects of variables relevant to observational learning. *Child Development,* 1971, 42(5), 1509–1516.

Leifer, A. D., & Roberts, D. F. Children's responses to television violence. In J. P. Murray, E. A. Rubenstein, & G. A. Comstock (Eds.), *Television and social behavior* (Vol. 2). *Television and Social Learning.* Washington, D.C.: US Govt. Printing Office, 1972.

Lesser, H. *Television and the preschool child: A psychological theory of instruction and curriculum development.* New York: Academic Press, 1977.

Li, G. P. Chinese and the media. In C.-T. Wu (Ed.), *"Chink!" A documentary history of anti-Chinese prejudice in America.* New York: World Publishing, 1972. (Originally published in *East/West, The Chinese American Journal,* June 24, 1970.)

Liebert, R. M., Neale, J. M., & Davidson, E. S. *The early window: Effects of television on children and youth.* New York: Pergamon, 1973.

Lind, A. *Hawaii's People.* Honolulu: Univ. of Hawaii Press, 1967.

Lippmann, W. *Public opinion.* New York: Harcourt, Brace, 1922.

Lorch, E. P., Anderson, D. R., & Levin, S. R. The relationship of visual attention to children's comprehension of television. *Child Development,* 1979, 50(3), 722–727.

Lum, G. Heard, but not seen. In C.-T. Wu (Ed.), *"Chink!" A documentary history of anti-Chinese prejudice in America.* New York, World Publishing, 1972. (Originally published in *East/West, The Chinese American Journal,* July 15, 1970.)

Lyle, J. Television in daily life: Patterns of use overview. In E. A. Rubenstein, G. A. Comstock, & J. P. Murray (Eds.), *Television and social behavior* (Vol. 4). *Television in day-to-day life: Patterns of use.* Washington, D.C.: US Govt. Printing Office, 1972.

Lyle, J., & Hoffman, H. R. *Children's use of television and other media.* Los Angeles: University of California, Los Angeles, Department of Journalism, 1971.

Lyle, J., & Hoffman, H. R. Children's use of television and other media. In E. A. Rubenstein, G. A. Comstock, & J. P. Murray (Eds.), *Television and social behavior* (Vol. 4). *Television in day-to-day life: Patterns of use.* Washington, D.C.: US Govt. Printing Office, 1972. (a)

Lyle, J., & Hoffman, H. R. Explorations in patterns of television viewing by preschool-age children. In E. A. Rubenstein, G. A. Comstock, & J. P. Murray (Eds.), *Television and social behavior* (Vol. 4). *Television in day-to-day life: Patterns of use.* Washington, D.C.: US Govt. Printing Office, 1972. (b)

McAllister-Johnson, P. *Interpersonal communication effects of viewing "Roots."* Unpublished doctoral dissertation, University of Wisconsin, Madison, School of Journalism and Communication, 1977.

McIntyre, J. J., & Teevan, J. J., Jr. Television violence and deviant behavior. In G. A. Comstock & E. A. Rubenstein (Eds.), *Television and social behavior* (Vol. 3). *Television and Adolescent Aggressiveness.* Washington, D.C.: US Govt. Printing Office, 1972.

McLeod, J. M., Atkin, C. K., & Chaffee, S. H. Adolescents, parents, and television use: Adolescent self-report measures from Maryland and Wisconsin samples. In G. A. Comstock & E. A. Rubenstein (Eds.), *Television and social behavior* (Vol. 3). *Television and Adolescent Aggressiveness.* Washington, D.C.: US Govt. Printing Office, 1972. (a)

McLeod, J. M., Atkin, C. K., & Chaffee, S. H. Adolescents, parents and television use:

Self-report and other measures from the Wisconsin sample. In G. A. Comstock & E. A. Rubenstein (Eds.), *Television and social behavior* (Vol. 3). *Television and Adolescent Aggressiveness*. Washington, D.C.: US Govt. Printing Office, 1972. (b)

Maykovitch, M. K. *Japanese American identity dilemma*. Tokyo: Waseda Univ. Press, 1972.

Medrich, E. A. *The serious business of growing up: A study of children's lives outside of school*. Children's Time Study, Berkeley: University of California, Berkeley, School of Law, 1977.

Medrich, E. A. Constant television: A background to daily life. *Journal of Communication*, 1979, *29*(3), 171–176.

Moley, R. *The Hays Office*. New York: Bobbs-Merrill, 1945.

Morison, P., McCarthy, M., & Gardner, H. Exploring the realities of television with children. *Journal of Broadcasting*, 1979, *23*(4), 453–463.

Murphy, J. P. *Attributional and inferential strategies in the interpretation of visual communications: A developmental study*. Unpublished doctoral dissertation, University of Pennsylvania, 1973.

Murray, J. P. Television in inner-city homes: Viewing behavior of young boys. In E. A. Rubenstein, G. A. Comstock, & J. P. Murray (Eds.), *Television and social behavior* (Vol. 4). *Television in day-to-day life: Patterns of use*. Washington, D.C.: US Govt. Printing Office, 1972.

Murray, R. L., Cole, R. R., & Fedler, F. Teen-agers and tv violence: How they rate it and view it. *Journalism Quarterly*, 1970, *47*(2), 247–255.

Nagata, K. *A statistical approach to the study of acculturation of an ethnic group based on communication-oriented variables: The case of Japanese Americans in Chicago*. Unpublished doctoral dissertation, University of Illinois at Urbana-Champagne, 1969.

Neely, J. J., Heckel, R. V., & Leichtman, H. M. The effect of race of model and response consequences to the model on imitation in children. *Journal of Social Psychology*, 1973, *89*(2), 225–231.

Nicholas, K. B., McCarter, R. E., & Heckel, R. V. The effects of race and sex on the imitation of television models. *Journal of Social Psychology*, 1971, *85*(2), 315–316.

Ogawa, D. M. *From Japs to Japanese: An evolution of Japanese-American stereotypes*. Berkeley, California: McCutchen, 1971.

Okamura, R. Y. *Farewell to Manzanar*: A case of sublimal racism. *Amerasia Journal*, 1976, *3*(2), 143–148.

Ormiston, L. H., & Williams, S. *Saturday children's programming in San Francisco, California: An analysis of the presentation of racial and cultural groups on three network-affiliated San Francisco television stations*. Speech presented to the Federal Communications Commission's Hearing on Children's Television, Washington, D.C., January 1973.

Paik, I. That Oriental feeling: A look at the caricatures of the Asians as sketched by American movies. In A. Tachiki, E. Wong, F. Odo, & B. Wong (Eds.), *Roots: An Asian American reader*. Los Angeles: University of California, Los Angeles, Asian American Studies Center, 1971.

Parker, E. B. *The functions of television for children*. Unpublished doctoral dissertation, Stanford University, 1960.

Peterson, R. C. & Thurstone, L. L. *Motion pictures and the social attitudes of children*. New York: MacMillan, 1933.

Price, F. T. *Some effects of film mediated professional models on the self-perceptions of black school children*. Unpublished doctoral dissertation, Wayne State University, 1970.

Reeves, B. Children's understanding of television people. In E. Wartella (Ed.), *Children communicating: Media and development of thought, speech, understanding.* Beverly Hills, California: Sage, 1979.

Roberts, D. F., Herold, C., Hornby, M., King, S., Sterne, D., Whiteley, S., & Silverman, L. T. *"Earth's a Big Blue Marble:" A report of the impact of a children's television series on children's opinions.* Palo Alto: Stanford University, California Institute for Communication Research, 1974.

Robinson, J. P. Toward defining the functions of television. In E. A. Rubenstein, G. A. Comstock, & J. P. Murray (Eds.), *Television and social behavior* (Vol. 4). *Television in day-to-day-life: Patterns of use.* Washington, D.C.: US Govt. Printing Office, 1972.

Robinson, J. P., & Bachman, J. G. Television viewing habits and aggression. In G. A. Comstock & E. A. Rubenstein (Eds.), *Television and social behavior* (Vol. 3). *Television and adolescent aggressiveness.* Washington, D.C.: US Govt. Printing Office, 1972.

Rosekrans, M. A. Imitation in children as a function of perceived similarity to a social model and vicarious reinforcement. *Journal of Personality and Social Psychology,* 1967, 7(3), 307–315.

Rubin, V. Personal communication, May 7, 1981.

Ryu, J. S. *Mass media's role in the assimilation process: A study of Korean immigrants in the Los Angeles area.* Paper presented at the Annual Meeting of the International Communication Association, Chicago, Illinois, April 1978.

Scherer, K. R. Stereotype change following exposure to counter-stereotypical media heroes. *Journal of Broadcasting,* 1970–1971, 15(1), 91–100.

Schramm, W., Lyle, J., & Parker, E. B. *Television in the lives of our children.* Palo Alto, California: Stanford Univ. Press, 1961.

Singer, B. D. Mass society, mass media and the transformation of minority identity. *British Journal of Sociology,* 1973, 24(2), 140–150.

Springer, D. V. Awareness of racial differences in pre-school children in Hawaii. *Genetic Psychology Monographs,* 1950, 41(2), 214–270.

Springer, D. V. National-racial preferences of fifth grade children in Hawaii. *Journal of Genetic Psychology,* 1953, 83, 121–136.

Stein, A. H., & Friedrich, L. K. Television content and young children's behavior. In J. P. Murray, E. A. Rubenstein, & G. A. Comstock (Eds.), *Television and social behavior* (Vol. 2). *Television and social learning.* Washington, D.C.: US Govt. Printing Office, 1972.

Su, S. G. *The Chinese family system.* New York: Columbia Univ. Press, 1922.

Surgeon General's Scientific Advisory Committee on Television and Social Behavior. *Television and growing up: The impact of televised violence.* Report to the Surgeon General, United States Public Health Service. Washington, D.C.: US Govt. Printing Office, 1972.

Surlin, S. H. Bigotry on air and in life: The Archie Bunker case. *Public Communications Review,* 1974, 2, 34–41.

Surlin, S. H. *Roots* research: A summary of findings. *Journal of Broadcasting,* 1978, 22(3), 309–320.

Surlin, S. H., & Cooper, C. F. *"The Jeffersons" and their racially integrated neighbors: Who watches and who is offended?* Paper presented at the Annual Meeting of the Southern Speech Communication Association, San Antonio, Texas, April 1976.

Surlin, S. H., & Dominick, J. R. Television's function as a "third parent" for black and white teenagers. *Journal of Broadcasting,* 1970–1971, 15(1), 55–64.

Surlin, S. H., & Tate, E. D. *All in the Family:* Is Archie Bunker funny? *Journal of Communication,* 1976, *26*(4), 61–68.

Tan, A. S., & Tan, G. Television use and self-esteem of blacks. *Journal of Communication,* 1979, *29*(1), 129–135.

Tate, E. D., & Surlin, S. H. Agreement with opinionated television characters across cultures. *Journalism Quarterly,* 1976, *53*(2), 199–203.

Teahan, J. E., & Podany, E. C. Some effects of films of successful blacks on racial self-concept. *International Journal of Social Psychiatry,* 1974, *20*(3–4), 274–280.

Tolley, H., Jr. *Children and war: Political socialization to international conflict.* New York: Columbia University, Teachers College Press, 1973.

U.S. Commission on Civil Rights. *Window dressing on the set: Women and minorities in television.* Washington, D.C.: US Govt. Printing Office, 1977.

Vidmar, N., & Rokeach, M. Archie Bunker's bigotry: A study in selective perception and exposure. *Journal of Communication,* 1974, *24*(2), 36–47.

Ward, S., Robertson, T. S., & Wackman, D. *Children's attention to television advertising.* Proceedings of the Association for Consumer Research Conference, College Park, Maryland, 1971.

Ward, S., & Wackman, D. Children's information processing of television advertising. In P. Clarke (Ed.), *Annual reviews of communication research* (Vol. 2). *New models for mass communication research.* Beverly Hills, California: Sage, 1973.

Whiting, B. B. (Ed.). *Six cultures, Studies of child rearing.* New York: Wiley, 1963.

Winick, M. P., & Winick, C. *The television experience: What children see.* Beverly Hills, California: Sage, 1979.

Wolf, M. *House of Lim.* New York: Appleton-Century-Crofts, 1968.

Wu, C.-T. (Ed.). *"Chink!" A documentary history of anti-Chinese prejudice in America.* New York: World, 1972.

Yankelovich, Skelly and White, Inc. *A trend report on the role and penetration of "Sesame Street" in ghetto communities (Bedford Stuyvesant, East Harlem, Chicago, and Washington, D.C.).* New York: Children's Television Workshop, 1978.

Yee, A. H. Myopic perceptions and textbooks: Chinese Americans' search for identity. *Journal of Social Issues,* 1973, *29*(2), 99–113.

Joann Sebastian Morris

Television Portrayal and the Socialization of the American Indian Child

Many hundreds of years ago, at the beginning of history, our wise men foretold of the coming of other peoples to this land. They foresaw a time of rapid change and confusion in which our youth would be growing into adulthood unprepared to cope with these new conditions. We, the Native American people, are now at that very point in our history and we must take account of our responsibility to our young.
—Coalition of Indian Controlled School Boards, 1975, p. 2.

After 20 years of research, social scientists recognized that television viewing shapes children's values, attitudes, and, subsequently, their behaviors. Psychologist Albert Bandura has demonstrated that children learn by observation and readily imitate complex behavior patterns, even without reinforcement (Baran & Meyer, 1974). The extent to which the prosocial and antisocial behaviors of children are affected by television continues to be a growing concern (Moore, 1977).

The study by Coates, Pusser, and Goodman (1976) on the effect of television viewing on the free-play behavior of preschool children demonstrated that children who viewed programs that displayed only positive behaviors increased significantly their positive social behavior and total social contacts. More importantly, for those interested in the behavioral effects on ethnic minorities, particularly American Indian

TELEVISION AND
THE SOCIALIZATION OF THE MINORITY CHILD

youngsters, it was found that those children who were more reluctant to participate socially were even more positively affected by viewing sociable behavior on television. This finding confirms an earlier study by O'Connor (1972) in which it was found that the behavior of children who were reluctant to interact with others was positively influenced by viewing curriculum films depicting sociable models. These two studies have a direct bearing on American Indians since native youngsters are frequently more hesitant to interact socially with others, particularly with those not of their ethnic group and occasionally even with those not of their tribal group.

Attitudes likewise are affected by television viewing. Positive changes in attitudes toward ethnically different children were found in a study by Gorn, Goldberg, and Kanungo (1976), wherein white Canadian preschool children, who viewed *Sesame Street* with segments depicting minority children at play added, showed a greater preference for minority children to visit their school in contrast with the preschoolers who did not view the special segments. This particular study is also significant to American Indians since it demonstrates the benefits that could be derived from increased and improved television programming that would portray American Indians and their culture in a positive, or even neutral, manner.

There is scant data in social science literature that records the effects of television portrayal specifically on American Indian youngsters. Little if any research has been conducted with American Indian children in spite of the fact that, of all ethnic groups, American Indians are probably the most underrepresented and negatively depicted in the alternate reality created by television.

STEREOTYPES AND AMERICAN INDIANS

It is interesting to note that many people still consider research into the effects of television viewing to be relatively new. The general public is itself basically unaware of the actions of numerous researchers and community action groups concerned with this issue. As early as 1960, American Indian groups began protesting the television portrayal of tribal peoples. In that year the Oklahoma Legislature, after receiving considerable pressure from its large American Indian population, denounced the portrayal of American Indians in a resolution which read in part,

> There is no excuse for TV producers to ignore the harm that may be done the children of America by repetitious distortion of historical facts per-

taining to the way of life of any race or creed, including the American Indian. Many television programs show Indians as bloodthirsty marauders and murderers [U.S. Commission on Civil Rights, 1977, p. 6].

To the extent that children's behavior and values are affected by television, relations between Indian and non-Indian youngsters are affected by television's narrow and usually stereotyped portrayal of American Indians. The most common Indian characters viewed on the television screen are depicted as simple, lazy, wasteful, and humorless; they are shown as lacking intelligence and English-speaking skills and as believing in heathenistic nonsense for a religion. This portrayal was begun in the cheaply made western films and later carried over into television westerns.

The stereotype's visual image is generally that of a Plains Indian. There are hundreds of tribes still in existence, each with its own housing style, language, religion, and other distinguishing cultural aspects. Yet the differences are obscured by the monotonous image ascribed to American Indians by television producers, directors, and writers. American Indians are all visualized as wearing beaded and fringed leather garb, hunting buffalo, living in tipis, and moving constantly. Those tribal groups who wore woven cotton garments, those who ate fish or acorns as their staple, those who resided in open-air or subterranean houses, along with those who moved only once a year or were sedentary are all obscured in the name of simplifying someone's concept of an American Indian for a television audience. Tribal diversity is especially lacking when American Indian characters are used in historical scenes in which they play minor roles. The unimportance of their individual and collective identity is underscored. They become faceless, nameless, and tribeless.

American Indian women are either ignored altogether or included solely as background characters. They are relegated to lesser roles in which they generally depict quiet, passive, dull, and hard-working women. The respect and independence experienced by many American Indian women from numerous tribes is never delineated for television audiences. One does not see portrayals of Navajo or Mohawk women who live in matrilineal societies and wield considerable power in the governmental affairs and economics of the tribe.

Other negative and erroneous stereotypes continue to surface in television programming. In television programs depicting the time immediately after the taming of the West, American Indian characters are rarely seen. When included, their role is still not a positive or popular one. They are frequently represented as half-breeds, perhaps in an attempt to depict the merging of two cultures. That many American

Indian people who survived the transition period underwent massive cultural shock is never addressed. When the culture conflict is acknowledged, it is generally represented by a character who is pathetic, alcoholic, and occasionally begging.

Even when contemporary American Indians are shown on television, the majority of programs including them continue to be of a documentary style. They may discuss life on a particular reservation, but most do not relay information about American Indians residing in urban areas, even though one-half of the American Indian population currently resides in nonreservation settings. On those rare occasions when American Indians are depicted in a contemporary setting, they are too often stereotyped as militant activists. Although this is one reality for some American Indians, the portrayal is still a negative one, particularly in the eyes of non-Indian viewers.

Rarely have Indian portrayals been positive or contemporary with their time. Whether the time period illustrated is historical or depicts the period of contact and cultural confusion or whether it stresses contemporary life, the role of the American Indian is generally not a positive one. Few social scientists have attempted to explain this overall negative image of the American Indian. Some American Indians argue that in order to justify the unfair treatment afforded most American Indian groups, even those considered "friendly," early American leaders had to convince the uninformed majority to believe that all Indians were untrustworthy, uncivilized, and unworthy of fair treatment. In such a climate was born the first anti-Indian public relations campaign.

Negative references to American Indians was the easiest way to influence public attitudes. Another tactic was to simply ignore American Indians as members of American society to keep them out of the national conscience of sympathetic Americans. Either way, the result remained the same: An unfair and inaccurate image of American Indians was created.

During interviews with a variety of television industry personnel conducted by Thomas Baldwin and Colby Lewis, it was discovered that among the networks' guidelines regarding the portrayal of minorities there exist many specific "do's" and "don'ts" regarding American Indians. Baldwin and Lewis learned that in westerns, certain types of violence are not to be inflicted on Indians. One such guideline states that "Your Indians have to decide to give up before a fight [U.S. Commission on Civil Rights, 1977, p. 69]." Not only are American Indians shown as savages, but as inept savages at that, helpless victims of the white man's superiority.

The limitations imposed on television producers are acknowledged, but not condoned, by informed American Indian community members.

We recognize that most television producers feel that they do not have sufficient time to develop complex situations or characters. We further understand their need to move the action rapidly and to simplify characters for easy viewer identification. Yet, by oversimplifying situations and stereotyping characters, television creates a distorted view of reality. This is dangerous since it has been found that children, particularly the very young, believe that television presents them with a valid picture of the real world (Paul, 1971).

For American Indians, who are generally portrayed negatively and only in an historical context, this spells disaster. It is little wonder that so many elementary-school-age children believe that American Indians are bad and, thankfully, do not exist any longer. It is hard for them to make the transition from the forest creature they have always heard about to the American Indian guest lecturer standing before them in the classroom wearing everyday clothes and speaking Standard English. This contradiction between the television image and the real world should not exist today.

TRAITS OF TELEVISION CHARACTERS

It may be helpful to review the data gathered by the U.S. Commission on Civil Rights regarding minorities and women in television (1977) to acquire an objective reporting on recent practices. The data used in their analysis was compiled by the University of Pennsylvania. The sample programs consisted of those telecast between 8 A.M. and 11 P.M. daily and children's noncartoon programs broadcast on Saturdays. One week of fall season programming was videotaped and carefully coded for each year of the study (1969–1974); however, ethnic breakdown of the nonwhite characters was only available for 1973 and 1974. To be included in the analysis, characters had to play a speaking role. Major characters were those in leading roles central to the story; all others were considered minor.

Some enlightening statistics about minority characterization in general are worth mentioning before speaking directly to the limited data on American Indians. The total number of major and minor characters in the 6-year sample was 5624. The largest proportion of all characters, 65.3%, were white males. White females constituted 23.8% of all characters, nonwhite males 8.6%, and nonwhite females only 2.3%. These statistics alone point out the discrepancy between the world depicted on television and the real world. Whereas males (white and nonwhite) actually constitute only 48.6% of the United States population, on television they represent 73.9% of the characters depicted.

Women were gravely underrepresented in contrast with reality, particularly minority women. When the ages of television characters were considered, it was found that again the television world differs from reality. Although 21- to 50-year-olds are frequently portrayed, both the very young and the elderly are ignored. Whereas white males were most often portrayed as older and more mature, minority males and all females were most often depicted as younger and less mature. It was also demonstrated that television showed a middle-class world where the characters were more likely to be rich than poor. Among the few characters who were very poor, 7.4% were minority males and 5.0% were minority females; only .6% were white males and none were white females.

After 1973, the data gathered on nonwhite television characters could be identified by ethnic group. In the 1973 sample, the total number of American Indian characters was only 4 of a total 109, or 3.7%. The following year, the total number of characters portraying Indians was only 8 of 115, or 7.0%. Although the figures doubled, it would be erroneous to conclude that American Indians were being portrayed in twice as many programs. Table 9.1 demonstrates that although larger numbers of American Indians appeared, they were still only depicted in two different series in each sample year. Television producers may attempt to increase their overall count of minorities, but these minority characters are frequently shown in groups and are all involved in the same activity.

Table 9.1 also points to another area of concern to American Indians, and that is the occupations in which they are depicted. In the 1973–1974 sample, only six distinct occupational roles were assigned to American Indian characters. Of the six, four were historical occupations (chief, guide, adventurer, and hunter) while only two were contemporary (ranch foreman and sheriff's deputy). Yet even the two contemporary roles still smack of stereotyping since they were occupations set in the West and out of doors. All too frequently, when American Indians are finally being portrayed in a contemporary setting, their roles are either as militants, at one end of the social spectrum, or at the opposite end, as "regulators"; that is, as supporters of the status quo. It should also be noted that two native characters were cast as unemployed and the occupations of two others were unknown or unspecified.

The issue of how American Indians are typecast into particular stereotyped occupations is of central importance since research has shown that children learn from television occupational portrayals (DeFleur & DeFleur, 1967). The damage done to American Indian children

TABLE 9.1
Sex and Occupation of American Indian Characters in Prime-Time Television Sample, 1973–1974[a]

Year	Importance of character	Total minority characters	Total Indian characters	Male Indians			Female Indians		
				Number	Role	Program	Number	Role	Program
1973	Major	21	1 (4.8%)	1	Ranch foreman	Walt Disney	0	—	—
	Minor	88	3 (3.4%)	2	Chief Guide	Buck and the Preacher	1	Unknown	Buck and the Preacher
1974	Major	29	3 (10.3%)	2	Sheriff's deputy Adventurer	Nakia Walt Disney	1	Unemployed (Eskimo)	Walt Disney
	Minor	86	5 (5.8%)	5	Hunters (3) (Eskimo) Unemployed Unknown	Walt Disney Nakia	0	—	—

[a] Compiled from data from the U.S. Commission on Civil Rights (1977).

who consistently see their people in noncontemporary, nonprofessional roles could be great indeed. One must keep in mind that thus far the discussion has centered solely on the number and occupations of American Indians portrayed in the 1973–1974 samples. No data was available to determine if the Indian characters were portraying positive or negative personalities. Nor was data provided to allow a discussion of who played American Indian roles. Too often, tribal peoples are still being played by non-Indian actors and actresses.

LACK OF AMERICAN INDIAN VISIBILITY

If we take a look at other aspects of the television industry, one can easily see that American Indians are still grossly underrepresented or simply ignored. In television commercials it is rare that American Indians are depicted. Only recently does one occasionally see a young Indian woman advertising a brand of corn oil, but here again stereotyping is evident due to the suggestive mental association between American Indians and *maize*. Rarely does an American Indian child view an American Indian playmate on television, even in toy commercials. Nor are American Indian mothers or family groups seen in commercials. Children's programs, including those on educational television stations, rarely include American Indian characters nor do they interview or film real American Indian children, even in settings purported to be multi-ethnic. Within the last few years a Cree singer, Buffy Sainte-Marie, has involved herself with the *Sesame Street* series. She has appeared with her Sioux husband and their son in order to allow all children, especially American Indian youngsters to see a contemporary American Indian family, a definite rarity on television.

Although situation comedies have been written for other ethnic groups, none have been developed for American Indians. How are people ever going to begin seeing American Indians as regular human beings if they are never portrayed as such. Although there is a vast array of religious programs on the air, rarely does one find so much as a discussion of the various American Indian religions. That Congress finally passed the Indian Religious Freedom Act in August, 1978, never even made the news.

Although there are occasional musical salutes on television or specials highlighting serious music, traditional American Indian music and the works of contemporary American Indian musicians are rarely heard. Neither the ballet or opera composed by Quapaw musician Louis

Ballard has ever been performed on television. From where are talented American Indian children to gain their inspiration? Although there is a wide variety of talk shows on the air, it is the exception to find an American Indian as guest. Does this say to American Indian youngsters that their people are not interesting or newsworthy?

There is today more interest in and emphasis on television news programs. Networks vie for status as the station with the best news coverage. Yet there appears to be something akin to a blackout on American Indian news. Although energy is the topic of the times, there is little news time devoted to understanding the complex relationship between the United States government and the Council of Energy Resource Tribes (CERT), a coalition of 25 Indian tribes that still hold important mineral resources on their reservation lands. On those infrequent occasions when CERT has been alluded to, it is erroneously labeled an OPEC-like organization. Although uranium has been mined for years in the Southwest, the high incidence of uranium poisoning among Navajos is not disclosed on the news. Nor do we hear of the fluoride pollution of Mohawks on the St. Regis Reservation on the New York–Canada border. Nor are the disputes over Chippewa hunting and fishing regulations on reservations in Michigan and Minnesota ever reported. When major demonstrations are taking place across the nation, American Indian parents and their children do not hear about it on television. Generally, these communities must rely on American Indian newspapers to inform them. When American Indians attempt to gain television coverage of a march or demonstration, the hardest task is to convince the media to focus on the issues involved rather than to sensationalize the demonstration itself.

In their 1977 report, the U.S. Commission on Civil Rights summarized, "women and minorities rarely make the news. Most newsmakers are white male government officials and public figures [p. 54]." Their comment came after analyzing the news programs broadcast on ABC, CBS, and NBC on randomly selected dates between March, 1974 and February, 1975. A total of 230 news stories were analyzed; of these only two related to American Indians. The stories reported a denial of American Indians' voting rights and the evacuation of American Indians from a monastery in Wisconsin. Although the Indians had occupied the monastery for 34 days and wanted to present the issues underlying the takeover, no Americans Indians appeared in the news story. How are American Indian children to know the events that are shaping their lives? How will they ever feel a part of this society if they never hear about their people on the news? And how can they be instilled with a sense of pride when what little news coverage exists is slanted or sensationalized?

Not only is the image of the American Indian in the news a serious concern, but so is the lack of native newscasters. In a study conducted by the U.S. Commission on Civil Rights (1977), the ethnicity of the 85 correspondents in sampled newscasts was identified, and not one was an American Indian. Within the entire television industry, the number of American Indian employees is minimal. During the U.S. Commission on Civil Rights' investigation into the race, sex, and job classification of employees at 40 television stations across the nation in 1975, it was found that American Indians accounted for only 22 (.3%) of the 8176 employees sampled. These 13 males and 9 females were divided among the job classifications in the following manner: 2 female professionals, 9 male technicians, 1 male sales worker, 1 male and 7 females in office and clerical staff, and 2 male craftsmen. There were no American Indian officials or managers. Although that study was published in 1977, it is doubtful that these figures have changed significantly.

A final area not yet elaborated on, and one that usually provides a negative characterization of American Indians, is the television western. It is probably most responsible for maintaining America's negative attitude toward its American Indian population. Nowhere else are we so consistently and callously shown as whooping savages bent only on destruction. The disorienting effect on young American Indian children has been seen time and again. Due to the propagandizing in these films and the extreme oversimplification of who are the good and the bad guys, very young American Indian children have been observed cheering for the cavalry! Once American Indian youngsters recognize what they are doing, their behavior frequently follows a patterned sequence: from naivete to confusion, disillusionment and eventually distrust. American Indian children should not have to undergo such ego-shattering experiences. They should not have doubts placed in their minds about their own self-worth and value.

If one were required to summarize the two greatest deficiencies within the television industry in its relationship with American Indians, they would be in the areas of recognition and respect. Television writers and producers must recognize the very existence of American Indians in our society today; they can no longer be ignored. Although Los Angeles is known as the entertainment capital of the world, those involved in the industry are unaware that Los Angeles also houses the largest concentration of American Indians (approximately 90,000) of any urban center in the country. It is an injustice to continue to ignore

American Indians as a discrete segment of the United States population. This recognition must be forthcoming from the television networks.

The television industry must also learn respect for American Indian people and for their tribal cultures and customs. They must be allowed, at least in the media, to function totally within American society and not on the periphery as outsiders. Television decision makers can no longer justify depicting American Indians in stereotyped images. It has long been time to present an updated, positive, and factual image of American Indians to viewing audiences. The American Indian people should have a voice in determining what material is culturally accurate and what is sensationalized or stereotyped. This affected the 1980 battle that raged between the American Indian community and Warner Bros. Studios, which was unwilling to listen to respected American Indian leaders and elders, particularly from the Sioux nations. Warner Bros. wanted to produce a mini-series based on the book *Hanta Yo*, which had been shown to be erroneous, damaging to the image of American Indians, and a distorted account of traditional Sioux life (Deloria, 1980). Respect for American Indian people, and particularly for the Sioux nations, would dictate that an alternate program be considered. To obtain such respect, sensitivity to issues revolving around the image of American Indians must be increased.

IMPLICATIONS FOR AMERICAN INDIAN CHILDREN

If American Indian children spend many hours of their youthful lives watching television programs that tell them that their own tribe and entire race are to be despised and ignored, there is little doubt that the mental health of these children will be gravely affected. In most American Indian homes, parents attempt to instill a sense of pride in their young ones. And many American Indian communities across the country are revitalizing their ceremonies, languages, and customs. Yet all the work of community and parents can be undermined from within the home by television. The view of themselves and their race that American Indian children receive from their parents is generally one that incorporates many positive characteristics. Yet that viewpoint is not compatible with the way the children see their tribesmen depicted by television networks. Many adult American Indians will admit to a sense of personal disorientation in childhood. They recall wondering why nonIndians treated them as if it was not acceptable to be an American Indian. Future generations of American Indian children should not have to grow up with similar doubts.

The primary message conveyed by television is that to be an American Indian is neither good nor valued. Under this influence American Indian children are unable to perceive themselves or their tribesmen in a positive manner and their sense of self-worth is lessened. If one's self-esteem is low, one's desire and ability to improve, grow, and accept challenges are hampered. If one does not feel worthy, life holds few positive adventures. Educators have seen the dramatic effects of a low sense of self-esteem in the statistics available on the high school drop-out rate for American Indian youth, which is at least three times higher than the national average. A major reason for this is the feeling of alienation from and rejection by the majority culture (Demmert, 1976).

Television is harmful to American Indian children in another, less overt way. Either directly or indirectly, television espouses the values of the dominant society. Yet many white values have been demonstrated to be in almost direct opposition to traditional American Indian values. While most American Indian cultures revere cooperation, sharing, the wisdom that comes with old age, and living in balance with nature, for example, television programming instills the opposing white values of competition, materialism, youthfulness, and progress at the expense of nature. Such a conflict in values causes further frustration and personality disorientation. American Indian children question which values they should adhere to and live by. The television industry should take a hard look at the values they impose on the public and ask whether other values are not deserving of equal time.

Since television is a visual media, it may have an even more profound effect on American Indian children than has ever been imagined or fully documented, particularly those living in the Southwest. Many social scientists and educators agree that American Indian children are visual, rather than verbal, in their approach to the world. During a study on a southwestern tribe (John, 1972), it was observed that in the classroom, Navajo children, although attentive to the teacher's voice, tend more to observe her actions. Whereas middle-class urban children are expected to display their knowledge and growing skills verbally, southwestern American Indian children make primary use of their observational skills. In the traditional American Indian home, little emphasis is placed on being verbose. It appears obvious, then, that although improved scripts and narratives relating to American Indians are imperative, the visual image must also be updated and made more positive since American Indian youth are more strongly influenced by visual media than by verbal ones. This inclination toward visual stimuli raises concerns about the full extent to which American Indian youngsters are daily influenced by television programs. Further research in this area is indicated.

American Indian children are also indirectly affected by television's stereotypes about American Indians since the teachers instructing and influencing them have usually been raised on a diet of the same negative television programs. These educators frequently make erroneous and invalid assumptions about American Indian culture and pass them on to their students during class lessons. Many teachers still consider American Indian life to be alien and undesirable and therefore work with renewed vigor to steer American Indian students away from it. Teachers' attitudes are particularly important since 99% of American Indian children are taught by non-Indian instructors (Demmert, 1976). As sensitive as American Indian children are to nonverbal actions and attitudes, they easily sense the teacher's inherent, albeit possibly unconscious, racism and prejudice toward their race. Consider also the trauma imposed on some American Indian children who feel the need to speak up in defense of their culture. The intestinal fortitude required of a young American Indian to stand up in a classroom or an auditorium to correct an adult, particularly an authority figure, is considerable. If television would improve its recognition of and respect for American Indian life, fewer children would have to suffer these indignations.

It is not enough to speak solely about the effects that television portrayals of American Indians may have on the American Indian child; one must also consider the effects on non-Indian children. Although the consequences to the American Indian child are more personal and immediate, non-Indian youngsters are affected nonetheless. They, too, ingest the negative messages delivered on the television screen. Some of these ill-informed youngsters are likely to taunt and tease American Indian classmates. Many are the instances where native children begin denying they are American Indian after such altercations. Non-Indian youths eventually grow up and, if no one has provided them with alternative, positive attitudes toward American Indians, they may go through their entire adult life harboring negative feelings toward them.

It would be erroneous to blame television programming and its poor portrayal of American Indians for all identity problems facing American Indian children and adults; television alone is not the culprit. American Indian tribes are unfortunate enough to also have to combat the negative stereotyping still found in certain newspapers; in outdated, racist texts and other books; in films, pictures, study prints, and other materials, even those specifically designed for classroom use, such as record albums that patronizingly attempt to teach Indian song and dance. All these factors work together to reinforce a negative image of the American Indian. It is, therefore, crucial to focus attention on this issue and to work toward the eventual eradication of these false and unhealthy attitudes.

SUMMARY AND RECOMMENDATIONS

The main goal of this chapter was to bring attention to information about research into the effects of television as it relates to American Indians, to demonstrate the almost total lack of positive portrayals on the television screen, and to indicate some of the damage done to the mental health of American Indian children due to the industry-induced negative visual image of their race.

It is equally as important to speak to the issue of altering this present pattern. The two major functions of television are to entertain and to inform. Yet in neither of these areas are American Indians accurately or positively depicted, if they are shown at all. Television networks must, therefore, be made to become more responsible, to the American Indian community, particularly, and to the general public. Researchers and educators must also involve themselves further to make their influence and pressure felt.

It is difficult to present scientific data relative to the effects of television portrayal on the American Indian child due to the paucity of research with an American Indian sample population. Not only is this type of research badly needed, but there is also a great need for research into ways to mitigate stereotypes. Additionally, researchers might consider looking at what specific factors (societal, environmental, etc.) will reinforce positive behavior in American Indian children.

Given that television teaches primarily white, middle-class values, that it influences attitudes and behaviors, and that not all cultures adhere to those same values, it would be helpful to American Indian and non-Indian parents alike if networks would make programs available that would promote the cultural values of other ethnic groups, thereby demonstrating the diversity that realistically exists in this country. In this way, the television industry would make its programming more compatible with reality, rather than perpetuating its own biased version of reality.

It has also been demonstrated that instructional television programs can be developed to teach children more accepting attitudes toward people whose cultures differ from theirs. More work in this area is needed, particularly in the development of curriculum materials that would teach self-esteem. Friedrich and Stein (1975) found that children's television programs can have greater impact when followed up with additional activities and discussion. This thought needs to be carried back to the classroom. If teachers utilize television programs that cultivate appreciation for other cultures as a part of their regular program, and if they discuss these aspects with their students, the program and its message become imbued with special importance. This approach needs to be spread throughout all educational institutions across the country.

Colleges and universities that educate the future leaders of the television networks likewise have a responsibility to promote the positive aspects of cultural diversity and the need for an improved image of the American Indian, as well as other ethnic minorities. College-level courses must also promote the two ideals of respect for and recognition of others, those ideals disclosed earlier as being desperately needed within the television industry.

REFERENCES

Baran, S. J., & Meyer, T. P. Imitation and identification: Two compatible approaches to social learning from the electronic media. *AV Communication Review*, 1974, 22, 167–179.

Coalition of Indian Controlled School Boards. *Newsletter*, 1975, 4, 2.

Coates, B., Pusser, E., & Goodman, I. The influence of *Sesame Street* and *Mister Roger's Neighborhood* on children's social behavior in the preschool. *Child Development*, 1976, 47, 138–144.

De Fleur, M. L., & De Fleur, L. B. The relative contribution of television as a learning source for children's occupational knowledge. *American Sociological Review*, 1967, 32, 789.

Deloria, V. Jr. The twisted world of Hanta Yo. *Minority Notes*, 1980, 8–9.

Demmert, W. G., Jr. Indian education: Where and whither. *American Education*, 1976, 12, 6–9.

Friedrich, L. K., & Stein, A. H. Aggressive and prosocial television programs and the natural behavior of preschool children. *Monographs of the Society for Research in Child Development*, 1975, 38(4, Serial No. 151).

Gorn, G. J., Goldberg, M. E., & Kanungo, R. N. The role of educational television in changing the intergroup attitudes of children. *Child Development*, 1976, 47, 277–280.

John, C. P. Style of learning—styles of teaching: Reflections on the education of Navajo children. In C. B. Cazden, V. P. John, & D. Hymes (Eds.), *Functions of language in the classroom*. New York: Columbia Univ. Press, 1972.

Moore, S. G. Effects of television on the prosocial behavior of young children. *Young Children*, 1977, 32, 60–65.

O'Connor, R. C. Modification of social withdrawal through symbolic modeling. In K. D.
    O'Leary & S. G. O'Leary (Eds.), *Classroom management*. New York: Pergamon,
    1972.
Paul, N. L. Invisible factors in a child's reaction to television. *Childhood Education*,
    1971, *47*, 303–306.
U.S. Commission on Civil Rights. *Window dressing on the set: Women and minorities in
    television*. Washington, D.C.: US Govt. Printing Office, 1977.

M. Beatriz Arias

Educational Television: Impact on the Socialization of the Hispanic Child

According to the 1978 report of the Bureau of the Census (U.S. Department of Commerce, 1979), there are over 3 million students of Hispanic origin enrolled in elementary and secondary public education programs in the United States. This large population of children—over 7% of the total school-age population—offers many challenges to the more traditional forms of classroom instruction as a result of the linguistic and cultural dissimilarities between these students' home and school settings. Educators have looked to innovations found in bilingual and bicultural programs, specialized teacher education programs, and multicultural curriculum development as methods of modifying the existing classroom for the educational needs of children from Hispanic backgrounds. They have also looked to educational television as one way of supplementing and enhancing these new programs.

Children are heavy consumers of television programming and there is some evidence that children of Hispanic backgrounds also follow this general trend. Comstock et al. (1978) note that children aged 2–11 view on an average of 27.6 hr of television per week and teenagers 12–17 view an average of 21.9 hr per week. They also note that there seems to be an inverse relationship between income level and amount of formal education that the head of the household obtained and

203

TELEVISION AND
THE SOCIALIZATION OF THE MINORITY CHILD

the amount of television a child in that household views. Lyle and Hoffman (1972), conducted a study of television viewing patterns by preschool-age children in Los Angeles, California, that included a sample of Chicano children. They found that 98% of the children liked to watch television. Chicano preschoolers in this sample seemed also to watch slightly more television than their black or white peers.

This chapter examines the role educational television has played in addressing the linguistic and attitudinal needs of Hispanic students. It includes:

1. An overview of the Hispanic image on television
2. A review of educational television programs specifically targeted for a bilingual/bicultural audience
3. A synthesis of research findings regarding the impact of such programming on students socialization

In the 1970s, there has been an increasing recognition among researchers that although television may play an effective role in the socialization of children, it cannot be considered the direct and only cause of social behavior. Comstock and Colbey (1978) emphasize that socialization is a process of many interactions and that television is only one contending force among a full array of other socializing agents. The difficulty of isolating and demonstrating a causal relationship between television and socialization among the numerous uncontrollable variables of the cultural environment surrounding a child is underscored in a discussion by Asante (1978) on television's impact on black children's language. This difficulty should not lead researchers to totally discount the effect of television on socialization but to study further the compounding effects of television and other socializing agents. Nevertheless, television has come to be viewed as the most prominent medium for the socialization of children in contemporary society. Leifer and Roberts (1972) note that the large amount of time children spend viewing television, compounded with the fact that children learn by observing behavior, requires that television be acknowledged as having a significant impact on children's social behavior. Valdez (1978) augments this discussion by asserting that television serves as a special case of socialization for the young child. This "enculturation" inculcates values, reinforces habits, and creates expectations. The characters portrayed become models for behavior of the young viewer. Media socialization is viewed by Valdez as a process through which values, attitudes, and roles are transmitted, acquired, and internalized by the audience. It is especially with this quasi-prescriptive role of television that researchers concerned with the media socialization of the minority child are particularly concerned.

THE HISPANIC IMAGE
TRANSMITTED BY TELEVISION

One of the most important facets of the portrayals of characters through the media, especially for minority children, is that they become validated as models by virtue of the fact that they are on the screen. Although it is not the purpose of educational programming to offset the stereotypes offered by the networks, a discussion of the impact of educational television on Hispanic children must perforce make note of the total media context in which it is offered. An analysis of the image–message structure of the television content reveals the cultural assumptions of the dominant groups in American society. The media offer a very limited range of Hispanic models with which the Hispanic child can identify. Cortés (1979) has discussed the development of the Chicano media stereotype on commercial television: It is one that portrays Chicanos as violent law-breakers and misfits. Supporting evidence is provided by Greenberg and Baptista-Fernandez (1979), who analyzed network television series for their content and characterization of Hispanics. They found that three categories accounted for the majority of Hispanic characters in network television series from 1975 to 1978: law-breakers, law enforcers, and comic characters. The first two areas involve the use or threat of violence. It is precisely this type of stereotype that educators assert contributes to the maintenance of Hispanics' low self-esteem. At the same time that the major networks have been focusing on the violent and law-breaking aspects of the Hispanic, educational programs have been developed that attempt to give positive value and status to the cultural characteristics of the Hispanic.

With the creation of the Children's Television Workshop (CTW) in 1968, the systematic use of television in educational programs for children reached national prominence. Although the CTW's first program series, *Sesame Street*, was designed to help prepare minority students for the mainstream classroom (Cooney, 1970), several researchers (Flores, 1974; Williams & Natalicio, 1972) were quick to note that the new educational television series were not specifically meeting the needs of children of Hispanic background for appropriate language instruction and cultural maintenance. Funds from Title VII of the Bilingual Education Act and from several other sources in the government and in foundations were used to develop educational programs to supplement instruction in bilingual classes. Programs such as *Carrascolendas*, *Villa Alegre*, and *Sonidos Míos* were developed to serve a bilingual population of Hispanic children, and *Sesame Street* and *The Electric Company* began to increase Spanish-language content in their programs (Children's Television Workshop, 1973). Other programs series, such as *Rebop* and *Vegetable Soup* were developed in the mid-1970s with a multicultural but not a multilingual emphasis.

The use of educational television as a teaching tool for children of Hispanic background rested on the assumptions that (a) children are attracted to television programs (Comstock *et al.* 1978), and (b) that children can learn effectively from television series (Chu & Schramm, 1967). It was further assumed that the pervasive nature of television in homes, specifically in Hispanic homes, would allow television to serve as instruction at school and in the home (Wood & Wylie, 1977).

According to Dr. René Cardenas, director of Bilingual Children's Television and the *Villa Alegre* program, the primary objective of the use of television programming was twofold: to reinforce Hispanic children's cultural awareness and to provide positive role models. Thus, educational television was seen early on as a supplement for bilingual education in the schools. Programs such as *Carrascolendas* and *Villa Alegre* were designed to increase skills in both English and Spanish and to promote biculturalism for students from Hispanic backgrounds (Fleck, 1974; Williams & Natalicio, 1972).

EDUCATIONAL TELEVISION PROGRAMS DEVELOPED FOR A BILINGUAL AND BICULTURAL AUDIENCE

The initial years of *Sesame Street* were more concerned, by design, with cognitive goals rather than with affective goals such as socialization. *Sesame Street* did not concentrate strongly on the cultural values of the different groups in its audience during its first seasons. There were some attempts at providing a strong black image for the program by introducing black performers into the counting and reading segments in the program and by having black characters as part of the regular cast (Cooney, 1970). There was no strong emphasis on other ethnic groups during this first year.

Consequently, during the first few years after the initiation of *Sesame Street*, limited Spanish content was provided. Filep, Millar, and Gillette (1970) and Flores (1974) reviewed viewing patterns and parental opinions to conclude that *Sesame Street* did not meet the social needs of Hispanic children. In an independent review of scripts from the program series during its third season, it was found that the limited Spanish segments were frequently direct translations of English segments and had little cultural sensitivity to Spanish language or content.

Hispanic and other ethnic characters in the programs were found to be sometimes stereotypic and insulting.

In response to these observations and others, *Sesame Street* added a bilingual and bicultural curriculum component in its fourth season, June 1972–June 1973. By introducing "sight words" in Spanish and two bilingual/bicultural characters, María and Luis, *Sesame Street* hoped to "reinforce cultural identity and self-pride in viewers from Spanish-speaking backgrounds [Children's Television Workshop, 1973]."

Concurrent with this addition of cultural content in *Sesame Street*, two other program series, *Carrascolendas* and *Villa Alegre*, were developed specifically to meet the needs of children of Hispanic background for bicultural information. Williams and Natalicio (1972) note that the Chicano child suffers from the dual disadvantage of seldom seeing a positive bilingual and bicultural model on television. To redress this, the producers of *Carrascolendas* developed a multicultural social component in their series. The goals for socialization were similar to those for *Villa Alegre* in that the program was designed "to develop in children a desire to become a bilingual and have the best of both worlds [Fleck, 1974, p. 31]." An emphasis was placed on the instruction of human relations skills through the modeling of the valued, prosocial behavior of the characters in *Villa Alegre*, Happy City.

The task of developing interesting, captivating educational programming appropriate for the bilingual child is a challenging task primarily because two languages are involved. It is essential to consider the following issues in bilingual programming: (a) how to reinforce both languages without invoking the boredom that such redundancy could entail; (b) the varieties and styles of Spanish and Spanish–English combinations chosen; and (c) the type of Spanish or English used by the role models.

Most studies of bilingual programming have not evaluated the use of language and its role in reinforcing stereotypes. Researchers have asked, What has been the impact of educational television programming on Hispanic children? This impact has been defined with respect to the cognitive and affective changes that resulted from viewing *Sesame Street* and *Carrascolendas*. For example, several studies have evaluated the educational effectiveness of *Carrascolendas*, a bilingual program for students in kindergarten through Grade 2. Williams and Natalicio (1978), in order to test the series pilot in Austin, Texas, used a battery of five tests in Spanish and five in English. By testing the students on the following instructional components—multicultural, social environment, language skills, numbers and figures, the physical environment, and concept development—they found that consistent viewers significantly outscored nonviewers on all of the English subtests and on Spanish language usage. They explain these results by suggesting that the students might be more receptive to new knowledge in English language content areas because of the social and cultural climate in the Austin environment. An increase in fluency of use of both languages was also noted among the consistent viewers. Williams and Natalicio add that using *Carrascolendas* in the classroom as an alternative or addition to *Sesame Street* represents a difference in philosophy to the approach popular at the Children's Television Workshop at the time. *Carrascolendas* gets the school ready for the Spanish-speaking child instead of getting the child ready for school.

When *Carrascolendas* was broadcast nationwide, Siebert (1973) conducted a national evaluation of the series. He found that the material presented had a significant impact on student learning in history and culture and increased the children's pride in Mexican culture. First-grade viewers benefited in English and Spanish language skills, mathematics, history, and culture. Second-grade viewers only benefited significantly in Spanish content areas and in English-language fluency. These results were supported by Van Wort (1974). The two studies differ in that Van Wort found that there were no significant gains for viewers as compared to nonviewers in the areas of mathematics and self-concept.

Laosa (1976) selected 15 boys and 15 girls in kindergarten through Grade 2 who watched *Carrascolendas*. The sample included Puerto Ricans, Cuban Americans, Chicanos, and whites for comparative study. The results suggested that all the students comprehended and recalled over two-thirds of the material presented on the programs and that the Chicanos, as a group, had higher mean scores on the posttests than the other two groups. This supports the notion that there may be a difference between language and ethnic groups and that all Hispanic children may not be most effectively served by the same approach to educational television (Gibson, 1976).

The findings for *Sesame Street* and *Carrascolendas* support the general assumption that television can be an effective tool for education if it is designed for and targeted to a specific audience. The studies also suggest that not only must the audience be considered but the social and cultural forces in the child's surroundings need to be taken into account in order to make the most effective use of television as an educational medium.

EDUCATIONAL TELEVISION AS A SOCIALIZING AGENT FOR HISPANIC CHILDREN

This section will focus on one specific program—*Villa Alegre*—as an example of educational programming targeted primarily to Hispanic children with a multicultural approach.

The first episode of *Villa Alegre* was aired in the fall of 1974. It was developed primarily to help Hispanic children 4- to 8-years-old to bridge the linguistic and cultural gap that exists between home and school. As the director of the educational effort, Dr. René Cardenas (1980) stated that the goals of the program were to facilitate bilingualism, to help Hispanic children to learn Spanish and to help eradicate the negative stereotype of the Hispanic by presenting cultural differences in a very positive way. Cardenas notes: "Early on we wanted to convey the humanistic notion that there are more cultural commonalities between Anglo and Latino than differences". This positive approach has been fundamental to *Villa Alegre's* format; there are no dehumanizing characteristics, or stereotypes, or winning at someone else's expense as the hidden message (deAvila, cited in Fleck, 1974, *personal communication*).

The *Villa Alegre* format combines video, animation, and film to explore five curricular themes: human relations, natural environment, nutrition, energy, and man-made objects. Both English and Spanish are used in the dialogue, but they are not mixed by the same character. Ball, Helmrick, and Torres (1977) note: "Each character translates the dialogue of the others' response so that viewers who were either English or Spanish-speaking could understand the story's dialogues and messages [p. 8]."

Using Spanish has its problems; although a large segment of the target population is Spanish-speaking, not all Hispanic children are Spanish-speaking. Interestingly, a 1975 evaluation of *Villa Alegre* found a drop in English-speakers' attention when the segment was primarily in Spanish. Yet the attention of Spanish-speaking subjects did not diminish during English-only segments. This suggests that children at a very early age have internalized the dominant society's valuation of the preeminence of English over Spanish.

Some support for the early internalization of the dominant society's language attitudes is provided by Ball, Helmrick, and Torres's (1977) evaluation of *Villa Alegre's* Series C. Research with a sample of 245 kindergarten, second-, and fourth-graders (Hispanics 130, non-Hispanics

115) revealed interesting patterns in the students' affective reactions to the segments.

Although there were no sex or ethnic–racial differences in the children's liking and acceptance of the show, major differences emerged within the Hispanic group due to language dominance. The more English-dominant the Hispanic child, the less enthusiastic he or she was about the show. Interestingly enough, this negative attitude toward the Spanish segments was more evident in the kindergarten sample than in the higher grades. Based on these limited data, the evaluators found that within the Hispanic sample there was a small subgroup already rejecting its cultural background. This last finding, although tentative, suggests the importance educational television can have on forming children's attitudes toward their mother tongue. More conclusive information is needed however, before the data from one educational television program can be generalized.

The dominant culture consistently reinforces the belief that Spanish is a second-class language. How this reflects on students' self-perceptions is obvious by the preponderance of studies that show that second-generation Hispanics tend to forget Spanish. Programs that depict Spanish-speakers as positive role models have the potential to offset the negative Chicano media stereotype to which Cortes (1979) has alluded. In this manner, educational television can reinforce an equitable portrayal and reflection of Hispanics.

REFERENCES

Arias, B. Comments on television impact on children's language: An exploration. Paper presented at the Invitational Conference on Television and the Socialization of the Minority Child, Los Angeles, California, April 1978.

Asante, M. Television's impact on black children's Language: An exploration. Paper presented at the conference on Television and the Socialization of the Minority Child, Los Angeles, California, April 1978.

deAvila, E. Personal communication, April 1980.

Ball, S., Gerry, A., Creech, R., Ellworth, R., & Landes, S. The first year of Sesame Street. Princeton, New Jersey: Educational Testing Service, 1970.

Ball, S., Helmrick, L., and Torres, Y. A formative evaluation of Villa Alegre: Series C. Oakland, California: Bilingual Children's Television, 1977.

Dr. Rene Cardenas. Personal communication, May 1980.

Children's Television Workshop. Children's television workshop annual report. New York: 1973.

Comstock, G., Chaffee, S., Katzman, N., McCombs, M., and Roberts, D. Television and human behavior. New York: Columbia University Press, 1978.

Comstock, G., & Colbey, Research directors for the study of television and ethnicity: Methodological considerations. Paper presented at the Invitational Conference on

Television and the Socialization of the Minority Child, Los Angeles, California, April 1978.

Cooney, J. *The first year of* Sesame Street: *A history and overview* (Vol. 1). *Final report.* New York: 1970.

Cortes, C. *The media curriculum on Mexican Americans: Educational challenge in the 80's.* Paper presented at the Fourteenth Annual Convention of the Association of Mexican American Educators, Los Angeles, Nov., 1979.

Chu, G. C., & Schramm, W. *Learning from television: What the research says.* Palo Alto, California: Stanford Univ. Press, 1967.

Diaz-Guerrero, R., & Holtzman, W. H. Learning by televised *Plaza Sesamo* in Mexico. *Journal of Educational Psychology,* 1974, 66, 632–643.

Filep, R. T., Millar, G. R., & Gillete, P. T. Sesame Street: *A survey of two cities viewing patterns in inner city Los Angeles and Chicago.* New York: Institute for Educational Development, 1970.

Filep, R. T., Millar, G. R., & Gillette, P. T. *The Sesame Mother Project.* El Segundo, California: Institute for Educational Development, 1971.

Fleck, M. *Villa Alegre:* An experiment in bilingual education. *Sundance,* 1974, *12,* 31–33.

Flores, B. *The observation and testing report on the* Sesame Street *programs.* Los Angeles: University of California, Los Angeles, Chicano Studies Center, 1974.

Gibson, M. Approaches to multicultural education in the United States. *Anthropology and Education Quarterly,* 1976, 3(4), 7–17.

Greenberg, B., & Baptista-Fernandez, P. *Hispanic Americans: The new minority on television* (Project Castle Report, No. 12). East Lansing: Michigan State University, Department of Communication, 1979.

Laosa, L. M. Viewing bilingual multicultural educational television: An empirical analysis of children's behaviors during television viewing. *Journal of Educational Psychology,* 1976, 68(2), 133–142.

Leifer, A. D. & Roberts, D. Childrens' response to television violence. In John P. Murray, *et al.,* (Eds.), *Television and Social Behavior* (Vol.11). Washington, D.C.: U.S. Government Printing Office, 1972.

Lyle, J., & Hoffman, H. Children's use of television and other media. In E. A. Rubinstein, G. A. Comstock, & J. P. Murray (Eds.), *Television and social behavior:*(Vol. 4). *Television in day-to-day life: Patterns of use.* Washington D.C.: US Govt. Printing Office, 1972.

Siebert, W. *Instructional television: The best of ERIC.* Stanford, California: Stanford Univ. Press, 1973. (ERIC Document Reproduction Service No. ED 08253S)

Summative Report on Activities and Findings by Bilingual Childrens' Television, Inc. Internal Document BCTV, Oakland, California 1975.

U.S. Department of Commerce, Bureau of the Census. *School enrollment—social and economic characteristics of students: October 1978* (Current Population Reports, Series P-20, No. 346). Washington, D.C. US Govt. Printing Office, 1979.

Valdez, A. Socialization influences of television commercials on pre-school age children. Doctoral dissertation, Stanford University, 1978.

Van Wort, G. Carrascolendas: *Evaluation of a Spanish/English educational television series within Region XIII: Final Report.* Evaluation Component October 1974, in ERIC 092089.

Williams, F., & Natalicio, D. Evaluating Carrascolendas: A television series for Mexican American children. *Journal of Broadcasting,* 1972, 16, 299–307.

Wood, D. N., & Wylie, D. G. *Educational Telecommunications.* Belmont, California: Wadsworth, 1977.

TELEVISION, MINORITY CHILDREN, AND PERSPECTIVES FROM RESEARCH AND PRACTICE

Bradley S. Greenberg
Charles K. Atkin

Learning about Minorities from Television: A Research Agenda

This chapter will move among three intersecting research questions that have emerged throughout various sections of this book. The research questions are the following: First, what content about minorities appears on television that may shape beliefs and expectations about minorities? Second, what impacts of television that have been identified for children in general may have special significance for minority children in particular? Third, how do the portrayals of minorities on television impact on the self-concept and on the race-related expectations of minority children?

Although the chapter will not attempt to look at these questions in a comprehensive fashion, it will search for critical issues in each. To do so, we will identify what commercial television is now programming about minorities and what appear to be the special vulnerabilities of the minority child to television programming. We also will review the available research evidence as to television's impact on minority youngsters. Finally, we will pose a research agenda that consolidates the several research questions into a scheme that permits a more comprehensive analysis than is currently available.

TELEVISION AND
THE SOCIALIZATION OF THE MINORITY CHILD

MINORITY ROLE PORTRAYALS

Numerous content analysis studies have documented the amount and nature of minority group portrayals in the mass media. Blacks have been the most widely studied minority group. These descriptions provide a basis for developing predictions about the possible impact of such content on audiences, particularly children and adolescents.

Entertainment Portrayals

Until the middle to late 1960s, blacks and other minorities were most notable for their invisibility in the mass media. Minorities were largely absent in movies, and this practice carried over into television; radio dramas seldom presented minority performers. Even *Playboy* cartoons contained fewer than 1% black figures (Greenberg & Kahn, 1971).

When minorities were portrayed, it was usually in an unflattering fashion. Classic films from *Birth of a Nation* to *Gone with the Wind* offered narrow and disparaging stereotypes of blacks (Colle, 1968). The popular *Amos 'n Andy* radio program featured exaggerated black roles—lazy, dumb, crooked, conniving, clowning characters played in dialect by white actors. This caricature was transferred intact to the television series, albeit with black actors. Blacks played menial servant roles presumably acceptable to white audiences. The short-lived television program starring Nat King Cole never attracted sufficient advertising support; the first successful black television star was Bill Cosby in *I Spy* in 1965 (U.S. Commission on Civil Rights, 1977).

The stereotypes of American Indians (blood-thirsty, drunken savages who seldom won battles) and Asian Americans (evil villains, laundry workers, or nonaggressive, superwise Charlie Chan) are also familiar. Recent studies of television images of Hispanics indicate that they fare no better.

The growth of the Civil Rights movement during the 1960s was eventually accompanied by a trend toward more frequent and positive media representation of minorities. By 1969, one-half of all television dramas contained a black performer (Dominick & Greenberg, 1970). Since that time, about 6–9% of all characters in television shows have been black (Seggar, 1977). Although they are relegated to more minor roles and are in less prestigious occupations (Northcott, Seggar & Hinton, 1975; Seggar & Wheeler, 1973), blacks are portrayed as equally industrious, competent, and physically attractive as whites. Blacks are more moral and kind, whereas whites are more dominant in relationships (Hinton, Seggar, Northcott, & Fontes, 1974).

Professional sports is one area where blacks have achieved success and prominence. However, a content analysis of commentary by the all-white announcers of pro-football games shows a subtle bias against black players. Researchers transcribed comments about 33 pairs of black and white players who were matched by position and accomplishments (e.g., running backs O. J. Simpson and Larry Csonka; receivers Paul Warfield and Fred Biletnikoff). White players received more favorable references about physical ability, mental ability, and achievement off the field; announcers also expressed more sympathy and praise for whites. Announcers more often discussed negative past activities of blacks, and made unfavorable comparisons. Whites were described as more aggressive, with blacks represented as recipients of aggression (Rainville & McCormick, 1977).

There are a number of interesting findings from our recent research project (project Castle) at Michigan State University. For 3 years, we videotaped a single episode of each fictional prime-time, and Saturday morning series available early in the fall season. This sample week of episodes has then been systematically content-analyzed on a number of dimensions, including racial, sexual, and family portrayals; some innovative efforts at analyzing pro- and antisocial behaviors have been made. It remains true that when we speak of minorities on television, the only minority available for any sort of intensive analysis are blacks. Other minorities, for example Hispanics, are still invisible. No minority other than blacks has been able to sufficiently gain access to television programming content; the infrequent television portrayals of other minorities can not be expected to have much direct impact. The absence of portrayals of other minorities could contribute to a weakened self-concept among their young people.

For the 1977–1978 television season, our sample week encompassed 81 different television entertainment series, of which 43 had one or more black characters; thus, half of the television shows had a black. In all, 101 different blacks were identified on these shows. For other minorities, there were 12 American Indians and 13 Hispanics. The population of speaking characters with identifiable ethnic origins numbered 1100. So the population of television blacks comprised a little more than 9% of the population. The surge to include blacks on commercial television in the late 1960s resulted in an increase to this level by 1968 or 1969; it has remained there since that time. You can virtually count on the fact that 1 in every 10 or 11 television characters will be black.

Regardless of whether you consider this proportion adequate or not, its stability over time is remarkable. Furthermore, the population of blacks exhibits a peculiar density pattern. There is a distinct black ghetto on television. Nearly one-half (N = 44) of the 1977–1978 season's blacks existed on just six shows (*Muhammed Ali, Fat Albert, The Jeffersons, Good Times, What's Happening?*, and *Sanford Arms*). Thus, one-half the television blacks was segregated, and the other one-half was widely diffused. Furthermore, two-thirds of all the black characters were in situation comedies or in Saturday cartoons.

In a special analysis, we drew a sample of 101 white characters from the same shows that had yielded our black population. Prior studies typically compared the available blacks with all whites on television. It seemed important to determine if the blacks were at least similar to those whites appearing on the same show with them, for they provided the most accessible comparative references for young viewers in terms of potential role models. First, two-thirds of the blacks and three-fourths of the whites are males. The white characters thus contain the same sex bias that has been demonstrated in repeated content analyses since 1970; the black characters, more typically found in family settings, are somewhat more likely than white characters to be women. Second, the sample of black characters is strikingly younger than the white sample; two-thirds of the former were in their 20's or younger, compared to less than one-half the white sample in these age groups. Television ignores elderly blacks even more than elderly whites, but television also ignores middle-aged blacks in its standard programming.

Regarding occupations, one-third of the television blacks versus one-half of the whites have an identifiable job, and whites are more likely to be professionals, administrators and managers. Blacks also have a substantially lower ranking in general SES assessments.

In terms of programming context, nearly one-half of the blacks are cast in situation comedies and an additional one-fifth in Saturday cartoons, more than double the rate for white characters.

We also examined the social interaction patterns of blacks and whites on television. There is no significant racial difference in giving, seeking, or receiving advice, information, or orders. The topics of conversation do not differ substantially, although whites are more likely to talk about business and about crime.

So this attempt to compare television black characterizations with *same-show* whites is promising; it may provide a new dimension for making comparative statements about television content.

Advertising Portrayals

Blacks were once even more rarely found in advertising than in entertainment content. In the 1940s and 1950s, they appeared in less than 1% of major magazine advertisements (Kassarjian, 1969; Shuey, King, & Griffith, 1953), although this proportion crept up to 2% during the 1960s (Cox, 1969–1970; Kassarjian, 1969; Stempel, 1971). The few blacks who did appear were entertainers, athletes, or menial servants (Colfax & Steinberg, 1972; Shuey et al., 1953). Newspaper advertisements showed blacks very sparingly; one researcher searched through 20,000 ads in the New York Times during 1963–1964 and found 11 black faces (Boyenton, 1965).

The big jump occurred from 1967 to 1969, from 2 to 5% in magazine advertisements (Cox, 1970), and from 5 to 11% in television commercials (Dominick & Greenberg, 1970). There was little increase beyond this in the 1970s. These studies show that blacks tend to appear in "crowd scenes" with whites rather than alone or with other blacks in print and broadcast advertisements (Culley & Bennett, 1976; Dominick & Greenberg, 1970). The situation in children's Saturday morning shows is quite different, as one-fifth of the commercials contain black characters (Atkin & Heald, 1977).

News Portrayals

The visibility of blacks in the news has been more prominent. By 1970, blacks appeared in 13% of newsmagazine pictures (Stempel, 1971). An analysis of newspaper coverage of comparable fatal campus shootings of white and black students (Kent State versus Jackson State and Southern University) found approximately equal amounts of space devoted to each incident (Baran, 1973). Blacks appeared in almost one-fourth of network newscast film segments in the early 1970s, although mostly in nonspeaking roles pertaining to busing, desegregation and other Civil Rights issues (Roberts, 1975). Nevertheless, there are few black television news correspondents, and they seldom handle the lead stories (U.S. Commission on Civil Rights, 1977).

MINORITY STATUS AND POVERTY

Let us now move from an examination of television content to issues regarding child viewers of television, with particular emphasis on

minority children and their special susceptibility to being socialized by
television programs.

It is our thesis here that the question of minority children's vulnerability to television content can best focus on that very large subset of
minority children who are simultaneously economically disadvantaged. In 1970, the census counted 23 million black Americans; 9.5
million were under 18, and 4 million of these were below defined
poverty levels. These 4 million black children constituted 40% of all
American children below the poverty line (U.S. Department of Commerce, 1970). Despite some expected gains during this decade, it is still
possible to claim that this special intersection of black children and
poor children provides a legitimate and appropriate target group for
studies of television's effects. If one were slightly more expansive in
considering economic needs, it would be possible to stipulate that
one-half of all black children under 18 are economically disadvantaged. This is not done to tightly link the attributes of race and economics. Rather, it is done to facilitate our understanding of the potential
impacts of television on minority children, especially when those
minority children also face economic deprivation.

The environment of the poor black child carries a set of psychological and social orientations that should be identified here (cf. Chilman,
1966; Epstein, 1961; Gottlieb, 1964; Irelan & Besner, 1965; Keller, 1963;
Lewis, 1966; Minuchin, Montaluo, Guerney, Rosman, & Schumer,
1967). If one wishes to analyze television, it must be done within the
child's existing context of potential and actual needs. As these children
watch television, one must account for the following major life perceptions which typify many disadvantaged black viewers:

> *Emphasis on short-term goals.* There is little opportunity to plan
> ahead. Even stronger-than-average preferences for immediate
> gratifications are related to the realities of being poor.
>
> *Emphasis on the concrete.* Events and people are less likely to be
> judged in abstract terms. Emphasis is on the here-and-now in terms
> of observable attributes and behaviors. Practical actions hold forth;
> intellectuality may be rejected.
>
> *Lack of efficacy.* Whether labeled alienation, powerlessness,
> anomie, isolation, or fatalism, a lesser belief that one can influence
> one's own destiny more likely characterizes minority group mem-
> bers, especially impoverished ones.
>
> *Low self-esteem.* The adult poor see themselves as incapable and
> inefficient. This self-assessment is transmitted to the children. For
> black children low self-esteem is exacerbated if there are few and/or
> inadequate black role models available.

Nonachievement. To the extent that hopes and aspirations are thwarted or do not develop because the environment does not nurture them, a typical response is to stop attempting to achieve.

Aspiration–achievement discrepancy. Given a culture that glories in and constantly transmits messages about societal achievements, and given some sense of a higher probability of failure, a paradox results. One aspires to and values the same things as the major society—more luxuries, better lives, more education—but the discrepancy perceived between self-achievement and these aspirations is large and increasingly frustrating.

Illusion. Illusion and fantasy become more common among the poor. Men talk of imagined conquests; women talk of material things they do not have. Illusion provides a self-protective coping mechanism.

Restricted options and experiences. Lack of resources clearly limits alternative responses to life situations; experiences in the home and at work are of a much different nature so that contact and empathy with and understanding of the values and behaviors of other races or other economic groups is limited.

These are not universal characteristics, nor are they mutually exclusive; there are many within-group differences. However, as appropriate as these attributes are for characterizing both the black poor and the nonblack poor, they are intensified for the former.

It is in this context, then, that we may begin to examine what and how television becomes an integral part of the black child's daily life, and continue with a special emphasis on the poor black child.

THE ECONOMICALLY DISADVANTAGED CHILD

The Television Experiences of the Economically Disadvantaged Child

Here, the use the child makes of television both in terms of gross exposure and content selections will be examined. Furthermore, it is important to understand the child's perceptions of television content and their impacts on cognitions, desires, and behaviors. A preliminary "propositional inventory" will be offered in order to categorize the research. Selected findings from a recent research project, where 600 students in the fourth, sixth, and eighth grades were interviewed about television will be presented. There were 250 blacks and 350 whites in the samples, drawn from the Detroit, Michigan and San Jose, California areas.

One final introductory note is important. Many studies have made comparisons between black and white youngsters without considering family-income discrepancies. This is not synonymous with comparing economically advantaged with disadvantaged youngsters, although in many cases it may be a fairly good approximation of that difference. Any sample of black children is going to include a far greater proportion of the economically disadvantaged than a comparable-size sample of white children. The point is that racial and economic differences are often confounded both because many studies do not differentiate between them and because there is a correlation between the two attributes. There is the additional fact that the poor black is even poorer than the poor white. So when racial differences are noted, for example, in television exposure time, the difference may as much represent an intensification of the poverty condition and its consequences.

GREATER DEPENDENCY ON TELEVISION IN LEISURE-TIME ALLOCATION

Studies from both academic and commercial sources persistently demonstrate the greater time allocation to television among the poor, both for adults and for children. The typical poor home has two working television sets. In a Cleveland study with 400 9- to 10-year-olds, poor white youngsters reported daily viewing that averaged 6 hr per weekday, compared to 4 hr for the better-off children; the poor black children averaged 7 hr. The poor children were more likely to watch television before going to school in the morning, during their lunch hour, after school, and in the late evening. In a Philadelphia study with 300 ghetto and suburban high school students, the middle-class white teenager was giving 3½ hr on Sunday to television, in contrast to 4½ hr for the poorer whites, and 6 hr for the poor black adolescents (Greenberg & Dervin, 1972).

National data confirm this pattern and demonstrate an additional point as well. In the last decade, Nielsen data show that overall television watching has increased among all homes (Comstock, Chaffee, Katzman, McCombs & Roberts, 1978). But what is the state of national viewing within low-income households? In the Nielsen household sample, four income stratifications are made: Income less than $5000 annually; $5000–$9000; $10,000–$14,999; and $15,000+. A comparison was made of homes with children, by household income. The poorest homes averaged 4 hr more per week (200 hr more per year) than the wealthiest families. Among teenagers 12–17 years of age the relationship is even stronger. The poorest homes average 12½ hr more per week of television watching than those more well-to-do, or some 600 additional television hours a year. These estimates may be low. The data from the youngsters in the Nielsen sample are derived from their parents' estimates. Parental estimates of their children's viewing behaviors are consistently lower than self-reports of the children. The mother may underestimate the child's viewing time because her values so direct; the child may overestimate for the same reason.

Some claim that the context of viewing television is one that stimulates conversation among family members. Surely some conversation occurs, but there is little evidence to suggest it is either important or constructive (Lyle & Hoffman, 1971). The interaction between parent and child is perhaps more likely to be negative than positive. "Shut-up so I can hear," "Go to bed," "It's bad—don't watch." The increasing incidence of multiple-set households further eliminates the opportunity for social interaction among family members during common viewing times. And low-income houses are almost as likely as others to have two working television sets.

Consider, then, the typical school-age disadvantaged child. Each day, 7 hr are spent going to, coming from, and being in school; 8–9 hr are spent sleeping; and 4–5 hr are spent watching television. If we consider these to be primary activities rather than secondary ones, which appears to be the case, we are reduced to identifying what is done with the remaining three to five hours.

LESS CONTENT SELECTIVITY

The child we are focusing on is more likely to watch more of whatever is available (Greenberg, 1972). This child is in the audience for more different times of the day and for more varied programs. These are not preference statements, they do not bear on what the child likes to see. But it is conclusive that disadvantaged children watch more of almost everything rather than concentrating their greater exposure on a select set of programming categories.

In Nielsen audience data, the audience size among low-income 2- to 11-year-olds, as compared with all 2- to 11-year-olds, is larger for 8 of 10 programming categories and the same for the remaining 2. It is impressively larger for news shows, in particular (Comstock *et al.*

1978). There are some useful distinctions to be made, however, in terms of what low-income children would prefer to watch, even though preferences may be less important than actual behavior.

Racial differences predominate in program preference studies more than income differences. Minority children (and adults) express a strong affinity for those shows that regularly feature minority actors and actresses. For example, in Washington, D.C., *Sanford and Son* received a metropolitan black-household rating of 69 for 8 weeks in 1974 but a total metropolitan household rating of 35. In Chicago, Illinois, the same show had respective ratings of 69 and 34; in Detroit, Michigan they were 74 and 41. In all three cities, *Flip Wilson* was among the top six shows for black households and not in the top 10 among total households.

There are some interesting differences that have been identified between the program type preferences of lower- and middle-income children. One focuses on affinity for violence-filled shows: The economically disadvantaged child watches more of these shows and likes them more. In perhaps a more constructive sense, the favorite shows of lower-class children are far more likely to be shows in which a family setting exists, in which a parent and child function together. These appear high on the list of favorite program choices for the disadvantaged youngster, and are most often in the family situation-comedy genre. However, inasmuch as black characters are predominantly cast in such shows (e.g., *Good Times*), it is difficult to isolate whether this is a preference for television families or for television minority characters.

MORE ACCEPTING OF TELEVISION MESSAGES

Across several studies, the proposition that the more disadvantaged are less critical of television content is supported with near-uniform consistency (Greenberg & Reeves, 1976). Here are some samplings of these findings:

• The economically disadvantaged child is more likely to believe a television report than a report from any other mass medium.
• The same child is more willing to forego other media behaviors if a choice must be made among media.
• The same child attributes more credibility to television news people than to news people from other media.
• Minority students perceive television to be more fair to minority groups than do majority group children.

Television commercials are more likely to be believed among lower-income and/or minority youngsters. For instance, a study by Atkin (1980) presented two breakfast cereal commercials to 4- and 7-year-old children. One-half the children were from low-income Mexican-American neighborhoods, one-half were from white middle-class homes. The Mexican-American children were far more likely to trust in the nutritional expertise of the cartoon characters (Fred Flintstone and Barney Rubble) who endorsed a presweetened cereal, were more likely to believe the implied claim that sugared cereal would make them big and strong, were more likely to feel that these cereals were more fun and healthful than others, and were more influenced by the persuasive arguments presented in the commercials.

Running throughout these discrete findings is the general idea that television entertainment content in general is more likely to be judged as true to life. Some responses from our survey of Detroit and San Jose youth illustrate the extent to which minority children perceive that fictional portrayals are realistic. The question asked if the child agreed with each statement; the percentages indicate how many children of each race said "yes" (approximately 30–40% indicated that they were "not sure").

	Blacks (%)	Whites (%)
Black men/women I see on television are like black men/women in real life	29	25
Blacks on television talk like blacks in real life	46	42
Blacks on television behave like blacks in real life	26	15
Black teenagers on television are like black teenagers in real life	41	33
The jobs men/women do on television are like the jobs men/women do in real life	60	52
Mothers/fathers on television are like mothers/fathers in real life	38	25
Wives/husbands . . . like real life	26	17
Teenage boys/girls . . . like real life	41	31
Police officers/doctors/secretaries/nurses . . . like real life	44	37

It can be seen that black youth consistently felt that the television portrayals were more real, although the differences are not large. Why? The restrictions of home and environment permit fewer alternative personal and communication experiences. Fewer activities take place outside the school grounds. Direct contacts with the outside world are limited. Many primary contacts with outside phenomena are likely to be television contacts, against which few standards of comparison are available.

MORE VIEWING TO "LEARN" SOMETHING

Watching television serves many functions for viewers. Among these are an opportunity to relax, to get some excitement, to find diversion from in-home or out-of-home unpleasantries, to pass time, and to combat loneliness (Greenberg, 1974). But the most repeated finding is that low-income children expect to learn something from their television experiences. These children anticipate that learning will occur primarily in ways that will be socially adaptive. The results of our survey illustrate this basic point: Proportion of youth saying that they watch television to learn how different people behave, talk, dress, and look (whites: 38%; blacks: 50%); Proportion saying that they watch television to learn what police, doctors, secretaries, and nurses are like (whites: 39%; blacks: 52%). Learning is a motivation that undoubtedly interacts with the other experiences and psychological postures of these children's attitude toward television. The children are receptive, positive, eager, and believing.

GREATER INVOLVEMENT WITH TELEVISION PROGRAMS

Children from disadvantaged backgrounds tend to be more emotionally involved in the plots of programs and to identify more closely with characters. This is especially true for responses to black characters on television by black youngsters. Black youths were approximately three times as likely to express identification with black characters, compared to white youths. These findings are from the social role survey:

Percentage saying YES	Black children (%)	White children (%)
Freddy Washington	57	27
Lamont Sanford	45	13
J. J. Evans	45	19
Bill Cosby	43	15
Thelma Evans	43	7
George Jefferson	41	8
Dee Thomas	37	17
Louise Jefferson	30	6
Roger Thomas	28	11
James Evans	29	4
Mrs. Thomas	22	5
Florida Evans	21	3
Average for 12 black characters	37	11

Blacks and whites are equally likely to identify with white television characters. Across 26 white television characters, an average 17% of black youth versus 16% of white youth say they want to be like the character. Thus, black children relate to a larger number of characters because they identify with both black and white actors. It should be noted that white children, although seldom identifying with black characters, are also less likely than blacks to identify with same-race characters. Relatively few white or black children want to be like most of the white models they see on television.

WHAT IS LEARNED FROM TELEVISION

There is no disagreement among researchers or educators about the premise that economically disadvantaged children learn from watching television. The arguments begin when one turns to such questions as whether they learn more or less than others, whether it is constructive learning or not, and just what the content of the learning is.

Cognitive learning from television has been most ably demonstrated by research done in conjunction with the Sesame Street programs (Bogatz & Ball, 1971). This program was created for the disadvantaged youngster. Research results from the first and second years of the show clearly indicate that the more a disadvantaged youngster watched the program, the more that child learned the skills and information emphasized in the programs. Furthermore, this large amount of learning did not require adult supervision, was picked up as well by home viewing as by in-school viewing, and was even more impressive among the younger viewers than the older ones. But each of these results was obtained among the more advantaged child viewers as well. That is, Sesame Street was not a teacher solely for the disadvantaged; it taught the more advantaged child at least equally. The paradox is this: If a disadvantaged child watches more of Sesame Street than an advantaged one, the former learns more, and the cognitive gap between them tends to lessen; however, if an advantaged and a disadvantaged child both watch a large number of programs, the former—because of what has already gone into making that child an advantaged one—learns more of what is available and the gap between them may increase. Analyses by Cook, Appleton, Connor, Shaffer, Tamkin & Weber (1975) indicate that Sesame Street may indeed serve to widen the gap.

Another instance of the widespread use of television for straightforward learning was the creation of The Electric Company. Significant positive gains in reading skills were found in Grades 1–4 among viewers. Gains were largest in Grades 1 and 2 presumably because of higher entry-level skills in the upper grades. The impact of in-school viewing of *The Electric Company* was similar for several subgroups tested, including Chicano, black, and white children, boys and girls (Ball & Bogatz, 1973). Parallel programs specially designed for ethnic subgroups, for example, *Carrascolendas,* have been equally impressive in their ability to teach rudimentary learning skills to the very young.

Often these same shows teach other things as well. *Sesame Street* and *Mister Rogers' Neighborhood,* for example, have had such specific prosocial consequences as increased co-operation and sharing behaviors, task persistence, and tolerance for delay among more regular viewers. More positive attitudes toward school and toward other races have been also documented among viewers. In one major study, prosocial interpersonal behavior (co-operative play, nurturance, verbalization of feeling) increased only among children from poor families. The higher SES children did not increase their prosocial behavior from watching *Mister Rogers Neighborhood* (Stein & Friedrich, 1972).

Greenberg (1972) asked white elementary-school children to identify the source of most of their knowledge about the physical appearance, talk, and dress of blacks. Those with infrequent personal contact with black people relied principally on television. Among rural children who seldom lived near or attended school with blacks, two-thirds reported that television was their basic information source. One-third of suburban children cited television; urban children, who had extensive contact with blacks, were least likely to report reliance on television input.

According to the self-reports of young blacks and whites, television is a major source of learning about the world. In particular, job roles and behavior patterns are learned from television.

Contemporary researchers have focused attention on the top-rated television program of the 1970s, *All in the Family.* A secondary objec-

Proportion of youth saying that they learn most of what they know about these topics from television

	Blacks (%)	Whites (%)
Jobs that men and women have	47	35
How men and women make decisions	34	21
How men and women solve problems	42	29
How parents and children interact	57	44
How husbands and wives interact	45	33
How teenagers act	48	37
How black people dress, behave, talk	40	23

tive of this program was to combat bigotry by poking fun at it and by helping viewers gain insight into their own prejudices. However, the selective perception process seems to prevail with this type of satirical content. Several investigators have reported that authoritarian, prejudiced individuals tend to *literally* interpret the actions of the bigoted character, Archie Bunker. When Archie expresses an ethnic or racial slur, these viewers agree with him and feel he is "telling it like it is." Less prejudiced members of the audience perceive Archie as a foolish, narrow-minded bigot and interpret his comments as satire. Thus, there is a tendency for selective perception to distort the intended message toward the predispositions of viewers, resulting in reinforcement of prior prejudices or tolerances (Brigham, 1975; Brigham & Giesbrecht, 1976; Chapko & Lewis, 1975; Surlin, 1974; Tate & Surlin, 1976; Vidmar & Rokeach, 1974; Wilhoit & de Bock, 1976). The producers cast Archie as lovable, allowing many individuals to identify with him. Even so, only a small proportion of watchers feel that Archie's views are valid and appropriate, which minimizes the unintended effect. Furthermore, a substantial number of viewers report that the program helps them to recognize their own prejudices (Vidmar & Rokeach, 1974) and makes them less certain about their ethnocentric ideas (Wilhoit & de Bock, 1976). Finally, the reinforcement effect also works to reduce prejudice for those who are already predisposed toward tolerance.

Two studies of young viewers of *Sesame Street* suggest that positive racial attitude change can be produced. This program seeks to foster favorable affect toward American Indians, Asian Americans, and blacks by frequently presenting appealing models from these minority groups. A field survey indicated that white children who viewed 2 years of *Sesame Street* became more positive toward other races (Bogatz & Ball, 1971). An experiment in an all-white nursery school manipulated exposure to *Sesame Street* segments containing nonwhite persons. When asked if they wanted to play with white or nonwhite children pictured in photographs, just one-third of the unexposed control group picked the minority playmates. More than two-thirds of those who had seen the multiracial segments preferred to play with the minority children; the vicarious contact appears to have heightened interest and increased familiarity with these minority groups (Gorn, Goldberg, & Kanungo, 1976).

Some observers have predicted that black children who are exposed to white-dominated media content will develop destructive self-images and perceptions of white superiority, but no evidence of this is available (Hinton *et al.* 1974). There are experiments showing that young black children are more likely to imitate the play behavior of televised white models than black models (Atkin, 1975; Neely, Heckel, & Leichtman, 1973). Similarly, others have expressed concern about the effects of certain types of black portrayals, such as the Super Fly characterizations in "blaxploitation" films. They argue that ghetto youth who have few positive real-life models to emulate are susceptible to the superficially glamorous portrayals of violence, sex, and drugs in such black-oriented films. Clearly, some viewers copy hair and dress styles and mimic distinctive "hip" words and deeds of movie heroes, but systematic data on this influence is lacking (Poussaint, 1974). On a more positive note, one experimenter found that the self-concept of black children was enhanced after watching a 1-hr movie depicting successful black athletes, entertainers, soldiers, and families (Dimas, 1970).

Children learn some less desirable things from a steady diet of commercial television. They learn more aggressive traits if they watch a steady diet of televised violence, and research demonstrates that the programs that contain heavier doses of such content are among the show categories more favored and watched by the disadvantaged. The child who views regularly is more likely to accept violence as a mode of conflict resolution, is more likely to consider violence an effective means of solving problems, and expresses greater willingness to use it. Furthermore, the disadvantaged (by either race or income) perceive less violence in a given unit of content, judge it to be more acceptable, enjoy it more, find it more humorous, and judge it as more true to life than do the advantaged.

In conclusion, television is a most powerful teacher, both formally and informally. For entertainment content, incidental learning is particularly impressive in those areas in which the viewer has a particular void. And the less advantaged child clearly has more voids than the more advantaged child.

PARENTAL INVOLVEMENT

Young black people in our sample experience closer control over television exposure than do white respondents. One-third of the black youngsters said that their parents "make more rules about television" compared to most kids their age, while one-fifth of the whites reported this. One-half of each group said that their parents "almost always" knew what programs they are watching, but a higher proportion of blacks said their parents "care very much" about the shows they watch. In addition, the black youth are no more likely than white youth to be allowed to stay up late to watch television on school days and they are subject to just as many prohibitions against watching programs of which parents do not approve. Parents of black youngsters are more likely to guide their children toward approved minority programs on television. For a set of four programs featuring black performers (*Good Times, Sanford and Son, The Jeffersons,* and *Fat Albert*), an average of 40% of the black parents versus 22% of the white parents suggested that their child should watch. For other prosocial programs (e.g., *Little House on the Prairie, The Waltons, Rhoda*), about one-fifth of both the white and black youth received guidance. The percent of black parents suggesting their children watch black shows was at a much higher level than the proportion of white parents offering guidance for any show type.

Third, black parents are somewhat more likely to actually sit down and watch television programs with their children. This is especially the case for black programs, where more than 80% of the black parents watch with their child. For 37 of 46 programs studied, a higher proportion of black than white youth reported that their parents watched with them. The difference averaged 10–15% higher for black youth.

Finally, black and white parents provide equivalent amounts of interpretation of television depictions. About two-fifths of the black and white youth said that their parents tell them about the real and unreal elements in televised portrayals of occupations, family roles, racial roles, and sex roles.

A RESEARCH AGENDA

Having isolated critical factors about television and the minority and/or disadvantaged child, we can begin to isolate focal research issues. The research program we propose addresses this question: What do youngsters acquire from fictional portrayals that may establish or alter cognitions, aspirations, expectations, and beliefs about specific social roles? Understanding the social role learning that occurs as a function of television portrayals will serve (a) to underscore the significance of social learning by young people, and (b) to identify a research process that can be replicated with other social role content areas of national import, for example, portrayals of the elderly, portrayals of the sexes.

These are the specific social role attitude consequences of television viewing that are of central interest:

Cognitions about a particular role. What does the viewer believe to be true about that social role, and why? How much variance does the

youngster perceive to exist or to be permitted for a specific social
role?

Valuation of roles and role attributes. What role attributes or behaviors does the youngster value, and for what reason? What preferences develop?

Development of role aspirations. What roles are aspired to, from
television, through anticipatory socialization? Why?

Expectations about role-appropriate behaviors. How is a role-holder
expected to behave? How is this expectation affected by the discrepancy between the television role-holder and what role-holders experience directly?

Behavior toward role holders. In what ways do youngsters behave
differently toward role-holders because of images shaped by television?

There are two basic rationales for studying social role learning about
blacks. The first is to demonstrate the need for understanding white
children's responses to black portrayals and the second is to examine
black children's responses to black portrayals.

To the extent that whites develop impressions, expectations, and
beliefs about black people from television portrayals of blacks, there are
important implications for the cross-racial socialization of young
people in this country. In the context of planned integration of schools
in urban areas and some accompanying conflicts between white and
black youths, it seems imperative to examine if, and how, the media
contribute to a lessening or heightening of interracial tensions. To what
extent is the urban white child's beliefs about blacks shaped conjointly
by personal and television experiences? Are the television portrayals
generally reacted to as realistic or ridiculous? Do these youngsters find
any of the black portrayals particularly attractive and worthy of emula-
tion? To what extent is there cross-race identification with television
characters and the behaviors of those characters? These are the issues
for whites who live in urban areas, who have direct experiences with
black youths, and who are exposed to fictional television portrayals of
blacks.

At the same time, millions of white children are growing up in a
nonintegrated environment, in small and medium-sized cities with no
appreciable minority population and virtually no minority peers in
their schools. It is here that we would expect maximum minority role
information to be transmitted by the media and by television in particular. Television far exceeds all other media in terms of time allocation
among adolescents. Racial impressions may not be very important until

such young people reach adolescence and begin to be aware of people who look and perhaps behave in ways different from those to which they are accustomed. Thus, the extent to which television "teaches" segregated white children about the way blacks behave, interact, look, and think can have significant implications for what these white youngsters expect and believe to be true about blacks. For this white subgroup, isolated from direct experiences with substantial numbers of minority people, it is particularly important to determine the quantity and quality of vicarious information received through the mass medium that they deem very real-to-life and with which they share so much of their leisure time.

Equally, if not more, important, to what extent are the black models aspired to by black youngsters? This third focus of concern deals with the issue of racial self-concept. It is important to determine if black children identify with and choose as role models some of those black heroes and heroines or other main characters portrayed on television programs. Do blacks exposed to such role models believe that the industry is making an effort at integration through such presentations? Does persistent exposure to such models instill greater racial awareness and an increment in racial pride or in self-pride? Does it generate more positive expectations about the social and professional acceptance of blacks by whites? Does it make for more cordial relations with white schoolmates? If those characters are judged to be negative, to be counterproductive to black goals for self-achievement, then it is equally important to determine whether the perceptions of black television portrayals generate increased hostile attitudes toward whites. If the characters are judged by black adolescents to be stereotypical of black people, then the social learning can result in more negative interracial responses.

Some other issues might also be examined. Do black children increase or decrease personal efficacy after seeing minority characters in dominant or subordinate roles on television? Does television provide access to varied social roles (e.g., occupational options, geographic mobility, middle-class lifestyles) beyond the direct experience of the disadvantaged child and thus facilitate the development of empathy with a wider range of social roles? Can this empathy extend to a greater understanding of the attitudes and actions of whites? Do television portrayals heighten aspirations? If so, will unfulfilled aspirations result in eventual dissatisfaction and frustration if access remains or appears to remain unavailable? Finally, how do minority children respond when their race is an object of ridicule, as in programs such as *All in the Family* that ostensibly satirize bigotry? How do they respond when minority television characters display negative feelings toward white characters?

Our conceptualization of the general process of acquiring social role orientations from television is derived primarily from Bandura's (1977) social learning theory. This perspective posits imitative performance of vicariously reinforced stimuli observed directly or via television. According to Bandura, many role models presented on television are highly effective in attracting children's attention because they are relevant, powerful, competent, distinctive, attractive, and readily accessible. Since these models are featured frequently and pervasively, children's retention of images and symbols is also enhanced. The learned messages are likely to be activated into overt expression to the extent that portrayed reinforcement contingencies provide cues which indicate the context in which they are likely to be rewarded. Three modeling functions constitute significant mechanisms for learning from television:*Observational learning* is the transmission of information about ways of organizing component responses into new patterns of behavior; observers acquire novel responses by watching the performances of televised models. The pictoral demonstrations available on television are particularly powerful for younger viewers with less developed conceptual skills and less motivation to learn from verbal sources. *Strengthening or weakening inhibitions* govern the expression of previously learned responses. The observation of reinforcement to a model helps determine how behavioral restraints are modified; vicariously punished responses tend to inhibit expression whereas normally prohibited responses that are rewarded or merely ignored reduce inhibitory constraints. *Response facilitation,* the third major function, occurs when the model performs a socially sanctioned behavior that serves as an external reminder, eliciting the performance of the viewer's existing responses in the same general class.

A large amount of research evidence compiled since 1960 has demonstrated that television has significant effects on youthful viewers; hundreds of these studies have been reviewed in annotated bibliographies by Atkin, Murray, and Nayman (1971) and Comstock, Lindsey, and Fisher (1975). The research yields a very complex picture of these effects. The characteristics that youth bring to television combine with the attributes of the television content to produce varying types of exposure, interpretation, and consequences. The social context of the viewer has important implications for the predispositions of viewers and their responses to television. The general proposition that consumption of televised messages will produce corresponding changes in the role orientations of adolescents is contingent on the juxtaposition of television content factors, viewer characteristics, social influences, and patterns of exposure and interpretation. A schematic outline of the key variables is presented in Figure 11.1.

A comprehensive and sensitive analysis of television effects must consider the components of this model. The first stage is a careful measurement of the qualitative and quantitative aspects of televised portrayals of social roles through content analytic techniques. Before

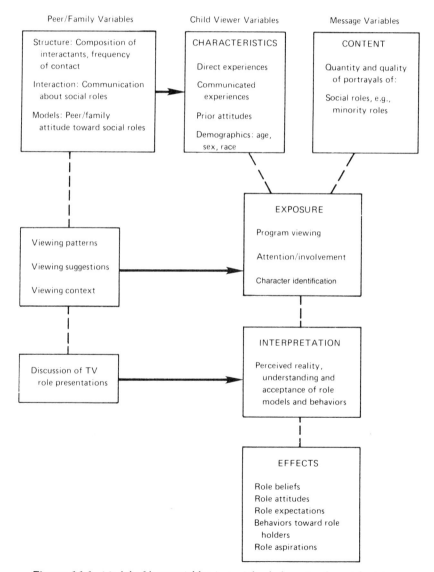

Figure 11.1. Model of key variables in social role learning from television.

one can determine the outcome of exposure, the exact dimensions of the message inputs must be assessed. The prior experiences, attitudes, and demographic attributes of the young viewer must also be considered, along with the interpersonal stimuli that shaped each predisposition. The measurement of exposure must include indices of message contact and psychological responses while viewing. Interpretive reactions that serve as intervening processes can also be ascertained. Social inputs that affect the nature of the viewing experience may be tapped. Finally, the rich array of cognitive, affective, and behavioral learning must be fully measured.

General Hypotheses

Five general predictions can be framed to guide research in social role learning from television. These are tied to the five dependent variables outlined previously.

H_1: Young people exposed to programs containing systematic portrayal of specific social roles will acquire cognitions reflecting the elements of the televised presentation; compared to nonexposed or light viewers, heavy viewers will hold perceptions of actual attributes and behavior patterns of role-holders that are consistent with the televised version. For instance, heavy viewers of programs featuring women police officers will be more likely than light viewers to perceive that a higher proportion of real-life police are female.

H_2: Young people exposed to programs containing role portrayals that systematically project favorable or unfavorable stereotypes will have a greater tendency to develop values of roles and role attributes that correspond to the televised presentation, than those less extensively exposed. For instance, those who regularly watch programs featuring a strong and hardworking black mother will be more likely to hold a favorable attitude toward black mothers.

H_3: Young people exposed to programs featuring consistently favorable portrayals of achieved roles will tend to aspire toward holding such role positions; exposed adolescents will tend to have lower aspirations from watching unfavorably portrayed roles. For instance, those who frequently watch programs presenting flattering depictions of defense attorneys will be more likely to aspire to this occupation than less heavily exposed adolescents.

H_4: Young people exposed to programs portraying regularities in behavior patterns of role-holders will tend to develop expectations that real-life role-holders will behave in that manner. For instance, those who often see black television judges acting fairly and authoritatively will be more likely to anticipate that actual black judges that they encounter will act that way.

H_5: Viewers' behavior toward real-life role-holders is expected to be influenced by the perceptions, attitudes, and expectations that are shaped by the television role portrayals.

Interaction Hypotheses

Beyond these main hypotheses, more precise predictions can be stated that take into account the attributes of the youngster who receives the message. The attributes central to this presentation are shown in Figure 11.1. Let us identify some illustrative hypotheses that a literature review would suggest as the expected role in the television exposure–social role learning relationship.

PARENTAL AND PEER INFLUENCE

Television's impact will be lessened if the youngster is exposed to interpersonal messages that are contradictory and frequent; its impact will be facilitated to the extent that such interpersonal messages do not exist at all; and its impact will be moderate if interpersonal sources input similar messages.

DIRECT EXPERIENCE

Prior personal experience with role-holders will be related to the impact of television in this fashion:

1. Limited or no prior experience will be related to maximum impact of television material.
2. Prior experiences that are consistent with the television material will reinforce the child's social attitudes and behaviors; attitudes and behaviors based on inconsistent prior experiences will be altered in the direction of the television presentation.

EXISTING ATTITUDES

The nature and direction of the young person's existing attitudes toward social roles and behaviors will be related to television learning in these ways:

1. The absence of prior attitudes, or the presence of only weakly-held prior attitudes, will be related to maximum acceptance of the social role emphases of the television content.

2. Directional prior attitudes will be strengthened if the television themes are consistent and weakened if the themes conflict.

NEEDS

The viewer with manifest or latent needs for information about particular roles and behaviors is more likely to accept what television offers than the child with less need for such information.

MOTIVATIONS

The more the child is psychologically dependent on television, the more impact from content:

1. The more the child is motivated to learn about life from television, the greater the impact.
2. The more the adolescent is motivated to learn about self-adaptive behaviors from television, the greater the impact.

INVOLVEMENT

Attention to and involvement with the television characterizations will be positively related to the degree of impact of that content.

PERCEIVED REALITY

Perceived reality of television content will be positively related to impact.

Overall Research Plan

A comprehensive and definitive examination of the influence of television on role learning requires a combination of controlled experimentation and field survey data. Experimental and quasi-experimental conditions provide for control over the key stimulus variables and a careful observation of dependent variables. Survey methods allow for an assessment of the levels and interrelationships of many variables in the naturalistic setting in which television is viewed and for an exploration of the cumulative impact of television content. A key prerequisite for these behavioral research phases is a thorough knowledge of the kinds of social role portrayals existing in current television programming; this is obtained through sophisticated content analytic techniques.

Let us exemplify a prototype research plan that extends over a 2-year period. This will permit the use of more sophisticated design procedures than the more typical, one-shot study and enable us to examine critical components of the proposed research model. For purposes of illustration, we shall focus on minority role learning by both black and white youngsters. The reader may conceptually substitute other role learning areas of greater personal or theoretic interest; the general approach is suitable to that kind of translation. We would begin with content analysis of specific television character portrayals, that is, all those black actors or actresses appearing in a continuing prime time (8–11 P.M.) or Saturday morning (8 A.M. to 1 P.M.) series or in commercials adjacent to or within these times. This content analysis would be conducted during the fall of a first year of study and repeated during the fall of the next year in order to be responsive to possible changes across the beginning of two different television seasons.

Furthermore, these general content analyses would be supplemented during Year 1 by intensive analyses of multiple episodes (3–5) of those shows featuring black characters that a viewing survey identifies as the most regularly watched among the targeted age groups. That is, the portrayals of favorite black characters would be examined across time to provide more reliable information as to the characteristic portrayals and behaviors of these characters.

Second, we would conduct a panel-design field survey in which black and white children (with age groups to be specified) are personally interviewed in order (a) to assess their levels of exposure to programs that regularly feature blacks; (b) to measure a set of mediating variables, for example, the perceived reality of blacks on fictional television shows, personal cross-race experiences by the respondents, their television dependency, and the credibility they place in television; and (c) to measure the subjects' cognitions, attitudes, and expectations regarding blacks. These data should be collected at two points in time, in concert with the results of the multiwave content analyses previously described. That is, the content analytic findings would be the basis for a large segment of the specific questioning of these respondents about television blacks.

Third, we would conduct a field experiment in which exposure to black portrayals on television is systematically manipulated for a subgroup of viewers. The basic experiment will be to induce, through incentives, viewing or nonviewing of a specific menu of television programs that feature black characters on a regular basis. The effects of this exposure on specific black image impressions would be assessed. A slightly different approach here would be to choose from syndicated series a pair of series that present quite different black role models. At one extreme, *Amos 'n' Andy* could be introducted to a group of respondents and viewed for four or five episodes; at a quite different level, *I Spy* might be introduced to a different group of respondents. The idea would be to utilize what appear to be both positive and negative content approaches in the presentation of television blacks and to determine whether, and in what ways, they may impact on the key dependent variables.

Fourth, we would conduct an in-school experiment that specifically manipulates the presentation of black characters in law-abiding, mixed, or neutral roles. Over a specific time period, one group would receive television stimuli that consistently depict blacks in law-abiding portrayals, a second control group would receive stimuli portraying blacks in roles irrelevant to law-breaking, and a third group would receive a combination of law-breaking and law-abiding portrayals. The specific purpose of this experiment would be to determine to what extent the expectations of white and black youngsters toward blacks in these specific social roles can be structured by such role portrayals. The choice of law-abiding or law-breaking contrasts is illustrative. Any number of other pairings is possible, for example, strong black women versus weak black women; blacks as professionals versus blacks in lesser occupational roles; blacks in integrated settings versus blacks in segregated settings.

SUMMARY

Our research plan is not the only one available, but it is offered as a promising option.

As Lee Barrow, (1975) now dean of the Howard University School of Communication, observed, "My tentative conclusions are that we know virtually nothing about either the short- or the long-term effects of television on minority children. . . If I were to place all of our knowledge in a thimble, I would probably still have room for my thumb."

Barrow's thumb is neither exceptionally small or large. It would still fit, except perhaps for his thumbnail. The research we have been able to assemble may be considered equivalent to the border pieces of a 1000-piece jigsaw puzzle. The remainder of that puzzle has yet to be collated. It is for that reason that this chapter has become more a tactical and strategic plan for solving that puzzle than a recitation of firm, demonstrable research results. Not a single comprehensive, longitudinal study effort has been directed at exploring television and the minority child or the impact of minority characters in television programs on either minority or nonminority children. We have proposed one extensive approach to those research issues; other options ought to be considered as well.

We believe that such evidence, when available, can inform media policy makers. It can also inform public interest groups and appropriate government agencies. At that time, these intersecting interests should be better able to apply relevant research findings. That goal should be expedited.

REFERENCES

Atkin, C. K. Effects of television advertising on children. E. Palmer & A. Dorr (Eds.). In *Children and the faces of television: Teaching, violence, selling.* New York: Academic Press, 1980.

Atkin, C. K. Effects of television advertising on children—First year experimental evidence. Technical report, Michigan State University, East Lansing, 1975.

Atkin, C. K. & Heald, G. The content of children's toy and food commercials. *Journal of Communication,* 1977, *27,* 107–114.

Atkin, C. K., Murray, J. P. & Nayman, O. B. (Eds.). *Television and social behavior: An annotated bibliography of research focusing on television's impact on children.* Washington, D.C.: US Govt. Printing Office, 1971.

Ball, S., & Bogatz, G. *Reading with television: An evaluation of* The Electric Company. Princeton, New Jersey: Educational Testing Service, 1973.

Bandura, A. *Social learning theory.* Englewood Cliffs, New Jersey: Prentice-Hall, 1977.

Baran, S. Dying black/dying white: Coverage of six newspapers. *Journalism Quarterly,* 1973, *50*(4), 761–763.

Barrow, L. Nonregulatory policy research. Speech delivered at the Research on Television and Children and Youth conference, Reston, Virginia, November, 1975.

Bogatz, G. A., & Ball, S. *The second year of* Sesame Street: *A continuing evaluation.* Princeton, New Jersey: Educational Testing Service, 1971.

Boyenton, W. The Negro turns to advertising. *Journalism Quarterly,* 1965, *42*(2), 227–235.

Brigham, J. *Ethnic humor on television: Does it reduce/reinforce racial prejudice?* Paper presented at Annual Conference of American Psychological Association, (NY, Sept.) 1975.

Brigham, J., & Giesbrecht, L. *All in the Family:* Racial attitudes. *Journal of Communication,* 1976, *26,* 69–74.

Chapko, M., & Lewis, M. Authoritarianism and *All in the Family. Journal of Psychology,* 1975, *90,* 245–248.

Chilman, C. S. *Growing up poor.* Washington, D.C.: US Govt. Printing Office, 1966.

Colfax, D., & Steinberg, S. The perpetuation of racial stereotypes: Blacks in mass circulation magazine advertisements. *Public Opinion Quarterly,* 1972, *35,* 8–18.

Colle, R. D. Negro image in the mass media: A case study in social change. *Journalism Quarterly,* 1968, *45,* 55–60.

Comstock, G., Chaffee, S., Katzman, N., McCombs, M., & Roberts, D. *Television and human behavior.* New York: Columbia University Press, 1978.

Comstock, G., Lindsey, G., & Fisher, M. *Television and human behavior*. Santa Monica, California: Rand Corporation, 1975.

Cook, T., Appleton, B. H. T., Conner, R., Shaffer, A., Tamkin, G., & Weber, S. *"Sesame Street" Revisited*. New York: Russell Sage Foundation, 1975.

Cox, K. Changes in stereotyping of Negroes and whites in magazine advertisements. *Public Opinion Quarterly*, 1969–1970, *33*, 603–606.

Cox, K. Social effects of integrated advertising. *Journal of Advertising Research*, 1970, *10*, 41–44.

Culley, J., & Bennett, R. Selling women, selling blacks. *Journal of Communication*, 1976, *26*(4), 160–174.

Dimas, D. *The effects of motion pictures portraying black models on the self-concept of black elementary school children*. Unpublished doctoral dissertation, Syracuse University, 1970.

Dominick, J., & Greenberg, B. Three seasons of blacks on television. *Journal of Advertising Research*, 1970, *10*(2), 21–27.

Epstein, L. A. Some effects of low income on children and their families. *Social Security Bulletin*, February 1961, pp. 12–17.

Gorn, G. J., Goldberg, M. E., & Kanungo, R. N. The role of educational television in changing the intergroup attitudes of children. *Child Development*, 1976, *47*, 277–280.

Gottlieb, D. Goal aspirations and goal fulfillments: Differences between deprived and affluent American adolescents. *American Journal of Orthopsychiatry*, 1964, *34*(5), 934–941.

Greenberg, B. Children's reactions to TV blacks. *Journalism Quarterly*, 1972, *49*(1), 5–14.

Greenberg, B. Gratifications of television viewing and their correlates for British children. In J. G. Blumler & E. Katz (Eds.), *The uses of mass communications*. Beverly Hills, California: Sage, 1974.

Greenberg, B., & Dervin, B. *Use of the mass media by the urban poor*. New York: Praeger, 1972.

Greenberg, B., & Kahn, S. Blacks in *Playboy* cartoons. *Journalism Quarterly*, 1970, *47*(3), 557–560.

Greenberg, B., & Reeves, B. Children and the perceived reality of television. *Journal of Social Issues*, 1976, *32*(4), 86–97.

Hinton. J., Seggar, J., Northcott, H., & Fontes, B. Tokenism and improving imagery of blacks in TV drama and comedy: 1973. *Journal of Broadcasting*, 1974, *18*(4), 423–432.

Irelan, L. M., & Besner, A. Low income outlook on life. *Welfare in Review*, 1965, *3*(9), 13–19.

Kassarjian, H. The Negro and American advertising: 1946–1965. *Journal of Marketing Research*, 1969, *6*, 29–39.

Keller, S. The social world of the urban slum child: Some early findings. *American Journal of Orthopsychiatry*, 1963, *23*(5), 823–831.

Lewis, O. The culture of poverty. *Scientific American*, October 1966, pp. 19–25.

Lyle, J., & Hoffman, H. R. Children's use of television and other media. In E. A. Rubinstein, G. A. Comstock, & J. P. Murray (Eds.), *Television and social behavior* (Vol. 4). *Television in day-to-day life: Patterns of use*. Washington, D.C.: US Govt. Printing Office, 1972.

Minuchin, S., Montaluo, B., Guerney, B., Jr., Rosman, B., & Schumer, F. *Families of the slums: An exploration of their structure and treatment*. New York: Basic Books, 1967.

Neely, J. J., Heckel, R. V., & Leichtman, H. M. The effect of race of model and response consequences to the model on imitation in children. *Journal of Social Psychology*, 1973, *89*, 225–231.

Northcott, H., Seggar, J., & Hinton, J. Trends in TV portrayal of blacks and women. *Journalism Quarterly*, 1975, *52*(4), 741–744.

Poussaint, A. Cheap thrills that degrade blacks. *Psychology Today*, 1974, pp. 22, 26, 27, 30, 32, 98.

Rainville, R., & McCormick, E. Extent of covert racial prejudice in pro-football announcers' speech. *Journalism Quarterly*, 1977, *54*(1), 20–26.

Roberts, C. The presentation of blacks in television network newscasts. *Journalism Quarterly*, 1975, *52*(1), 50–55.

Seggar, J. Television's portrayal of minorities and women, 1971–1975. *Journal of Broadcasting*, 1977, *21*, 435–446.

Seggar, J., & Wheeler, P. World of work on TV. *Journal of Broadcasting*, 1973, *17*, 201–214.

Shuey, A., King, N., & Griffith, B. Stereotyping of Negroes and whites: An analysis of magazine pictures. *Public Opinion Quarterly*, 1953, *27*, 281–287.

Stein, A., & Friedrich, L. K. Television content and young children's behavior. In J. P., Murray, E. A. Rubinstein, & G. A. Comstock (Eds.), *Television and social behavior* (Vol. 2). Washington D.C.: US Govt. Printing Office, 1972.

Stempel, G. Visibility of blacks in news and news-picture magazines. *Journalism Quarterly*, 1971, *48*(2), 337–339.

Surlin, S. Bigotry on air and in life: The Archie Bunker case. *Public Telecommunications Review*, 1974, *2*, 34–41.

Tate, E., & Surlin S. Agreement with opinionated TV characters across culture. *Journalism Quarterly*, 1976, *53*(2), 199–203.

U.S. Commission on Civil Rights. *Window dressing on the set: Women and minorities in television*. Washington, D.C.: US Govt. Printing Office, 1977.

U.S. Department of Commerce, Bureau of the Census. *General social and economic characteristics*. (Current Population Reports, Series PC, No. 1-c1). Washington, D.C.: US Govt. Printing Office, 1972.

Vidmar, N., & Rokeach, M. Archie Bunker's bigotry: A study in selective perception and exposure. *Journal of Communication*, 1974, *24*, 36–47.

Wilhoit, G. C., & de Bock, H. *All in the Family* in Holland. *Journal of Communication*, 1976, *26*, 75–84.

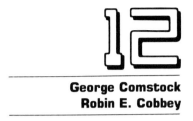

George Comstock
Robin E. Cobbey

Television and the Children of Ethnic Minorities: Perspectives from Research

The experience American television represents for the children of ethnic minorities commands attention precisely because of their minority status. American television is unabashedly profit-dominated and, because of this, it discriminates in its programming against minorities, whether defined by age, ethnicity, or otherwise, in favor of audiences whose hugeness rests on heterogeneity. It specializes only to the degree imposed by audience availability—children on Saturday mornings; housewives in the daytime, Monday through Friday. None of the innovative alternatives to commercial broadcasting to date—public television, cable, The Children's Television Workshop—have altered two facts: The public principally views commercial broadcast television, and children principally view television prepared for general audiences. In these circumstances, the children of ethnic minorities for the most part are either a minority within the majority for the modest portion of children's viewing represented by Saturday morning, or a minority within a minority most of the time. What should we think about the relationship that has evolved between this mass medium and this twice-over minority?

The available evidence leads us to propose four propositions whose value is as much heuristic as predictive. This circumstance derives not

245

solely from their generality but equally from the inadequacy of the evidence in their behalf, and particularly from the failure of that evidence to encompass a variety of ethnic minorities or to apply clearly to children.

MINORITY CHILDREN'S DISTINCTIVE ORIENTATION TOWARD TELEVISION

Ethnic minority children have a distinctive orientation toward television and other mass media. Support for such a proposition comes largely, but not wholly, from data reflecting adult—and therefore, parental—behavior, and almost wholly from data on blacks. We encounter such data in regard to use of television, attitudes toward television, and motives for viewing television.

The bulk of evidence suggests that blacks on the average are heavier viewers of television than are whites. This was initially interpreted as the result of the greater proportion of households of lower socioeconomic states (SES) among the black population, but the cumulative findings point toward a less commonplace explanation. Bogart (1972) examined a massive database—the 15,332 cases in the 1970 W. R. Simmons national sample on media use. He had previously concluded that differences between whites and blacks in media exposure could be explained entirely by disparities in income and differences in geographical location. He now concluded that the explanation held for newspaper reading and radio listening, but not for television viewing. "Television," he inferred, "plays a somewhat different role in the lives of Negroes than of whites at similar levels of income and education." What the Simmons data documented was that blacks on the average view more television than do whites. Greenberg and Dervin (1970) found the same ethnic difference in their 1968–1969 Cleveland, Ohio, Philadelphia, Pennsylvania, and East Lansing, Michigan samples—except that they found it to extend to high school and elementary school children. Our caution against embracing too quickly a conclusion applying generally to ethnic minorities or to all places is aroused, however, by Lyle and Hoffman's (1972) southern California sample in which viewing was greater among elementary and high school girls with Spanish surnames but not among the boys.

Blacks as a group rather definitely hold more favorable attitudes toward television than do whites. Bower (1973), in his 1970 national probability sample, found that blacks express greater liking for television, more frequently concur that, as individuals, they do not watch it enough, and are more likely to believe they are watching more than in past years. One of the most consistent patterns of mass media behavior in America has been an inverse relationship of SES to attitudes favorable toward television and to use of television (Bower, 1973; Robinson, 1972; Robinson & Converse, 1972; Steiner, 1963). This pattern dissolves in the black affinity for television. It is as if ethnic status carries with it a history, a set of needs, a body of motives, and a perspective that creates, from the same medium, distinctly different media. The inverse relationship so persistent among the white majority is, among blacks, either attenuated or reversed. Better-educated blacks appear to hold attitudes more favorable toward the medium than their less-educated peers, better-educated blacks do not appear to watch markedly less television than their less-educated peers (Bower, 1973). The stronger black affinity for television becomes visible early, for Greenberg and Dervin (1970) found that viewing was greater among black than among white children, as well as greater among black than among white adolescents when the black and white families appeared to be comparably low in SES.

The shift of blacks toward television and away from newspapers as a source of political information is a special instance of their distinctive orientation toward the medium. McCombs (1968) traces media use by blacks and whites during the four presidential elections between 1952 and 1964. These Michigan Survey Research Center national samples were divided into high versus low users of media when television and newspaper use were consistent, and into television versus newspaper users when they were not. The results mark one of the more social significant trends in media use. In 1952, the majority of blacks were low users of media during the campaign. By 1954, the majority were high users; and there was little difference between blacks and whites in the degree of principal reliance on newspapers. However, the proportion of blacks who relied principally on television increased sharply, but no such trend occurred among whites. The emerging black orientation toward television for political information was independent of education; it was not attributable to shifts in the distribution of education nor was it confined to any educational status.

Television is considered to be predominantly entertainment, whether the basis of that judgment is the content or the public's reception of the media (Comstock, Chaffee, Katzman, McCombs, & Roberts, 1978). Nevertheless, the evidence supports the view that ethnic minorities are motivated to a greater-than-average degree in their consumption of that entertainment by a desire for information. Bower (1973) found that persons of lower SES, which is more frequent among minorities, more often cited learning as a motive for television viewing. Greenberg and Dervin (1970) found that black elementary and high school students from families of lower SES more often cited learning as a motive for viewing and more frequently agreed that television portrays life accurately than did white peers of similar SES, although SES itself appeared to be inversely related to the holding of such beliefs. This heightened information motive is something ethnic minority youth and the disadvantaged share with the elderly, leading to the hypothesis that it is the product of isolation from the social mainstream.

There are a number of possible explanations for the apparently distinctive orientation of blacks toward television (Comstock, et al., 1978). The "political adaptation" explanation holds that the Civil Rights movement inspired blacks to seek information from television because the movement followed shortly after the medium's rise to prominence.The related "print stigma" explanation holds that a principal factor was the advantage accruing to the new medium from the history of inadequate and indifferent coverage from general circulation magazines and newspapers (Baker & Ball, 1969; Greenberg & Dervin, 1970; Lyle, 1967; National Advisory Commission on Civil Disorders, 1968). Both apply more plausibly to use of television news than to use of the medium generally, although certainly enhanced orientation toward the medium as a news source would be likely to lead to at least somewhat greater viewing of other programming. The "disparate values" explanation holds that blacks, exclusive of their differences from whites in educational differences in educational attainment aside, were less integrated into the nation's "book culture." Adherence to book culture values—exemplified most prominently in the emphasis of liberal arts education in both secondary and high education—has been advanced as one of the factors responsible for the greater hostility toward television associated with greater education among whites (Meyersohn, 1965). The "integration" explanation holds that television achieved its popularity and status among blacks by providing a symbol of assimilation—either through the information it offered or through the participation implied by its consumption. We do not have data that encourage us to choose among these alternatives. We suspect that transient factors related to black (and white) history have been at work, because the well known phenomenon of greater viewing by the elderly (Chaffe & Wilson, 1975; Comstock et al., 1978; Greenberg & Dervin, 1970; Schramm, 1968, 1969), does not appear among blacks in the data so far available. This leads us to believe that the correct explanation is dependent on the experience of specific black generations.

MINORITY CHILDREN'S TASTES
IN PROGRAMMING

Children of ethnic minorities have different tastes and preferences in television programming than do white children. American television is an enormously successful mass medium that attracts huge, diverse audiences nightly and less diverse, but sizable, audiences at other times. If we accept the evidence suggesting that they view television somewhat more than whites ethnic minority children presumably are at least proportionately represented in these audiences—60% of all 2- to 11-year-olds view between 9 and 11 A.M. on the typical fall or winter Saturday, 40% or more view between 7 and 9 A.M. during the surrounding weekdays, and 30% or more of all teenagers view between 7 and 10 P.M. on those weekdays. Disguised by the mass nature of television, however, are differences in tastes and preferences deriving from ethnic minority membership.

Lyle and Hoffman (1972), in comparing white, Hispanic, and black children in a Los Angeles, California basin community, found differences among these groups in which programs were cited as favorites. The differences, not discernible among first-graders, became increasingly apparent between the sixth and tenth grades. Greenberg and Dervin (1970) found differences in favorite programs between white and black elementary and high school students in the Midwest. Fletcher (1969) found that the declared favorite programs of black and white Atlanta, Georgia children in the sixth through twelfth grades differed. Surlin and Dominick (1970) found differences in the favorites of black and white Philadelphia teenagers.

There is also evidence that differences occur among adults. Greenberg and Hanneman (1970) found that in Michigan, sample blacks reported viewing somewhat different programming than did whites. Carey (1966) compared viewing data for blacks and whites in national samples of about 5000 families in each of 2 years; in both cases, only slightly more than one-half of the top 25 most popular programs were the same for blacks and whites. However, Greenberg and Dervin (1970) found sufficient similarity in the ranking of favorite programs by blacks and whites of low SES to conclude that they had quite similar preferences.

There is not a readily discernible pattern of elaborate character in the data. Several of the studies have taken SES into account (Greenberg & Dervin, 1970; Surlin & Dominick, 1970), and the findings, which are inconsistent as to the role of socioeconomic differences, do not lead us to accept SES as entirely responsible for differences in program preferences. There seems to be little doubt that ethnic minority children prefer programs featuring performers from their ethnic groups (Greenberg, 1972; Greenberg & Dervin 1970; Lyle, 1972; Lyle & Hoffman 1972). There is evidence that black children are especially drawn to programs featuring families (Greenberg & Dervin, 1970; Surlin & Dominick, 1970). Adult blacks also favor black television performers (Greenberg & Hanneman, 1970), but they do not appear to share the same inclination toward family programs (Carey, 1966). The ethnic differences found by Greenberg and Dervin (1970) for children and adolescents and their absence in the same investigative context among adults, even with socioeconomic influences taken into account, the disinterest of black adults toward family programs found by Carey (1966) and the appeal of such programs to black teenagers found by Surlin and Dominick (1970), and the increase in differentiation found by Lyle and Hoffman (1972) to occur with age—these findings combine to suggest that differences in taste emerge progressively as children grow older, then become modified and possibly sharply attentuated in adulthood.

BEHAVIORAL RESPONSE TO TELEVISION

The behavioral response of children and adolescents to television portrayals is in part dependent on ethnic minority membership. The experiments involving ethnicity decidedly encourage the view that it influences the way television affects behavior (Bandura, 1969, 1971, 1973; Berkowitz, 1962, 1964, 1973). Nicholas, McCarter, and Heckel (1971a) examined the effects of sex, race, and competency of models on children's imitation of televised portrayals. A sex and race-balanced group of 60 second-grade children responded to multiple-choice questions, one-half of which were purposefully too difficult for them, while viewing a videotape of four peers matched in sex and race who displayed answers to the same questions. White girls imitated boys, white or black, most frequently, and black girls imitated black boys most frequently, and white boys least frequently. Girls imitated boys more than boys imitated girls. Nicholas and colleagues (1971b) then examined the effects of adult versus peer status. The procedures were identical to those used for their first experiment except that white models were used. They included an adult male, an adult female, a boy, and a girl as models. Overall, children chose to imitate the adult over the peer model. Additionally, boys imitated males more faithfully than girls imitated the woman. The sole ethnic difference was that black children imitated the woman less often than did white children.

Neely, Heckel, and Leichtman (1973) investigated the effects of reinforcement and of race of model on the imitative behavior of black children aged 3–5. The children viewed a videotaped black or white peeraged model performing a task for which a verbal reward or punishment was given. The children then performed the same series of tasks. Children imitated the white more than the black model and the rewarded more than the punished model. Race appeared to be as important as reinforcement of behavior, for the punished white model was imitated about as frequently as the rewarded black model. These results are constent with those of Liebert, Sobol, and Copemann (1972) who employed live adult models; black children were again more likely to imitate the responses of rewarded models and white models. Neely *et al.* (1973) suggested that the greater tendency to imitate a white model is attributable to the status discrepancy that favors whites in American society, which ostensibly would make black children more likely to follow the example of a white than that of a black model.

Thelan and Soltz (1969) reported somewhat different results. Black children who observed a televised white adult male model receiving verbal reward showed less imitative behavior than black children observing the model receiving no consequences for his behavior. In a subsequent experiment, the opposite results were found among white children. The investigators speculated that the black children had previously learned that reward or praise to a white model will not necessarily apply to their own similar behavior. Thelan (1971) later tested this interpretation by introducing race of subject and model. Groups of black and white 5- and 6-year-olds of equivalent SES viewed televised portrayals of praised or unpraised white or black adults performing aggressive acts toward an inflated bear. Dependent measures were verbal and physical imitation and recall of aggressive behavior. White children viewing the black model displayed more imitative behavior than any other group. Both black and white children were able to recall more of the white model's behavior than the black model's. Black children had higher recall scores in the nonreinforced condition, a finding consistent with the earlier experiment (Thelan & Soltz, 1969). However, the author argued that differential reinforcement history is not the correct interpretation because black children viewing the praised white model exhibited as much imitative behavior as white children in the same condition.

On the whole, the findings are reminiscent of those by Bandura and others (Bandura, 1965, 1973; Bandura, Ross & Ross, 1961, 1963a, 1963b) concerning the relationship between sex of model and sex of the viewing child. Portrayals of aggressive models more readily elicited imitative aggression in males, presumably because aggression is more

socially accepted on the part of males. However, females later repro-
duced the observed behavior when a reward was offered, thus demonstrating that learning may have occurred even when its contribution is
not readily observable in performance. Portrayals of males had the most
impact on boys whereas portrayals of females were not similarly effective with girls.

These findings encourage an interpretation of the results for ethnicity in which similarity of model and viewer become subordinate to
ascribed status. Rosekrans (1967) demonstrated that young viewers'
perceptions of similarity between themselves and a portrayed person
increased the likelihood that the children would emulate that portrayal. The findings for ethnicity do not contradict the inference that
perceived similarity enhances the likelihood of behavioral influence.
However, the detectable pattern favors emphasis on the social status
normally ascribed to the portrayed personages. Males, of whatever race,
enjoy an advantage over females. Whites, in most instances, enjoy some
advantage over ethnic minorities. These generalizations become confounded, as the early findings on sex and aggressiveness hint, when
behavior is more normative for a demographic category; similiarity
may then play a larger role. The early findings on increased behavioral
capability, despite the absence of evidence from immediate performance, similarly lead us to be skeptical that the experimental outcomes
attributable to ethnicity fully reflect learning resulting from viewing.

TELEVISION AS A SOURCE OF GUIDANCE
FOR MINORITY CHILDREN

Ethnic minority children have information needs that give particular
prominence to television as a source of guidance. All children have
similar needs for information. What sets ethnic minority children apart
is their relative isolation from sources that can satisfy those needs. This
circumstance arises in part from their ethnicity, and in part from the
socioeconomic disadvantage that is frequently associated with being a
minority member. Lower SES generally induces a particular reliance on
television because it brings information that is not otherwise readily
available.

Gerson (1966) found that black teenagers relied more on the mass
media than did white teenagers for information about how to behave
with the opposite sex, which, given the preeminence of television in
media use among young persons in general and ethnic minority young
persons in particular implies reliance in particular on television. Reliance on the media was expressed both in the verifying of present

practices and in the seeking of new practices, or, in the authors terms, both in "reinforcement" and "norm acquisition." Two relationships emphasize the degree to which the television-dominated media use is rooted in the social relationships: (a) the reversal, among blacks, of an inverse relationship for whites between integration into the peer culture and reliance on the media, and (b) the divergence between the races in the role of sex, with white girls but black boys most reliant on the media within their ethnic groups. What these two relationships most likely reflect is the influence of differential need based on sex-related interests and on isolation from alternative sources of information. For the whites, media reliance apparently was a substitute for peers; for blacks, a complement, because their peers could not supply information as readily. Within this context, boys among blacks, but girls among whites, apparently were left with the greatest information deficits: the black boys, because of the male responsibility for initiating social interaction and the inadequacy of peer information, and the white girls, because of the very adequacy of peer information among white boys. These relationships, like those between age, race, and SES in regard to programs featuring families (Comstock et al., 1978; Greenberg & Dervin, 1970; Surlin and Dominick, 1970) in which such preference is greater among black teenagers than black adults, among black than white teenagers, and among lower than higher SES teenagers, exemplify information deficits attributable to social circumstances that many individuals feel can be redressed in some way by the mass media.

These varied findings conform to the explanation applied by DeFleur and DeFleur (1967) to their data on children's knowledge of occupations. Television appeared to provide knowledge about occupations with which the children had no firsthand experience. Prestige rankings by the children were more consistent for portrayed but otherwise unfamiliar occupations than for those with which the children had had actual experience or those with which they had neither media nor firsthand experience. These findings imply that television has an effect when experience fails, and that television, because of the limited, stereotypic scope of its portrayals, may provide a homogenizing influence—an implication to which the data available on ethnic minority children would not by themselves lead.

RESEARCH ON TELEVISION
HAS NEGLECTED MINORITIES

The egalitarian principle of proportionate representation of all persons regardless of race, creed, or political beliefs has not been honored in research on television and behavior. Only about 7% of publicly available studies provided noteworthy data on ethnic minorities or persons of lower SES (Comstock & Fisher, 1975). In any event, proportional representation would fail to provide parity in accrued knowledge. The past nevertheless establishes several priorities for future research.

The most obvious of these unaddressed issues is the importance that should be ascribed to television as compared to other agents of socialization. The emphasis we tentatively assign to television among the children of ethnic minorities derives solely from the relatively more prominent place—in terms of exposure, credibility, and as a source of information—that it appears to occupy in their lives. We do not begin with any yardstick of relative influence for children in general, and the most that can be said is that, as among ethnic minority children, average hours of viewing per week is substantial, and substantial proportions assign it credulity, employ it as a source for various kinds of information, and that it is most influential when other sources are absent (Comstock et al., 1978). Neither for children in general nor for ethnic minority children can much be said about the weight of television's influence compared to other socializing agents. The lack of a methodology that would provide a convincing answer does not make the question less important. It is entirely possible that television's influence is minor among all children, or that, despite the evidence that would suggest otherwise, that among ethnic minority children its relative contribution in fact is less than among white children.

A second issue to which the present findings lead us is the feasibility of intervention by parents and by schools in the communication flowing from television to the child. In the case of parents, the questions become those of focus: when might parents most effectively intervene, the technique they should use, and the constancy that is needed because childrearing is an everyday task, not a laboratory experiment, and the parents' efficacy will depend not only what they do but how consistently and regularly they do it. The finding by Greenberg and Atkin (1978) that parental involvement in children's viewing is somewhat more common in black than in white households encourages us to believe that among minority children parental intervention has particular promise. In the case of schools, we return to a theme as old as the empirical investigations of television's impact on children. Two decades ago, at the end of the two historic, large-scale investigations in England and the United States of the new medium's influence on children, Himmelweit, Oppenheim, and Vince (1958) argued that television is powerful principally when there is a vacuum of firsthand experience or alternative informational sources, and Schramm, Lyle, and Parker (1961) questioned whether schools were doing enough with and about the medium. These views remain pertinent today. Although certainly schools today use television more as an instrument of instruction, employ television seen outside of school more as an adjunct in the teaching of reading and other subjects, and more frequently focus on television—both news and entertainment—as subjects about which children and adolescents should be instructed so that they can respond more judiciously to what they view, the medium itself has become much more prominent in their lives—it consumes more time, and earlier inverse relationships between amount of television viewing and between television viewing and the child's intellectual ability appear to be diminishing (Comstock *et al.*, 1978; Louis Harris and Associates, 1975). Thus, the question of the who, when, and how of intervening in the communication that flows from television to children remains, and because of the somewhat greater role that it apparently assumes in their lives the question has special pertinence in regard to the children of ethnic minorities.

A third issue is the patterns of viewing and preferences that hold for ethnic minority children. The evidence that suggests a distinctive pattern for ethnic minority children is drawn almost wholly from blacks and rests on the accumulation of findings varying in place, time, quality, and sometimes outcome. The notion that minority children are attracted to performers who are alike or similar in ethnic background is plausible, but this apparent fact does not explain the determinants of their frequent but uneven subscription to majority tastes. We know very little about the current television viewing of black children, and less about that of Asian-American, American Indian, or Hispanic children. We certainly would like to know more accurately the ways in which minority children differ in their viewing, but we must also confront the particular instances in which they and other children concur in taste or our comprehension will have been entrapped by the lure of explaining differences to the detriment of understanding either those instances of perfect parallelism among ethnic groups or those in which apparent sameness is attributable to dissimilar factors. Such information would provide an important foundation for the design of intervention by parents and by schools, for interventions depend for efficacy not only on forcefulness and skills but on the accuracy of their application.

Fourth, we find ourselves dissatisfied with the exploration of the factors responsible for the differential behavioral response to televised portrayals associated with ethnicity. The evidence leads to the tentative conclusion that a principal factor in differential behavior outcomes is the ascribed status attached to ethnic membership. Race and sex, on the part both of who is portrayed and who views, make a difference. The failure of the scant data available to support the hypothesis that minorities may discount an observed reward of a nonminority child (Thelan, 1971) is intriguing, but not conclusive. The many other issues that might be raised have a similar status—the data are at best intriguing, more often nonexistent. Among these issues are (a) variation in outcome attributable conceivably to the class of behavior involved, with socially disapproved behavior possibly most enjoying enhancement from the ascribed status of a perpetrator; (b) the influence of portrayed prior association between models differing in ethnicity, for it is plausible that egalitarianism in portrayal might find a mirror in equivalent impact; and (c) the validity of the inferred processes, which even in regard to ascribed status rest on interpretations applied to observed behavior rather than on data—such as from the subjects themselves—that might disconfirm them. Ethnic group position will change, and ethnic groups themselves are hardly homogeneous in the attibutes that constitute status; attention, then, should focus on the variables responsible for effects related to ethnicity, rather than simply on ethnic differences.

There is also an issue raised by the data on ethnicity and television portrayals that has profound implications for the study of the medium. Greenberg (1972) found evidence of substantial identification of white children with black television characters. More interestingly, he found that such identification was associated with greater exposure to the medium, but was unrelated to greater everday contact with blacks. This suggests the hypothesis that television may, to some degree, operate independently in establishing the emulative potential of those portrayed models, whereas the real world determines status for live models. This would imply that portrayals of whites may enjoy an advantage because whites more frequently appear on the medium; thus, they have also been ascribed an elevated status on television.

Finally, there are the ambiguous roles of ethnicity and SES. For example, blacks as a demographic entity include a disproportionate quantity of households of lower SES. However, although blacks certainly can be spoken of as a group for which this is an attribute acknowledged, this does not excuse us from the necessity of distinguishing between relationships associated with ethnicity because of socioeconomic differences and those otherwise identified with ethnicity for cultural, historical, or other reasons. The research of the past very often fails by this criterion, sometimes by ignoring SES and sometimes by measuring it so crudely that one must be skeptical of the allegation that it has been taken into account.

The issues that are raised by ethnic status are not exclusive to ethnicity but represent circumstances that are much wider in occurrence but that appear more often among ethnic minorities. Isolation, economic disadvantage, and lack of alternative sources of information are not unique to minorities, nor is extensive use of television. The average child 2–11 years of age views more than the average adult between the ages of 18–49; minority status and economic disadvantage only amplify consumption of the medium. The children of ethnic minorities merit attention on theoretical grounds because of the particular circumstances they, as a group, sometimes exemplify; they merit attention on practical grounds because these circumstances probably do place them in a special relationship to television. In the end, however, what we examine in giving attention to ethnic minorities is the more general state of children and the mass media.

REFERENCES

Baker, R. K., & Ball, S. J. (Eds.) Violence and the media: A staff report to the National Commission on the Causes and Prevention of Violence. Washington, D.C.: U.S. Government Printing Office, 1969.

Bandura, A. Influence of models reinforcement contingencies on the acquisition of imitative responses. Journal of Personality and Social Psychology, 1965, 1, 589–595.

Bandura, A. Social-learning theory of identificatory processes. In D. A. Goshin (Ed.), Handbook of socialization theory and research. Chicago, Illinois: Rand McNally, 1969.

Bandura, A. Social learning theory. New York: General Learning, 1971.

Bandura, A. Aggression: A social learning analysis. Englewood Cliffs, New Jersey: Prentice-Hall, 1973.

Bandura, A., Ross, D., & Ross, S. A. Transmission of aggression through imitation of aggresive models. Journal of Abnormal and Social Psychology, 1961, 63, 575–582.

Bandura, A., Ross, D., & Ross, S. A. Imitation of film-mediated aggressive models. Journal of Abnormal and Social Psychology, 1963, 66, 3–11. (a)

Bandura, A., Ross, D., & Ross, S. A. Vicarious reinforcement and imitative learning. Journal of Abnormal and Social Psychology, 1963, 67, 601–607. (b)

Berkowitz, L. Aggression: A social psychological analysis. New York: McGraw-Hill, 1962.

Berkowitz, L. Aggressive cues in aggressive behavior and hostility catharsis. Psychology Review, 1964, 71, 104–122.

Berkowitz, L. Words and symbols as stimuli to aggressive responses. In J. F. Knutson (Ed.), Control of aggression: Implications from basic research. Chicago, Illinois: Aldine, 1973.

Bogart, L. Negro and white media exposure: New evidence. Journalism Quarterly, 1972, 49(1), 15–21.

Bower, R. T. Television and the public. New York: Holt, 1973.

Carey, J. W. Variations in Negro/white television preferences. Journal of Broadcasting, 1966, 199–212.

Chaffee, S. H., & Wilson, D. *Adult life cycle changes in mass media use.* Paper presented at the meeting of the Association for Education in Journalism, Ottawa, Ontario, Canada, August 1975.

Comstock, G., Chaffee, S., Katzman, N., McCombs, M., & Roberts, D. *Television and human behavior.* New York: Columbia Univ. Press, 1978.

Comstock, G., & Fisher, M. *Television and human behavior: A guide to the pertinent scientific literature.* Santa Monica, California: Rand Corporation, 1975.

DeFleur, M. L., & DeFleur, L. B. The relative contribution of television as a learning source for children's occupational knowledge. *American Sociological Review,* 1967, *32,* 777–789.

Fletcher, A. D. Negro and white children's television program preferences. *Journal of Broadcasting,* 1969, *13,* 359–366.

Gerson, W. M. Mass media socialization behavior: Negro–white differences. *Social Force,* 1966, *45,* 40–50.

Greenberg, B. S. Children's reactions to TV blacks. *Journalism Quarterly,* 1972, *49*(1), 5–14.

Greenberg, B. S., & Atkin, C. K. *Learning about minorities from television: The research agenda.* Paper presented at Television and the Minority Child, a conference sponsored by the Center for Afro-American Studies, University of California, Los Angeles, April 1978.

Greenberg, B. S., & Dervin, B. *Use of the mass media by the urban poor.* New York: Praeger, 1970.

Greenberg, B. S., & Hanneman, G. J. Racial attitudes and the impact of TV on blacks. *Educational Broadcasting Review,* 1970, *4*(2), 27–34.

Himmelweit, H. T., Oppenheim, A. N., & Vince, P. *Television and the child.* London and New York: Oxford Univ. Press, 1958.

Liebert, R. M., Sobol, M. P., & Copemann, C. D. Effects of vicarious consequences and race of model upon imitative performance by black children. *Developmental Psychology,* 1972, *6,* 453–456.

Louis Harris and Associates, Inc. *A survey on aging: Experience of older Americans vs. public expectation of old age.* Conducted for the National Council on the Aging, Inc. New York: Author, 1974.

Lyle, J. *The news in megalopolis.* San Francisco: Chandler, 1967.

Lyle, J. Television in daily life: Patterns of use. In E. A. Rubinstein, G. A. Comstock, & J. P. Murray (Eds.), *Television and social behavior* (Vol. 4): *Television in day-to-day life: Patterns of use.* Washington, D.C.: US Govt. Printing Office, 1972.

Lyle, J., & Hoffman, H. R. Children's use of television and other media. In E. A. Rubinstein, G. A. Comstock, & J. P. Murray (Eds.), *Television and social behavior* (Vol. 4): *Television in day-to-day life: Patterns of use.* Washington, D.C.: US Govt. Printing Office, 1972.

McCombs, M. E. Negro use of television and newspapers for political information, 1952–1964. *Journal of Broadcasting,* 1968, *12,* 261–266.

Meyersohn, R. B. *Leisure and television: A study in compatibility.* Unpublished doctoral dissertation, Columbia University, 1965.

National Advisory Commission on Civil Disorders. *Report.* New York: Bantam Books, 1968.

Neely, J. J., Heckel, R. V., & Leichtman, H. M. The effect of race of model and response consequences to the model on imitation in children. *Journal of Social Psychology,* 1973, *89,* 225–231.

Nicholas, K. B., McCarter, R. E., & Heckel, R. V. The effects of race and sex on the imitation of television models. *Journal of Social Psychology,* 1971, *85,* 315–316.(a)

Nicholas, K. B., McCarter, R. E., and Heckel, R. V. Imitation of adult and peer television models by white and Negro children. *Journal of Social Psychology*, 1971, *85*, 317–318. (b)

Robinson, J. P. Toward defining the functions of television. In E. A. Rubenstein, G. A. Comstock, & J. P. Murray (Eds), *Television and social behavior* (Vol. 4): *Television in day-to-day life: Patterns of use.* Washington, D.C.: US Govt. Printing Office, 1972, 568–603.

Robinson, J. P., & Converse, P. E. The impact of television on mass media usages: A cross-national comparison. In A. Szalai (Ed.), *The use of time: Daily activities of urban and suburban populations in twelve countries.* The Hague: Mouton, 1972.

Rosekrans, M. A. Imitation in children as a function of perceived similarities to a social model of vicarious reinforcement. *Journal of Personality and Social Psychology*, 1967, *7*, 307–315.

Schramm, W. Leisure roles. In M. W. Riley & A. Foner (Eds.), *Aging and society* (Vol. 1): *An inventory of research findings.* New York: Russell Sage Foundation, 1968.

Schramm, W. Aging and mass communication. In M. W. Riley, J. W. Riley, Jr., & M. E. Johnson (Eds.), *Aging and society* (Vol. 2): *Aging and the professions.* New York: Russell Sage Foundation, 1969.

Schramm, W., Lyle, J., & Parker, E. B. *Television in the lives of our children.* Stanford, California: Stanford Univ. Press, 1961.

Steiner, G. A. *The people look at television.* New York: Knopf, 1963.

Surlin, S. H., & Dominick, J. R. Television's function as a "third parent" for black and white teen-agers. *Journal of Broadcasting*, 1970, *15*, 55–64.

Thelen, M. H. The effect of subject race, model race, and vicarious praise on vicarious learning. *Child Development*, 1971, *42*, 972–977.

Thelen, M. H., & Soltz, W. The effect of vicarious reinforcement on imitation in two social–racial groups. *Child Development*, 1969, *40*, 879–887.

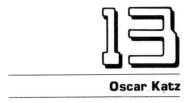

Oscar Katz

The Television Industry and Socialization: A Perspective

This chapter is the outgrowth of some ideas I presented at a conference on television and the socialization of minority children held at the
University of California, Los Angeles. It is also a reflection of a person
who has been a program executive for both a major network and a TV
production company; as well as having been involved in radio, the
theater, and the motion-picture industry. All of these activities are significant to mention because they provide a different background from
that of many of the other contributors to this book and place my comments in a different perspective. In short, as a programmer, I have been
involved in evaluating the impact of show business projects from a
different approach. At the same time, because I was a researcher who
became a programmer, I have tended to think and evaluate program
projects in terms of audience gratification, media characteristics, audience identification with dramatic characters, and similar factors. This
process has been true with most general-audience projects and my
background with children's programs such as *Captain Kangaroo*, *Fat
Albert and the Cosby Kids*, and the *CBS Festival of the Lively Arts for
Young People* all have been subjected to at least a part of this evaluation
process. My background with projects for children does tell me that

TELEVISION AND
THE SOCIALIZATION OF THE MINORITY CHILD

they are a special audience, and it is from this perspective that I would like to direct some of my comments.

TELEVISION:
SOME RELEVANT CHARACTERISTICS

The subject of this book interrelates two factors: television, on the one hand, and the socialization of the minority child, on the other. In other words, it interrelates a medium with a process or an objective. To put it still another way, the subject of socialization is complex; indeed, a complete exploration, one that I hope would lead to fuller understanding, must involve child development experts—particularly ones specifically involved with the problems of minority children— including educators, sociologists, anthropologists, psychologists, and psychiatrists, as well as media practitioners in the television field. And that is exactly where the catch comes in. These two groups, the broadcasters or the communicators and the experts or subject-matter specialists, have difficulty communicating with each other. It is almost as if they speak different languages and, obviously, this language barrier must first be removed before these two can bring their combined expertise to bear on the subject of television and the socialization of the minority child.

The broadcaster rarely fully understands the subject-matter specialists. This is partly the result of the use by the experts of difficult-to-understand terms. This is especially true in the social sciences, where a diversity of disciplines, viewpoints, approaches, and emphases has led to a variety of terminologies with a large degree of overlap. Thus, an educator may talk of the need to familiarize a child with an ever-widening environment, a sociologist may refer to the importance of socialization, and a psychiatrist may emphasize a child's identity needs. And yet, to a degree, these are overlapping and interrelated concerns.

Much more importantly, the broadcasters' confusion often stems from frequent and violent differences of opinion among the experts themselves on almost any question. In all the disciplines, the subject-matter specialists generally divide themselves into three groups: pro, con, and neutral. You can well imagine how confusing and discouraging this can be to nonexperts when they get involved in dialogue with such specialists. For those of us in broadcasting, it appears that this confusion, particularly in the child development field, results not from willfulness or sheer disorganization, but rather from the very complexity of the developmental process itself.

Conversely, the expert rarely understands the broadcaster. It seems to me that this is largely because specialists, although experts in their particular fields, are quite often not too well informed as to how television operates on various levels. Television has been called by some the "magic box," by others, the "boob tube." The first implies that television is so powerful it can do anything, the second that it is do-nothing, soporific. Neither, of course, is true. Television is neither omnipotent nor totally powerless. But in order to even approach using it with optimum effectiveness, we must take into account the nature of the medium itself, its characteristics and traits, and how it is perceived by its audience.

One obvious position to take is that the only way to eliminate the language barrier is for the broadcasters and social scientists to make a conscious attempt to understand the other. Broadcasters should turn to the expert or subject-matter specialist for guidance whenever advisable, knowing full well that they may suffer painful initial confusion, but recognizing that once the confusion stage is past, they will get some valuable input. The experts, on their part, should make a conscious effort to acquire a fuller understanding of television, its characteristics, and how it works.

As one who has spent practically all his professional life in television and radio, I would like to discuss some of television's relevant dynamics, as I see them. By this, I mean the medium's characteristics, the nature of its audience, its audience's frame of reference, and so forth. From this point of view, public television and commercial television are somewhat different media. Also, there are times when network television and local television may also be distinct and separate. In addition, if you take this approach, film is not a medium, but merely an audiovisual technique. In other words, a film dealing with a given subject may have to be constructed differently depending on whether it is designed primarily to be shown in the classroom or on television. Even more subtle possibilities exist. For example, a dramatic story, like *The Autobiography of Miss Jane Pittman* or *Queen of the Stardust Ballroom*, might be written and filmed one way for most effective showing as a television special but somewhat differently if the original intention was for presentation in a movie house.

One factor that should be recognized is that, considering both as media, school and television have vastly different characteristics. To mention a few, attendance in one is mandatory, in the other it is voluntary; many viewers of a particular program series do not watch it with anything approaching regularity. In addition, the classroom provides student–teacher feed-back, television does not. And there are other differences that will be touched on later. In my view, the important conclusion from these characteristics is that, to the extent that the school is considered a socialization force, television should not be looked on as an extension of the classroom. Television is simply not a substitute for traditional ways of teaching, and it should avoid objectives that can better be achieved by other institutions.

Another aspect of television is that, whether or not we like it, most people generally choose to watch it for entertainment. Mendelsohn (1966) has pointed out that considerable evidence adduced by researchers in mass communication has demonstrated what very well may be considered the First Law of Mass Entertainment; namely, when most people are confronted with a choice between deriving pleasure from "serious" nonentertainment fare or from nonserious entertainment fare, they will choose the latter in much greater proportions than the former. Maccoby (1963) has further added that the most important thing to remember concerning children's choice of programs is that they, like their elders, use television primarily for entertainment. Even when educational programs are available, few children watch them if there is an entertainment program available instead. In other words, this pattern of watching television for entertainment appears to apply equally to adults and children. Undoubtedly, this entertainment orientation was the main factor in the development of the formats for such programs as *Sesame Street* and *Captain Kangaroo*, to mention just two.

Related to this entertainment frame of reference, and perhaps growing out of it, is an aspect of television that never ceases to amaze me. In one sense, television is the largest of all the mass media. It has the broadest geographical reach, the widest demographics, and its audiences are astronomical in size when compared with those of other media. For example, a hit Broadway show would have to run seven performances a week, week in and week out, for well over 150 years to reach an audience equivalent in size to that of television's highest-rated single broadcasts.

Yet, in another sense, television is perhaps the smallest of the media. It is viewed on a small screen, alone or in small groups, and it is generally viewed in the privacy and intimacy of one's own home. This is an experiential conclusion, namely that these factors combined with the entertainment-orientation aspect seem to make television the most intimate of all of the media. By this, I mean that a necessary prerequisite for a successful television program or series appears to be a strong interpersonal relationship between the viewer and the characters in dramatic programs and between the viewer and the personalities in nondramatic programs. It even seems to apply to news and nonfiction broadcasts. This character–personality identification factor is probably responsible for programs such as *Fat Albert and the Cosby Kids* attracting larger audiences than, let us say, the *CBS Festival of Lively Arts for Young People,* even though both are produced with an eye to the entertainment-orientation aspect.

Another characteristic of this medium that I would like to touch on is television's mobility. Television is considered to have speed and mobility, and perhaps because of its recognized news function, it can generate a feeling of immediacy and currency. Thus, it is an ideal medium for bringing people to places, or rather for bringing places to people. This window-on-the-world function is, of course, served by specially designed for children programs like *In the News.* But beyond news, television can take children to the Lincoln Center in New York for a concert, to dramas shot on location, to other parts of the country and the world, and so forth. The reason I have spent so much time discussing television and its characteristics is that the child-development experts and media programmers must learn more about one another's fields in order to have a healthy and fruitful continuing dialogue.

TELEVISION AND THE MINORITY CHILD

It is important to appreciate the entertainment as well as educational aspects of television if professional broadcasters, social scientists, parents, and others hope to achieve an improved understanding of the impact of this medium on the socialization process. Neither the social science expert nor the professional communicator can come to any agreement unless there is some appreciation for the role of the medium in society. Without an understanding of television's role in society, our efforts to conceptualize the role of television on the socialization of the child in general, and the minority child in particular, may be impeded.

When we talk about television and the socialization of the child, particularly the minority child, we immediately confront an apparent major problem. This problem results from television's broad, almost universal reach, whereas America is made up of various subcultures. This was recognized in the Report to the President by the 1970 White House Conference on Children, which called America a mosaic in which the various tiles represent groups who have maintained their unique cultural or ethnic identities ("White House Conference on Children," 1970). Consequently, in attempting to teach cultural values, we come smack up against a dilemma, namely, whose values do we teach?

On closer examination, however, this dilemma quickly resolves itself. There is general agreement among the experts, and in the literature, that people are alike in more ways than they are different, that common cultural values far override cultural differences, and that hence the main emphasis should be on shared values, that is, on the traditional American values that have been associated with three dominant influences: a political commitment to constitutional democracy; an individualist, free-enterprise, profit-oriented economic philosophy; and a religious involvement in Judeo–Christian affirmations ("White House Conference on Children," 1970). This point of view was confirmed in a conversation I once had with Professor Seymour Feshback of the University of California, Los Angeles. During the course of our conversation, he suggested that commonality between people who feel, care, have emotions, etc. transcends differences, and if we want people to have empathy with each other, we must focus on similarities (Feshback, personal communication, 1971).

That the main focus should be on common values does not imply that subcultural differences should be ignored. Quite the contrary. Shaftel and Shaftel (1967) make this point, suggesting that perhaps one of the most crucial needs of our time is keen sensitivity to the feelings and perceptions of others. They further note that the ability to place oneself in another's shoes and to sense how he or she sees the world is a preliminary condition to the ability to move out of one's own "culture shell" to view events from the cultural outlook of someone raised in a subculture or national culture other than one's own.

Two examples of television programs that have attempted, successfully, I think, to deal with common problems or shared values are Fat Albert and the Cosby Kids and The Autobiography of Miss Jane Pittman. I consider Fat Albert and the Cosby Kids to be a most innovative television effort. To begin with, we decided to use animation, which to many of our critics was, per se, a dirty word. Second, the series gave us an opportunity to use Bill Cosby live as the adult authority figure that children need. Third, and most important, we decided that each episode of Fat Albert and the Cosby Kids would explore the concepts and precepts of growing up. That is to say, the series would deal with ethics and values, personal responsibility, values in conflict, and the like. As a result, individual episodes focused on telling lies, hookey playing, ganging up on a kid because he or she is different, interracial relationships, how to cope with authority, cheating on tests, and many other problems. That the kids in the series are black is neither minimized nor exploited. The important thing is that the behavior problems they confront are universal. Also important is that, to guide us in this effort, we gathered input from a panel of 11 experts selected from various academic disciplines that bear on child development.

One important note about *Fat Albert and the Cosby Kids* should be highlighted. Classroom teachers have some measure of their effectiveness because they have feedback. In television, feedback is almost nonexistent, so we are frequently flying by the seat of our pants, so to speak. This was especially true of *Fat Albert and the Cosby Kids* because of its innovative approach. So we asked the Office of Social Research of the CBS/Broadcast Group for help. They organized and executed a study designed to determine whether or not we were on the right track. Before I tell you the overall results, let me mention the study's limitations. Its primary objective was to determine whether the prosocial messages of *Fat Albert and the Cosby Kids* were being communicated to its audience of children. In other words, the study dealt with reception of messages. The findings do not indicate whether the messages were accepted or whether they did or did not modify the children's subsequent behavior. With this caveat, I must tell you that almost 9 out of 10 children received one or more specific prosocial messages from each episode of Fat Albert and the Cosby Kids. Furthermore, the average number of such messages received per episode ranged from just under two per child to close to four.

The Autobiography of Miss Jane Pittman is equally interesting. This program dealing with black history reached enormous audiences in its three showings on CBS. I attribute this primarily to two major factors. First, by using a fascinating central character, especially as portrayed by Cicely Tyson, the program made excellent use of television's character-identification aspect, which I mentioned earlier. Second, although black history was the subject matter with which the program dealt, it actually had a much broader theme. The program really dealt with human dignity, which has no color, but it did so using the life of a fictional black woman to illustrate this basic theme. Whatever the reasons for its success, the program gave blacks, including children, a feeling of pride in their own heritage, a necessary feeling of uniqueness and self-esteem. At the same time, the program was uplifting for nonblacks in the audience, hopefully giving them a better understanding of an important group of their fellow citizens. These two programs—*Fat Albert and the Cosby Kids* and *The Autobiography of*

Miss Jane Pittman have, in my opinion, made a contribution by inculcating shared values through diversity or by showing how to comprehend diversity within unity.

LIMITATIONS OF MASS MEDIA
EFFECTIVENESS RESEARCH

I should like to begin this section by pointing out that I tend to look carefully, perhaps even with mistrust, at most studies dealing with mass media effectiveness. Certainly, early radio and television effectiveness research was generally faulty. It all seemed to be derived from Psychology 1, in which we were taught that a stimulus operating on an object had a certain effect, illustrated diagrammatically by stimulus, or S, arrow, object, or O. It took many years for the researchers to learn that, as White has stated, people are not billiard balls manipulated by external cues. They have a life story and are members of groups, which means they interpret and modify the meaning of the stimuli they receive and are capable of integrating their responses to several more or less simultaneous stimuli so that the resultant action is quite different from what simple addition or subtraction would suggest (White, 1964).

In the early days of effectiveness research, social scientists, who to begin with had the biases of the social groups to which they belonged, would do a simple content analysis of a program or group of programs and, from this, would then predict or state the effect on the audience, usually with considerable definiteness. But researchers eventually learned that different people carry different predispositions with them when they serve as audience members for mass communications; that is, mass media operate within a total social context. So, people turned out to be a lot more complex than the O from Psychology 1. For example, I remember reading a study that found that a program dealing with prosocial parent–child relationships had disturbing effects when viewed by children in a home for children without parents.

At any rate, we have now learned that the O of the S→O formula was much more complex than we originally thought. Although this is a valuable lesson, I would like to suggest that there is an additional lesson that we have not yet fully absorbed. I am referring to my belief that the television program, or S itself, is much more complex than we appreciate. In this connection, F. Shaftel once told me of an experiment in which a group of ghetto children were taken on a field trip to Hawaii to study volcanoes, while a control group studied the same subject in class. Whatever the results with regard to which group learned more, the researchers learned accidentally, sometime later, that the students sent to the field were tremendously affected by the fact that the trip represented the first time most of them had traveled on a plane or stayed at a hotel. Thus, the stimulus, or trip, turned out to be much more complex than originally thought. Furthermore, the unanticipated effects could themselves have either socially desirable or undesirable end-results (F. Shaftel, personal communication, 1971).

I would argue, for example, that it is important to recognize that a single television picture, let alone a whole television program, has multitudinous images, and that the whole effectiveness process is further complicated by the fact that individual viewers select programs depending on their attitudes, predispositions, values and standards. In this connection, my own view of mass media effectiveness, which is a basic "gut" feeling for which I have absolutely no substantiation, consists of three theories: (a) a television program or series, if it has any effect at all, probably has multitudinous, almost infinite effects; (b) unanticipated effects are probably more important than the ones we expect; and (c) cumulative effects are probably more important than the effects of individual communications.

A program like *All in the Family* tells us things about family relationships, shows different value systems in conflict, and demonstrates how these can adapt and adjust to each other through discussion and process, rather than conflict. But consider the single question as whether or not it ridicules or reinforces bigotry. My own view is that it does some of each, although I am inclined to conclude that it ridicules it far more than it reinforces it, and thus its socially desirable effects outweigh its undesirable ones.

Take another example. Poussaint (1974) has observed that poor young blacks viewing television may see no representation of their community or lifestyle and get the impression that they do not count in this society. They may decide that "worthwhile" people live in the middle-class homes and neighborhoods shown in television commercials. To me, the key to evaluating this point of view is Poussaint's use of the word *may*. What he says may happen, may indeed happen. But then again, it may not. Perhaps many blacks subjected to the same series of stimuli have been motivated to take an active part in the movement to achieve equality for blacks, in the full sense of the word.

MISCELLANEOUS CONSIDERATIONS

It seems important at this point to briefly consider how broadcasters go about the creative decision-making process in television. For example, the creative person may desire to write a father or a mother out of a series, and I must confess that we have done both. Or the writer may decide to marry off the female lead in a series, and some time later to arrange for her to get a divorce. The professional sociologist may view these changes with alarm, considering them as tampering with such factors as parent–child relationships, the father image, the solidity of the family, and so forth. Considering their vantage point, the professionals are probably right in this point of view. The television programmer, however, is frequently faced with a different set of problems. For example, the decision to write a family member out of a series often results from some contractual or other difficulty with a particular performer; or the decision to divorce a couple previously married on the air may result from the fact that the marriage lowered the series' degree of audience identification. At any rate, the programmer and the sociologist are both probably right and are making their evaluations according to their different perspectives.

Next, I would like to mention briefly a pet suggestion of mine. Since the mid-1960s there has been an enormous growth in the size and number of communications schools, cinema schools, and television schools at American universities. These same universities, of course, also have various schools covering the social sciences, including education. All too often, the only connection between the communications school and those covering the social sciences is that they are located on the same campus. I feel that universities are missing a bet by not arranging for and insisting on closer collaboration between these schools. Why not start graduate programs jointly administered by the social scientists and the communications experts at the university? Perhaps, by taking such an approach, we will be able to turn out two new types of professionals for the future: the social scientist who is steeped in communications and its problems; and the communications expert who is steeped in social science and its lessons.

SUMMARY

I began this chapter by making a case for the fact that television is an important medium with many dimensions to its message and meaning. Furthermore, I argued that it is important for all of us, professionals, experts, critics, and parents, to understand the process and purpose of this medium so that we can have some common ground for appreciating its real and imagined impact on society.

The positions taken develop out of my concern for a "pass-the-buck" attitude concerning the role television plays in the socialization of minority and all children as well my concern to assist young people and adults to better understand the medium's strengths and weaknesses. It seems to me, that contemporary society faces problems of enormous magnitude, including those factors that influence in either a positive or a negative way the socialization of the minority child. It is therefore time for us to stop passing the buck among school, family, media, and church and to recognize instead that all the major institutions of our society have a shared responsibility in matters concerning our children.

REFERENCES

Invitational Conference on Television and the Socialization of the Minority Child, sponsored by the UCLA Center for Afro-American Studies, April 27–28, 1978.

Maccoby, E. E. The effects of television on children. In W. Schramm (Ed.), *The service of human communication.* New York: Basic Books, 1963.

Mendelsohn, H. *Mass entertainment.* New Haven: Connecticut College and University Press, 1966.

Office of Social Research. *A study of messages received by children who viewed an episode of fat albert and the cosby kids.* New York: CBS/Broadcast Group, February, 1974. (No author)

Poussaint, A. F. Building a strong self-image in the black child. *Ebony,* August 1974, pp. 138–143.

Shaftel, F. R., & Shaftel, G. *Role-playing for social values: Decision-making in the social studies.* Englewood Cliffs, New Jersey: Prentice-Hall, 1967.

White, D. M. Mass communications research: A view in perspective. In L. A. Dexler & D. M. White (Eds.), *People, society and mass communications.* New York: Free Press of Glencoe, 1964.

White House conference on children: Report to the President. Washington, D. C.: US Govt. Printing Office, 1970.

Author Index

Numbers in italics refer to the pages on which the complete references are listed.

A

Abbott, K., 166, *180*
Achelpohl, C., 169, *179*
Adler, R. P., 48, 59, *62*
Agee, W. K., 2, *10*
Akamatsu, T. J., 91, *100*
Akers, R., 169, *179*
Allen, V. L., 96, 97, *100*
Allport, G., 107, 117, 118, 119, 121, *129*
Alper, S. W., 48, *62*, 170, *178*
Anderson, D. R., 48, 65, 169, *178*, *182*
Andrews, L., 23, *33*, 53, 65, 170, *182*
Appleton, B. H., 42, 43, 44, 48, 54, 63, 170. *179*, 227, *242*
Arias, B., *210*
Arkoff, A., 166, *180*
Asante, M., 137. *148*, 204, *210*
Asher, S. R., 96, 97, *100*
Atkin, C. K., 20, 21, 22, 23, 24, 25, 29, *31*, *32*, *33*, 48, 49, 57, *63*, 179, *183*, 219, 225, 230, 234, *241*, 254, *258*
Attneave, C. L., 75, *79*
Ault, P. H., 2, *10*

B

Bachman, J. G., *184*
Baker, R. K., 248, *257*
Ball, S. J., 19, *31*, 42, 43, 45, 54, 55, 57, 58, 59, 60, 61, *63*, 82, *100*, 140, 146, *148*, 170, 175, *178*, *179*, 209, *210*, 227, 228, 229, *241*, 248, *257*
Balon, R. E., 175, 176, *179*
Bandura, A., 20, 26, *31*, 58, *63*, 91, *100*, 170, *179*, 234, *241*, 250, 251, *257*
Banks, J. A., 9, *10*
Baptista-Fernandez, P., 205, *211*
Baran, S. J., 187, *201*, 219, *241*
Barcus, F., 82, 84, 85, *100*
Barnouw, E., 75, *79*
Baron, R. A., 60, *64*
Barrow, L., 240, *241*
Bass, B., 118, *131*
Bechtel, R. B., 169, *179*
Benedict, R., 166, *179*
Bengen, B., 53, 54, *63*
Bennett, R., 219, *242*
Bentzen, M. M., 84, 86, 99, *100*

273

Subject Index

A

Academic achievement, 39, 119
Accessibility of television, 166
Acculturation of immigrants, 166–167
Achievement, 221
Actors, status of, 121
Adolescents, 50–51, 137, 167, 223, 232–233
Adult commentary, 58–59
Adult co-viewing, 54–55, 58–59, 231
Adult intervention, 50, 55
Advertisements, 48–49, 53–54, 57–58, 74, 89, 161–162, 219
and racial differences, 53–54
Affective development, 38, 59–62
Age, 52–54, 56, 88–89, 167
of television characters, 192
Agent of socialization, 4, 5
Aggressive behavior, 19, 60, 73, 170, 217, 230, 251
Alienation, 198
All in the Family, 91, 174, 228–229, 233, 269

Amalgamation, 115–116
The Amazing Chan and the Chan Clan, 157, 164
American Indian characters, 127, 188–191, 216
American Indian children, 115, 187–202
Americanization of Asian characters, 154–155
Amos 'n' Andy, 75, 216, 240
Analysis of ethnicity, 23–24
Approval of others, 107–108
Archie Bunker, 91, 174, 229
Asian American children, 164–178
Asian Americans, 115–116, 127, 151–185
Asian characters, 75, 127, 151–185
occupations of, 158
women's roles, 154
villains, 156
Aspiration-achievement discrepancy, 221
Assimilation, 115, 159, 167, 248
Attention to television, 169
Attitude change, 176
Attitude formation, 174
Attitudes of teachers, 199